MYTHIC ARCHETYPES IN
RALPH WALDO EMERSON

MYTHIC ARCHETYPES IN
RALPH WALDO EMERSON
ℰℭ

A Blakean Reading

RICHARD R. O'KEEFE

THE KENT STATE UNIVERSITY PRESS

Kent, Ohio, and London, England

© 1995 by The Kent State University Press, Kent, Ohio 44242
All rights reserved
Library of Congress Catalog Card Number 95-1707
ISBN 0-87338-518-7
Manufactured in the United States of America

02 01 00 99 98 97 96 95   5 4 3 2 1

Library of Congress Cataloging-in-Publication Data

O'Keefe, Richard R.
    Mythic archetypes in Ralph Waldo Emerson : a Blakean reading /
Richard R. O'Keefe.
        p.   cm.
    Inlcudes bibliographical references (p.) and index.
    ISBN 0-87338-518-7   ∞
        1. Emerson, Ralph Waldo, 1803–1882—Criticism and interpretation.
    2. Archetype (Psychology) in literature.   3. Blake, William,
    1757–1827—Aesthetics.   4. Romanticism—United States.   5. Myth in
    literature.   I. Title.
    PS1642.A62O38   1995
    814'.3—dc20   95-1707

British Library Cataloging-in-Publication data are available.

For Dale

CONTENTS

&ꙮ&

ACKNOWLEDGMENTS

ℬↃ℀

I OWE THANKS TO A number of persons who have helped me at various stages of this work. The reader of the following pages will see how often they refer to the books of Harold Bloom. Even more substantial is my intellectual debt to Barbara Packer, whose work showed me where I needed to go. The following scholars from Penn State University I have had the pleasure of not just reading but of knowing personally, and I am indebted to their assistance: Charles W. Mann, Jr., and Jerrold Maddox, who brought their respective disciplines of comparative literature and art to clarify my thinking; the late Philip Young, an inspiration to me in his teaching, his scholarship, his style, whose like I shall not see again; and especially to Robert E. Burkholder, Emersonian and friend, for both faith and works.

INTRODUCTION: "DISCIPLINE"

Names alter, things never alter.

—Blake

Good writing and brilliant discourse are perpetual allegories.

—Emerson

I SUGGEST IN THIS STUDY a new way of reading Emerson. The old ways have sagged library shelves and made monsters of bibliographies, but none seem to satisfy the reader who remains both admiring and critical of these strangest of all "essays." The critical complaint is as old as Emersonian criticism itself. In 1871 James Russell Lowell called Emerson "a chaos of shooting stars." The very recent critic who quotes that aptly styled early judgment, David Leverenz, cogently reviews the problem, recalling Jonathan Bishop's lament that "there is something at the heart of Emerson's message profoundly recalcitrant to the formulations of the discursive intelligence." Leverenz notes as well Eric Cheyfitz's candor: "Putting Emerson aside, we cannot remember what we have read or if we have read anything." Leverenz himself is troubled by Emerson's "fog of self," his "disengagements," his "unresolved tensions" within a set of "limitations that seem inseparable from his achievements" (71). He might also have included in this record of critical dissatisfactions Matthiessen's early worry about Emerson's "inveterate habit of stating things in opposites."[1]

I offer no solution to the problem, but I do indicate a different direction of inquiry that might lead to a more rewarding and less frustrated reading. Perhaps the problem is not Emerson's prose but our expectations of how that prose should work. Maybe the problem is not Emerson's writing but our "discursive intelligence." Possibly Bishop's mistake was looking for a "message" in the first place. Emerson's "essays" may not be "essays" at all, but poems. The language of those essays, from *Nature* in 1836 to "Works and Days" in 1870, is, as I shall demonstrate, poetic; in fact, Emerson's diction is considerably more poetic, from any post-Coleridgean critical viewpoint, than the language of Pope's *Essay on Man* or his *Essay on Criticism*. The difference is not that between Romantic and Neo-classic style. Poe's "The Philosophy of Composition" or "The Poetic Principle" can be read as discursive prose; Emerson's "The Poet" will frustrate any reader who attempts to translate it into the abstractions of conceptual discourse.

Much of Emersonian criticism and scholarship, past and present, from Stephen Whicher's *Freedom and Fate* in 1953 to David Van Leer's *Emerson's Epistemology* of 1986, remains unsatisfying in accounts of how Emerson's writing works, perhaps because of an explicit or implicit assumption that Emerson is a systematic thinker. I argue that he is not—but that he is a consistent poet—and that critical complaints about Emersonian contradiction or unresolved tensions are beside the point. An approach that reveals Emerson to be a literary artist, a writer who uses poetic devices and modes and tropes, may be more serviceable. Such devices, modes, and tropes appear in Emerson's work in the form of archetype and myth. Consequently, one cannot read Emerson as one reads Spinoza or Kant. Stylistically, formally, conventionally, Emerson's "essays" do not behave like abstract, conceptual discourse; in fact, they characteristically do not behave like discursive prose. *Nature* (1836) begins with a visionary experience ("I become a transparent eyeball; I am nothing; I see all") and ends with a "chant" by an "Orphic Poet." The world of discourse which includes autobiographical visionary epiphanies and Orphic chants is the rhetorical world of William Blake, and I use a few lyrics of Blake and some passages from his longer poems as models of this highly Romantic rhetoric. In emphasizing this particular Blakean mode of Romanticism, I derive some theoretical support from M. H. Abrams's concept of the secularization or psychological redefinition of traditional Christian thought; from Harold Bloom's explicit connections between Emerson and Blake; and from Northrop Frye's use of mythic archetypes as a tool of critical analysis.[2] The analysis of archetypal images has long been a productive tool for critics of the British Romantic poets (most notably in work on Blake); it is a method seldom employed on American Romantics, almost never on American Romantic prose. If Emerson is a "prophet," as both earlier and more recent criticism describe him, my method simply explores his language to find out what makes it prophetic: the mythic metaphors that characterize such poetic expression.

In these pages I attempt no contribution to critical theory. The first chapter analyzes the problem (how to read Emerson) and proposes a method that might help solve it (poetically). The next four chapters are essays in practical criticism, applying the method of poetic analysis to the reading of Emersonian texts. The theoretical support I derive from Abrams, Bloom, and Frye permits me to deal with the elements of those texts as archetypal images. Such images are nonlogical or metalogical—semantic synapses, not parts of syllogisms.

The archetypal models have been chosen from Blake precisely because there is no direct influence involved. Both Blake and Emerson, products of a Christian culture, found themselves forced, a generation apart and quite independently, to redefine and reinterpret the traditional body of Christian myth that they had inherited, a poetic task Shelley rejected and Wordsworth ignored.

An organizing device for the whole study has been the borrowing from Blake of the four archetypes of his central myth, ones that he derived from the traditional Christian culture that both Blake and Emerson shared and that both reacted against: Creation, Fall, Redemption, and Apocalypse. Here my study is not a virgin pioneer, for it follows and profits from two relevant trailblazers in Emersonian studies. Barbara Packer in her 1982 study, *Emerson's Fall,* draws a number of useful and illuminating parallels between Emerson and Blake in her exploration of the mythic concept of the Fall. More recently, Alan Hodder, in *Emerson's Rhetoric of Revelation: Nature, the*

Reader, and the Apocalypse Within (1989), explores parallels between Emerson's first book and the biblical Revelation. The suggestions in these two studies about Fall and Apocalypse in Emerson guided my investigation and made the chapters on Creation and Redemption not only feasible conceptually but schematically inevitable.

Ralph Waldo Emerson was never influenced by William Blake. This inquiry is not a source study. It explores parallels in the thought of Emerson and Blake only as those parallels appear in the two writers' use of archetypal images. I use Blake's texts here as models of how such imagery functions, and I throw no new light on Blake, nor do I intend to, attempting only an original analysis of Emerson in this Blakean archetypal mode.

Emerson came late to Blake, referred to him more often as "artist" or "painter" than "poet," and quoted from him only in his late essays and journals, after 1863, the year of the publication of Gilchrist's biography, facts documented by Armida Gilbert.[3] I find Emerson employing mythic archetypes analogous to those of Blake as early as *Nature* in 1836. This evidence does not suggest coincidences of literary history, which would have a merely minimal, historical interest as curiosities; rather, in terms of Frye's theory, they suggest an insight into how mythic archetypes work similarly in different contexts. The study of such archetypal tropes is now a traditional way of reading Blake. It constitutes a new way of reading Emerson.

The problem of Emerson's apparent contradictions or inconsistencies must be dealt with by every serious reader. My first chapter analyzes these polarities as "handles," to use Emerson's own term for them. I argue a dialectical method in Emerson's rhetoric rather than a dialectics of substance, a dialectic of rhetorical mode rather than of philosophical idea, and I see Emerson's dialectics, after the model of Blake's, as a structuring of images. To support this hypothesis, the chapter provides an extensive analysis of one of Emerson's major poems, "Hamatreya."

In the next four chapters I turn from rhetorical method to mythic substance. Chapter 2 explores Emerson's first book, *Nature,* in the context of the archetype of Creation. The next chapter examines "Circles," from *Essays: First Series,* as a mythic paradigm of the Fall. The fourth chapter studies Emerson's redefinition of the myth of Christian Redemption in his Divinity School "Address," in one early sermon, and in journal entries over a significant span of his career. Chapter 5 looks at poetic theory in "The Poet" and "Poetry and Imagination," but it reserves extended analysis for a late and neglected essay, "Works and Days," in terms of the mode of Apocalypse.

A final chapter draws a few conclusions derived from the method employed, and those conclusions suggest a different Emerson from the figure who emerges, central and self-contradictory, by turns, from most previous studies. Perhaps the most surprising conclusion is that the transcendental Emerson has largely disappeared. He is replaced in these pages by a radical existential prophet. The "apostle of culture" and the apologist for "Fate" may still lurk in the wings, the phantoms of other operas, but this stage is dominated by a poet, a visionary, and a prophet of personal revolution.

Any conclusions at all regarding Emerson are hazardous. Perhaps if the student had really learned from this master, he would not conclude at all. In these matters, as in others, Emerson is cautionary. "I know better than to claim any completeness for my picture," he warns us near the end of "Experience." And he goes on, with even more sobering qualifications: "I am a fragment, and this is a fragment of me." Yet he is able to affirm in the very next paragraph of that essay, "Life wears to me a visionary face" (*Complete Works* 3:83–84). The apparent logical contradiction is superficial, while the images reveal a profound truth: if the "fragment" of the "fragment" can still recognize the "visionary face," we may have all that we humanly need, possibly all that humanly matters.

1

THE DIALECTICAL IMAGINATION

ഇ൨ൟ

Without Contraries Is No Progression.

—Blake

Everything has two Handles.

—Emerson

"DID HE WHO MADE the Lamb make thee?" the speaker of Blake's "Tyger" asks that practical cat. Blake may be playing possum here. The answer, on one level, is autobiographically "yes." The "Author & Printer W Blake" certainly wrote and engraved both "The Lamb" of his *Songs of Innocence* in 1789 and "The Tyger" of his *Songs of Experience,* and after he printed the latter in 1794 he always produced the two sets together. Blake, in other words, was quite capable of holding together simultaneously in his mind the "Two Contrary States of the Human Soul."

A similar question might be asked about Ralph Waldo Emerson. Did he who made *Nature* in 1836, that prose poem of ecstatic radical optimism, make such essays as "Fate" and "Wealth" of 1860, with their dark implications of determinism? Emerson, too, seems capable of entertaining "contrary" concepts—"freedom" and "fate"—without either violating his intellectual integrity or surrendering to that "foolish consistency" which was for him "the hobgoblin of little minds."

How do "contrary" concepts function in the work of these two writers, the British poet, the American prose master? There is a great deal of evidence in the writings of both Blake and Emerson to suggest that both thought dialectically—that is, contraries for them were generative or creative. Dualism, polarity, dichotomy— these modes of perceiving and organizing human experience not only appear throughout the major literary productions of both writers, but they also seem to produce those works, both poems and prose. A list of titles is instructive in itself. Blake begins his own canon (the works he chose to engrave) with two prose "tractates," *All Religions are One* and *There is No Natural Religion,* which, as their titles indicate, form a logical and rhetorical pair. There are two versions or parts of *There is No Natural Religion,* an (a) and (b). He published an early *For Children: The Gates of Paradise,* a set of emblems with legends, and a later version, *For the Sexes: The Gates of Paradise.* The *Marriage of Heaven and Hell* brings the dialectical principle of organization into the same one work, which is, in addition, formally a combination of prose and verse. Among the early minor "prophetic books," *America* and *Europe* form a pair, and *The Song of Los* is divided into "Africa" and "Asia." The two major prophecies that Blake engraved are *Milton a Poem in 2 Books* (turning inward on an autobiographical incident) and *Jerusalem,* in four chapters (spinning outward as a mythic universal history). Clearly this poet thinks creatively much of the time in opposed pairs of images, motifs, or concepts.

Emerson also creates his own canon by revising and rewriting as essays works that were originally delivered as lectures, which themselves often began as entries in his journals. After three early and extraordinary works, *Nature* (1836), "The American Scholar" (1837), and the Divinity School "Address" (1838)—prose which has been called "prophetic" and which bears some analogies with Blake's early tractates as major pronouncements which later work qualifies and refines—Emerson typically works in pairs. He followed the *Essays* of 1841 with the *Essays: Second Series* of 1844. The two collections work together dialectically, but also within each occur dialectical pairs. "History" and "Self-Reliance," "Compensation" and "Spiritual Laws," "Love" and "Friendship," "Prudence" and "Heroism," "The Over-Soul" and "Circles," "Intellect" and "Art," make, directly or indirectly, subtly or obviously—six pairs that organize the whole first book.[1] The principle operates also in *Essays: Second Series,* though without hobgoblinish consistency. Thus "The Poet" and "Experience" make an ironic, contrasting pair; "Character" and "Manners" an obvious one; "Gifts" and "Nature" a possible one; or "Nature" and "Politics" an alternative. "Nominalist and Realist" brings the dialectic within the single essay, and also works with "New England Reformers" in an ironic way. Significantly, the second series produces an uneven number of essays: contraries have produced progression.

Representative Men (1850) gives us a variety of possible pairings among its six exemplars, though the author's order gives perhaps the most clear-cut sets: "Plato; Or, The Philosopher" with "Swedenborg; Or, The Mystic"; "Montaigne; Or, the Skeptic" with "Shakespeare; Or, the Poet"; "Napoleon; Or, The Man of the World" with "Goethe; Or, The Writer." The essays within *The Conduct of Life* (1860) could be shown to yield the same sorts of couplings as *Essays: Second Series,* there are nine of these, also, and "Fate," the first, and "Illusions," the last, make a dark bracketing of this late book's contents. And later still, as late as *Society and Solitude* (1870), the dialectical principle announced by its title can be seen at work among its twelve essays. Clearly, like Blake, Emerson thought much of the time in opposed or contrary concepts.

These dialectical pairings of Emerson's essays have not been observed often enough. An exception among his recent commentators is R. A. Yoder, who calls attention to the fact that Emerson "arrange[s] his essays in antithetical pairs" ("Emerson's Dialectic" 356).[2] The equivalent rhetorical structuring in Blake, especially in those complementary sets of lyrics, the *Songs of Innocence and of Experience,* is in those works too explicit to escape notice. There we see the "contrary states" clearly set up in the introductions of the two series, which feature, respectively, the "Piper" and the "Bard"; "The Lamb" and "The Tyger"; the two "Chimney Sweeper"'s, a ferociously ironic pairing; "The Little Boy Lost" and "The Little Boy Found" in *Innocence,* which pair with both "The Little Girl Lost" and "The Little Girl Found" and "A Little Boy Lost" and "A Little Girl Lost" in *Ex-*

perience, there being more losses in experience; "The Divine Image" and "A Divine Image"; the two "Holy Thursday"s; the two "Nurse's Song"s; and "Infant Joy" and "Infant Sorrow." There are other possible and more subtle couplings, always to one degree or another ironic. In looking at the interrelationships of these lyrics as dialectical, the reader may be helped by Northrop Frye's observation: "The *Songs of Experience* are satires, but one of the things they satirize is the state of innocence. . . . Conversely, the *Songs of Innocence* satirize the state of experience. . . . Hence the two sets of lyrics show two *contrary* states of the soul, and in their opposition there is a double edged irony" (237).

Analysis of examples can best lead to a working definition of the term "dialectical" for the purposes of this study, and though later chapters will deal extensively with Emerson's prose and Blake's verse, short lyric poems from both authors may make the clearest initial demonstration. The category of "love poems" suggests a dialectical potential. Blake's treatment of erotic relationships is ubiquitous and often explicit, Emerson's rare and indirect; but "The Clod and the Pebble" and "Give All To Love" reflect typical mental operations of both writers.

"The Clod and the Pebble" gives us two voices; the structure of the poem, by combining them in exactly equal space and time, creates its dialectic. The first voice is that of the "Clod of Clay":

> Love seeketh not Itself to please,
> Nor for itself hath any care;
> But for another gives its ease,
> And builds a Heaven in Hells despair.
> So sang a little Clod of Clay,
> Trodden with the cattles feet:

The exactly symmetrical second half of the poem gives us the contrary view of the pebble:

> But a Pebble of the brook,
> Warbled out these metres meet.
> Love seeketh only Self to please,
> To bind another to its delight:
> Joys in anothers loss of ease,
> And builds a Hell in Heavens despite.[3]

It is a poetic debate between the opposed and contradictory values of love as altruistic sacrifice and love as selfish pleasure. Perhaps nothing is so disconcerting about this poem as the fact that both voices occupy it equally. And both voices are *naturally* correct. Both are in character. Each speaks its view out of its own integrity. The clod in nature is made to be squashed by an external force, such as "cattles feet"; even the "gentle rain from heaven" could reduce it to mud. The pebble, just as naturally, disturbs and disrupts the force external to it, the rushing water of the brook. The clod expresses a traditional Christian concept of heaven-meriting virtue—self-sacrifice. The pebble advocates the equally traditional Christian concept of damnation, total self-satisfaction at the expense of the "other." But Blake's poem equates them structurally and rhetorically; both values are "natural" and "true." The poem is a miniature *Marriage of Heaven and Hell.*

Further, Blake's emphasis is insistently sexual, unsettling in a subversive and perverse way, and the sexual facts undermine the Christian allusions to "heaven" and "hell." Clearly, heaven and hell here are sexual experiences, with the clod's being masochism, the pebble's sadism. These sexual phenomena, then, are equated by the poem's rhetorical structure, and this sexual equation makes nonsense of the traditional Christian dichotomy. The dialectic of this poem creates a satire on singleness of viewpoint (may "God us keep / From Single vision & Newton's sleep" [*Poetry and Prose* 722], as Blake puts it elsewhere). It also puts the reader rather uncomfortably outside either viewpoint while he contemplates them both united in their perfect incompatibility. The poem is, quite obviously, a "Song of Experience," and it has no companion piece in *Innocence* (unless it be "The Blossom," where a repeatedly "happy" blossom "sees" a "merry Sparrow" and then "hears" a "sobbing Robin" without either observation altering its own happiness).

Emerson's "Give All To Love" is less "Freudian," or at least less explicitly sexual; but since it gives us not two voices but one voice that expresses opposite values, its dialectic may be even more radical than Blake's. Its one voice contradicts itself.

> Give all to love;
> Obey thy heart;
> Friends, kindred, days,
> Estate, good-fame,
> Plans, credit and the Muse,—
> Nothing refuse.
>
> 'Tis a brave master;
> Let it have scope:
> Follow it utterly,
> Hope beyond hope:
> High and more high
> It dives into noon,
> With wing unspent,
> Untold intent;
> But it is a god,
> Knows its own path
> And the outlets of the sky.
>
> It was never for the mean;
> It requireth courage stout.
> Souls above doubt,
> Valor unbending,
> It will reward,—
> They shall return
> More than they were,
> And ever ascending.

The speaker here—an anonymous, mysterious, or veiled persona met often again in Emerson's prose—in the first stanza urges upon the listener the unqualified value of love as greater than any other human value (greater than friendship, family, longevity, wealth, reputation, "plans," "credit," even poetry). In the second he praises love as a humanly divine value ("it is a god"). And in the third the speaker asserts that love elevates and improves humanity. At this midway point in the poem the reader must make quite a turn on Emerson's "stairway of surprise":

> Leave all for love;
> Yet, hear me, yet,
> One word more thy heart behoved,
> One pulse more of firm endeavor,—
> Keep thee to-day,
> To-morrow, forever,
> Free as an Arab
> Of thy beloved.
>
> Cling with life to the maid;
> But when the surprise,
> First vague shadow of surmise
> Flits across her bosom young,
> Of a joy apart from thee,
> Free be she, fancy-free;
> Nor thou detain her vesture's hem,
> Nor the palest rose she flung
> From her summer diadem.
>
> Though thou loved her as thyself,
> As a self of purer clay,
> Though her parting dims the day,
> Stealing grace from all alive;
> Heartily know,
> When half-gods go,
> The gods arrive. (*Complete Works* 9:90–92)

The speaker of the first half contradicts himself in the second half, the last three stanzas of this six-stanza poem. Its proportions, by the way, are cunning: the first half gives us a total of twenty-five lines in three stanzas of six, eleven, and eight lines; the second half delivers twenty-four lines in a complementarily shaped set of three stanzas of eight, nine, and seven lines. The poem opens out from its center like a binary fan.

The pivotal spine of that fan is the repeated qualifier "yet" in the second line.

In the following stanzas the speaker advocates freedom from the erotic attachment (fourth stanza), urges acceptance of the temporal or transitory nature of the relationship (fifth stanza), and finally asserts a divine value beyond love, in the light of which the previous value of love—in the first half of the poem a god—is now seen to be only a demigod. Further, this specific psychological or spiritual victory of the self, if achieved, is also the opening of the self to the arrival of real, true, or full "gods," and they are emphatically plural. That the love in question has been erotic is indicated by the contrasted relationships in stanza one and by the imagery in stanza five of "maid," "cling," "bosom young," "vesture's hem," and possibly the shed "rose" from "her summer diadem," if this last is a subtle metaphoric evocation of the loss of virginity.

What is most disturbing about this poem is that the same speaker who can attribute so much to love is able to change his mind so categorically and equally advocate its surrender. The reader is left thrown off balance, about as comfortable as at the end of Blake's "The Clod and the Pebble," and for an almost identical reason: the reader cannot come away from either poem with one view. If love in the Blake poem is both self-sacrifice and self-gratification, if in Emerson's it is an absolute value that discovers itself in the act of valuation to be relative, then both these poems express a "meaning" of "love" greater than the logical or rhetorical components that structure them.

That production of an original and larger insight emerging from the juxtaposition of contradictory points of view is what I shall describe as dialectical, and it is a poetic or imaginative, not a logical, mode of discourse. The same mode can be seen in two longer poems, poems more important in each of their canons, that deserve more detailed analyses, Emerson's "Hamatreya" and Blake's "The Mental Traveller."

If there was ever a poem that looked "deconstructed" on the printed page, that poem must surely be Ralph Waldo Emerson's "Hamatreya." The reader's untransparent eyeball discovers what appears to be, in fact, two different poems under one title. "Hamatreya" is a poem of sixty-three lines in two radically asymmetrical sections. The first section is untitled; the second is headed "Earth-Song." The first section contains twenty-seven lines, the second thirty-six. The lines of the two parts are very different kinds of lines: the first section is made up of blank verse, unrhymed iambic pentameter; the second has very short (two-stress or one-, two-, or three-foot) closely rhymed lines. The first section has two stanzas, the second five. There are lines in quotation in both parts (speakers within speakers), but the declaration of twelve lines in part one is unevenly matched by the Earth's Song of thirty-two lines. The number of lines outside of quotation marks is also unbalanced: fifteen in the first part, only four in the second. One does not expect Emerson to write sonnets or structurally balanced lyrics in the manner of Donne or Herbert; still, the asymmetries here are extreme. Is "Hamatreya" perhaps two different poems yoked by rhetorical violence together?

The discrepancies between the two sections are not merely structural; they are musical and prosodic as well. The blank verse Emerson employs in his first part is unorthodox, at times daringly contrapuntal, creating a conversational voice much more modern than Coleridge's in the "Conversation" poems and prosodically more modern than Frost's blank verse: "Hay, corn, roots, hemp, flax, apples, wool and wood" (1. 3).[4] The "Earth-Song," however, in its short, very heavily rhymed lines, is so obviously lyrical ("Mine and yours; / Mine, not yours. / Earth endures"; [ll. 28–30]) that this poet, who dismissed Poe as "the jingle man," might be said in this part of his poem to be pushing his lyrical luck. The whole poem not only looks like two different poems; it sounds like two different poems. There are lines in the first section that are so colloquial that they push the iambic pentameter almost (but not quite) beyond the possibilities of scansion: "Bulkeley, Hunt, Willard, Hosmer, Merriam, Flint" (1. 1).[5] On the other hand, much of the "Earth-Song" is so sing-songy it seems to burlesque the lyric mode.

In addition to structural and prosodic discrepancies between the two sections of "Hamatreya," there is a third and much more significant set of dichotomies, logical or rhetorical ones, and these begin with the title and continue to the last four lines of the poem.

What does the title mean? It has attracted more scholarly and critical attention than the poem itself. In the earliest study of "Hamatreya," Thomas Wentworth Higginson (1888) suggested the passage at the end of Book 4 of the *Vishnu Purana* as Emerson's source, where "Maitreya" is the disciple in the dialogue who seeks instruction. Emerson had copied out that passage in his "Journal Y" of 1845. Edward Waldo Emerson reprinted it as part of the notes to "Hamatreya" for the centenary edition (*Complete Works* 9:416–17). The source is not in question. But the source does not explain the fact that Emerson changed "Maitreya" to "Hamatreya," nor has there ever been any subsequent conclusive scholarly explanation of that change, a fact which suggests that the Hindu source is not the only possible identification of the name. Richard Bridgman in 1962 suggested a Greek etymology, *hama* for earth's surface and *treya* as a feminine suffix, deriving then an "awkward neologism" by Emerson, signifying "Earth-Mother." Kiffin Rockwell (1963) agreed with this theory (and with Bridgman's contention that there would have been no good reason to title the poem after a naive male novice); but citing Sanskrit dictionaries that would have been available to Emerson at the time of the poem's composition, he went on to offer "Children of Father Sky / Mother Earth" as a possible translation. Mohan Sharma (1968) used

"colloquial Hindustani" (not Emerson's most likely language com-
petence) as a purely Hindu signification that would play down the
idea of "mine" in favor of "thine." More relevant to the concern of this
study, Alice Hull Petry (1986) rejected an either Hindu or Greek reading and believed "that the title 'Hamatreya' is meant to be read both
ways" and that the duality of the title is in keeping with the duality of
the poem itself.[6]

There is a problem, however, if both etymologies work, as indeed
they seem to do. Again, we are confronted with dichotomy rather
than unity, because the Hindu and Hellenic cultural contexts are in
conflict here: the former, stressing epistemological illusion, disagrees
with the latter notion of pantheistic apotheosis. Was Emerson really
inventing a Joycean, multilingual portmanteau word to express both
meanings? Given the cultural and philosophical polarities in the two
significances (Hindu vs. Greek), the title can be said to contradict
itself.

If we accept both etymologies, it contradicts itself also in gender.
Maitreya was a male character in the *Vishnu Purana;* the Earth Mother
is, undoubtedly, female. Thus a curious rhetorical androgyny animates
the title.

There is a second rhetorical problem, that of the proper names
that constitute the first line of the poem. A superficial reading of
"Hamatreya" renders the landowners the villains of the piece, making
the poem a simplistic denunciation of private property in favor of
existential claims for Nature, a crude version of the Heideggerian
distinction between dominion and dwelling. (The poem is sometimes
anthologized in a context that seems to render it simply pro-environ-
mental, anticapitalist propaganda, as, for example, in *The Exploited
Eden,* an admirable, valuable text but one that does some disservice by
its contextualizing to the complexity of this poem.[7]) Emerson is not
exactly anti-capitalist, as his response to Brook Farm and his essay,
"Wealth," among other evidence, demonstrate. "Things" might be,
then and now, "in the saddle and ride mankind," but things—either
natural or man-made—are not in themselves evil for Emerson, and

THE DIALECTICAL IMAGINATION

neither is the human use of them. He extolled "Commodity" as early as *Nature* in 1836, and the Concord landowners in "Hamatreya" might be described as using their "self-reliance" to hitch their real wagons to their estate stars.

"Hamatreya" is too structurally and rhetorically complicated to be read merely as a question-and-answer, an error (the landlords') corrected by the Earth-Song. Further, although the anonymous speaker of the first section describes the landlords as "fond" (1. 12), "Boastful boys" (1. 13), who end up "lump[s] of mould" (1. 26), we need to recall that these names are not fictitious, but rather a litany of the first founders of Concord, beginning with the name of an ancestor of Emerson's on his mother's side, Peter Bulkeley, and Bulkeley was also the first name of Emerson's beloved retarded brother. In addition, Emerson had earlier used these names (plus a few more) in a highly favorable context, a locally patriotic and eulogistic speech, his "Historical Discourse at Concord on the Second Centennial of the Incorporation of the Town, September 12, 1835" (Waggoner 149). If he had wanted to summon up actual Concord landowners to heap abuse on them, he would hardly have chosen these particular historic names. It is the anonymous speaker of the first section of the poem who mocks these founding fathers (before Earth does later), not Emerson. But who is this speaker?

The Earth-Song is sung, of course, by Earth. The named landlords speak to us in their own words, the quoted section of part one. Who is the third speaker? Is, in fact, the anonymous speaker of the poem's beginning the same as the anonymous speaker who ends the poem after Earth's song is finished? Since he mocks the "fond" and "Boastful" landlords for their avarice (the "hot owner"), it is unsettling to discover him confessing avarice himself at the end: "My avarice cooled" (1. 62). If he has been earlier in the poem critically detached from the landlords, why is he now including himself as subject to their chief deadly sin? Or is the terminal anonymous speaker not the same as the one at the beginning? The poem itself does not provide an unambiguous answer to this question.

What does "Hamatreya" say about ownership in the face of mortality? It does not say one thing, but several things, in unresolved contraries. The two asymmetrical "halves" of the poem remain on the page in opposition; the words of the landlords continue as "brave" (perhaps braver since we see them as tragically doomed) as the scorn of the Earth, who is certainly as "boastful" as they are. The poem is structurally and rhetorically in dialogue with itself. The two sections, that of the landlords and that of the Earth, debate each other, but debate each other endlessly, since the second section of the poem in no way erases the first. The "messages" of the two sections are roughly equal, in spite of the structural difference, noted earlier, that accounts for discrepancies in their number of lines. What the landlords say occupies 105 words of this poem; what the Earth sings, 117. As messages they face and contradict each other in almost equal time, an asymmetrical poetic debate, but a quantitatively well-matched rhetorical fight, the Earth Mother's tit for the landowners' tat.

Further, each section betrays an internal dialogue within itself: the first, between the landlords and their skeptical, critical chronicler; the second, between the Earth and the acquiescent commentator who has, however, in acquiescing to Earth's wisdom, also discovered his common bond with the rest of the human community. The terminal speaker shares their avarice with the landlords he first disparages, and also, by implication and imagistic reference (1. 63), their mortality. If the last speaker is the first speaker, he has gone through a spiritual transformation effected by his listening to both the boasts of the landlords and the scorn of the Earth. Through the operation of the poem's dialectic, then, he has been brought to an awareness of himself, at the poem's end, that he lacked at its beginning. If the speaker's original persona and his concluding one are different voices, or different selves, there are four speakers instead of three. But a fourth speaker creates an unnecessary complication in the reading of the poem, and one that adds nothing to its meaning. The end of "Hamatreya" conveys a tone of most unambiguous finality:

When I heard the Earth-song,
I was no longer brave;
My avarice cooled
Like lust in the chill of the grave.

Assuming this final speaker to be the same as the first, there are only three voices. Through the collision of the opposing messages of the landlords and of the Earth, a dialectical demonstration, the speaker has achieved the concluding level of awareness that he lacked at the beginning.

It is certainly a poem that did not fare well at the hands of New Critics. Hyatt Waggoner, who regards "Hamatreya," "Merlin," and "Bacchus" as Emerson's "three greatest" poems, notes that "the chief New Critics themselves were silent on Emerson; he was not grist for their mill, his poems did not yield to their methods" (149). Yet Waggoner himself attempts to employ those very methods in his analysis of "Hamatreya," using, in fact, the terms "paradox" and "rhetorical irony" (154) in his effort to show how Emerson's "mixed feelings . . . toward Concord" (152) get expressed in the poem. His critique is sensitive, probing, and valuable, as is his whole book, but it does not explain very well the peculiar mix of this particular poem.

Ralph Waldo Emerson will help more. The poem can be seen as a single, short, concentrated example of an essential pattern of Emerson's thought, namely dialectical organization.

Stephen Whicher has familiarized us with the Emerson who is two Emersons, the radical younger, the "acquiescent" older, in a study whose evidence of dualisms and dichotomies is overwhelming.[8] Whicher, however, stops with the dualisms, while Perry Miller has detected something more, and qualitatively different—the presence of dialectical method:

In December 1841 and January 1842 Emerson delivered
at the Masonic Temple three lectures on the age; this

> was the first winter of Brook Farm, and of his con-
> sciousness that in Ripley's judgment the existence of
> the Farm was a standing rebuke to him. He worked
> out a subtle dialectic by opposing "the Times" of the
> first lecture to "the Conservative" of the second, and
> then finding a kind of synthesis of the two—or more
> accurately an escape from them both—in "The Tran-
> scendentalist." (471)

There seems to be always a push, in Emerson's thought, through contradictions toward qualified affirmation. But the contradictions must be dealt with first. "Without contraries is no progression," William Blake wrote, out of an analogous epistemology. Within one single essay, "Wealth," whose subject bears some relationship to "Hamatreya," Emerson offers both "The world is his who has money to go over it" and "If a man own land, the land owns him. Now let him leave home if he dare" (*Complete Works* 6:95, 115). His poem "Blight" begins, "Give me truths; / For I am weary of the surfaces, / And die of inanition" (*Complete Works* 9:139). It is important to note that truths is a plural; it is inanition that is "monological."

Waggoner gives the date of composition of "Hamatreya" as 1845–46 (109). Emerson bought the fourteen acres of land at Walden Pond in September 1844 (*Journals and Notebooks* 9:xix), and in January 1847 he bought "three acres of land adjoining his property to the east" (*Journals and Notebooks* 9:xxi). The creation of this poem "against" landownership is thus biographically bracketed between two acts of land acquisition by the poet. The contradictions are not just in the text; they are in Emerson. The text profoundly reveals them.

As dialectical organization, Emerson's "Hamatreya" retains enormous vitality as a poem. Part of that vitality surely stems from the fact that it resists simple or single interpretation. It is ornery but open. It resists and teases our aesthetic. It combines solidity with fluidness. Its earth is both the farm and the grave. The last word in this poetic debate between commodity and nature is simply the last word of the poem. The grave reminds us that, no matter who is speaking the line, whatever voice representing whatever value, human existence itself ends its dialectic in a synthesis of silence.

Blake's "The Mental Traveller," imagistically and conceptually, is a much more complex poem than Emerson's "Hamatreya." Formally and structurally, however, it is much simpler. Its 104 lines are arranged in twenty-six quatrains of iambic tetrameters, rhyming ABCB. It is thus a ballad, in one of the traditional variants of ballad measure. Its four-square stanzas of four-beat lines, though Blakean in numerology, suggest the strong, simple directness of the ballad tradition, and its simple, concrete diction adds to that impression. But though its form and diction are simple, the patterns of its imagery are not.

If Emerson's "Hamatreya" has suffered from a surprising degree of critical neglect, such has definitely not been the fate of Blake's "The Mental Traveller." In fact, so many scholarly hands have reached out to fondle this frowning babe that it is a wonder there are not more withered academic "arms" gesticulating about. But the poem continues turning on its own gyres in its own gnomic integrity, and though this study pretends no original "interpretation" of it, neither is the present context the appropriate one to sift through the slag heap of theories its flame has produced. Blake's images are certainly sexual; they are surely archetypal; they are doubtlessly religious and mythic, probably cultural and historical, possibly autobiographical, and, arguably, intentionally all of the above, given this poet's typical methods. This study will restrict itself to showing *dialectical movement* in the working out of whatever meanings the poem expresses.

In the very first stanza Blake emphasizes a dialectical structure in the poem by making explicit the sexual dichotomy that will operate throughout it: "I traveld thro' a Land of Men / A Land of Men & Women too." He is stressing the fact that whatever land this ironically is, it is the fallen world; here humanity is in sexual division. It is not unfallen humanity—in the singular—that he will be describing, but the divided and often opposed two sexes. Blake employs this explicitness of emphasis again in his last stanza, where the concluding line, "and all is done as I have told," reminds us emphatically of the cyclic nature of the action he has described. These first and last stanzas very deliberately frame the action of the poem.

Within it, as early as the second stanza, we find the opposed values of joy and woe ironically reversed relative to conception and birth. It should be noted that this little structure in stanza 2 relates conception and birth by opposition, not by cause and effect, and thus polarizes them along with joy and woe. The simile in this stanza enforces the dichotomy, reaping "fruit" in "joy" versus sowing in "bitter tears."

We then have the polarity of the baby Boy and the old Woman, complicated by its rich allusions, as the Boy is first Prometheus on his rock, then in stanza 4 Jesus in his crucifixion. Gold in these stanzas is consistently related in a neat paradox to misery—cups of gold catch shrieks in stanza 3; the woman numbering the Boy's every nerve with her fingers is compared to a miser counting his gold. The result of this activity gives us a further polarization: "She grows young as he grows old" (1. 20). The movement of the cycle then gives us the Boy as "Bleeding youth" (an Adonis figure) as the old woman has in turn become a "Virgin bright" in stanza 6, and his movement out of physical bondage and into sexual delight, where the sadomasochistic metaphor is reversed, the Boy now taking the sadistic role formerly enjoyed by the woman.

But the cycle continues inexorably to move. The Boy ages into a "Shadow" haunting the dwelling place or earthly cot in which he has accumulated his wealth of golden misery. These "gems & gold" are "meat" and "drink" with which he feeds his guests: "His grief is their eternal joy." Their celebration produces the polar opposite of the baby Boy at the beginning—namely, the "Female Babe" of the middle of the poem. She, it should be noted, is not sexually generated, but is made of those gems and that gold that are human misery. She, however, also couples (human culture is dichotomized because it is the product of the human condition, which is itself dichotomized). She seeks and finds her lover, and they turn out the former-Boy now "aged Host," a Lear figure, who becomes the opposite of a resident host, namely a wandering beggar. Wandering, he seeks a "Maiden" in ironic parallel to the Female Babe's seeking her lover, "young or old or rich or poor." When he finds his maiden, we have the antithesis of the opening situation of the poem: instead of male baby and old woman, old man and young girl. The landscape of the poem changes with their coupling, from fertility to waste, from rural "cottage" and "garden" to "desart."

The cycle continues as the aged ex-host grows younger on the love of the maiden (as the old woman grew younger on his love when he was a Boy), even to the point of infancy. Their infantile love-play is described in polarities of flight and pursuit and of not just "various arts of love," but "various arts of Love & Hate," the repetition echoing the poem's opening "land of men & women too."

In the final stage of the cycle the Boy is a "wayward Babe" again, and his maiden has become a "weeping Woman Old" once more. At this stage the wasteland is reversed to urban and rural civilization ("many a City there is Built / And many a pleasant Shepherds home"). As the reborn Babe, the Boy, however, functions as an object of terror who must be controlled (he cannot remain "wayward") by being subjected to crucifixion by the old woman. "And all is done as I have told" is Blake's version of the orthodox Christian, "as it was in the beginning, is now, and ever shall be, world without end, Amen."

These, indeed, are "dreadful things" that "The Mental Traveller" tells us. Blake had earlier written, "Without Contraries is no progression. Attraction and Repulsion, Reason and Energy, Love and Hate, are necessary to Human existence" (*Poetry and Prose* 34). Why is there no progression here? Here the contraries are locked into what Blake calls "Generation"; there is no redeeming vision here; the fallen world is presented as hopelessly fallen, and we have the same movement that Blake shows on the much larger canvas of the first eight of the nine nights of *The Four Zoas*. Here is the Fall without Redemption, without Apocalypse. "The Mental Traveller" is a nightmare vision of our world perceived as nothing but biological and historical determinism, a view of this world as hell divorced from any possible visionary marriage with heaven. The cycle as infinitely repeated is intolerable, and the emotional effect of the poem upon the reader should be wrath or indignation, liberating emotions for Blake. He had written very early on in *There is No Natural Religion:* "The bounded is loathed by its possessor. The same dull round even of a univer[s]e would soon become a mill with complicated wheels" (*Poetry and Prose* 2). "The Mental Traveller" is Blake's horrifying picture of such a mill, and it is indeed a "dark Satanic" one. The issues of this poem, as presented, cannot be resolved; the dialectical progression occurs in the mind of the reader (mentally traveling) who contemplates the fact that this poem presents "No Exit," and then realizes that his contemplation of it is outside of it, has escaped it. As a dramatization of the triumph of the natural cycle of death and rebirth, it is a celebration of human death (in Blake human and natural are opposed in the fallen world as they are united in the unfallen world or state of Eden). The poem ends, then, by not ending, but when the reader perceives that endless repetition (without creation, without freedom) is human death; such a reader is in very much the same state of mind as the one who reaches the end of Emerson's "Hamatreya," the only resolution of whose dialectic was "the grave."

This is no mere coincidence. "The Mental Traveller" and "Hamatreya" employ a similar strategy of poetic dialectic because they share the same theme. Furthermore, they present that same theme through the same three major characters—the narrator, the old woman, and the boy. The narrator in "Hamatreya" comes to his enlightenment through the operation of the poem's dialectic (listening to both the landowners and the Earth's Song) only at the end of the poem, while in "The Mental Traveller" the narrator is enlightened (by hearing and seeing) from the start. This narrator in Blake's poem does not interact with the other two major characters; in Emerson's the narrator's interaction with them is crucial to his coming to his enlightenment (or spiritual clarification) about his (and our) human condition. Emerson's use of the narrator is thus more dramatic than Blake's. This is unusual as Blake is almost always elsewhere the more dramatic poet. Emerson, however, employs a more dramatic dialectic in his essays than Blake does in his hortatory, polemical prose. In both these poems the reader is guided to the theme by the narrator, whose guidance is not ironic in either case; he is Wayne Booth's reliable narrator. The reader sees the meaning of both poems through the narrator's eyes.

Second, there is that "Woman Old," who dominates (quite literally) the initial and concluding phases of Blake's cyclical action. We have met her before, in "Hamatreya," where she was called "Earth," and where she was just as forceful. She is Gaea, the Earth Mother, and her power, expressed in contempt of humanity in "Hamatreya," is what she is exercising upon humanity without words in "The Mental Traveller." Elsewhere Blake calls her Vala when he thinks of her as material illusion, Tirzah when he regards her as the oppressive mother. Elsewhere Emerson calls her, in those same conceptual contexts, "Illusion" and "Fate." The idea of control—as sexual, as political, as biological—is essential to the confrontations with her in both poems: "They called me theirs, / Who so controlled me; / Yet every one / Wished to stay, and is gone, / How am I theirs, / If they cannot hold me, / But I hold them?" The holding, binding, and sadomasochistic coupling in Blake's poem is the same as the owning and controlling and holding in Emerson's. In Emerson's poem Mother Earth's brutality is verbal, expressed in her song; in Blake's it is described in dramatic action. In Blake, the old woman appears at the end as she does at the beginning. In Emerson, "Earth endures."

The third major character, the "Boy" in "The Mental Traveller," is that community of "boastful boys" in "Hamatreya." (Blake would appreciate Emerson's making his "Boy" a collective.) Emerson's humanity, like Blake's, is the victim of the cycle. The landowners "Possessed the land," but not for long; possession is metaphorically sexual as well as literally economic. Further, the Concord landlords as farmers are husbandmen (Blake's Boy "plants himself in all her Nerves / Just as a Husbandman his mould"), and the earth itself is the farmer's bride in which he sows his seed. By this possession on the part of the Concord landlords, by their industry, they produce wealth—not gems and gold but "hay, corn, roots, hemp, flax, apples, wool and wood," that have a certain market-exchange value in gems and gold. But the "boastful boys" disappear in the workings of the cycle; they are replaced by "strangers fond as they" ploughing their furrows (and Emerson would be as aware as Blake of the sexual metaphors here). But "Earth laughs in flowers"; the biological cycle itself mocks human endeavor, and when she sings her derision, she asks, "where are old men?" They fade like shadows. And when she holds them, finally, it is in her lap, the grave, her womb, and they are again the "Babe," and she, the eternally recurrent Mother.

The present study is by no means the first to observe dialectical structures in the writing of either Emerson or Blake; in fact, such critical observations are something of a commonplace for both authors. It may be the first, however, to attempt to relate their dialectical structures to each other.

Most commentators on Blake have been compelled to take account of dialectics in one way or another, whether they see Blake as a visionary monist with Northrop Frye, or as a dualistic Platonist with Kathleen Raine. From their various critical perspectives, Harold Bloom, Robert Gleckner, and Leopold Damrosch have all had to deal with Blake's dualities and dichotomies, whether these are seen as theological or psychological, historical or rhetorical.[9] Recent commentators on Blake who employ the term dialectic explicitly do so cautiously and flexibly. For David Gross, "the sense of dialectic I am using [is] open, fluid, and heuristic" (175–86). For Peter Thorslev it is "an emphasis on thinking as process" (44). But the dialectical impulse, once perceived, can even get into the style of scholarly titles, as in Mark Schorer's *William Blake: The Politics of Vision.*

Dialectical method was observed in Emerson as early as 1884, two years after his death, by W. T. Harris in "The Dialectical Unity in Emerson's Prose":

> There need be no formal syllogisms; the closest unity
> of the logical kind is the dialectic unity that begins
> with the simplest and most obvious phase of the sub-
> ject, and discovers by investigation the next phase that
> naturally follows. It is an unfolding of the subject ac-
> cording to its natural growth in experience. . . . Such
> development of a theme exhibits and expounds the
> genesis of conviction, and is the farthest removed from
> mere dogmatism. (Burkholder and Myerson 216)

And R. A. Yoder contributed an admirably detailed analysis in
"Emerson's Dialectic" (1969).

> To see the world as knowable and yet a mystery, to see
> both identity and diversity, this "double conscious-
> ness" is both the art and the achievement of the sage.
> An awareness of the "two sides" reaches to the heart of
> every philosophical problem. . . . This idea, that every-
> thing is two-sided, and that its polarity can be defined
> by a string of analogies based on the antithesis of
> identity and diversity, is the essence of Emerson's
> method. . . . And it is constantly his technique to di-
> chotomize within an essay, and even to arrange his
> essays in antithetical pairs. In this loose sense of set-
> ting opposing concepts against each other, dialectic
> was Emerson's device for organizing what he had to
> say. (Burkholder and Myerson 355–56)

Yoder also observed that "most interpreters of Emerson have agreed
that dialectic, in one sense or another, describes the structure of his
essays" (335) and names those interpreters as W. T. Harris, Walter
Blair and Clarence Faust, Stuart Gerry Brown, Sherman Paul,
and Charles Feidelson (366–67).[10] Though unmentioned by Yoder,
it should be recalled that when he begins his major discussion of

Emerson in *The American Renaissance,* F. O. Matthiessen observes, "The problem that confronts us in dealing with Emerson is the hardest we shall have to meet, because of his inveterate habit of stating things in opposites" (3).

Blake and Emerson are imaginative dialecticians. Dialectics, for both, is a literary means, not a philosophical end. I suggest that these two writers use dialectics to get beyond dialectics. The idea which is poetically realized by "Hamatreya" or by "The Mental Traveller" is one idea, not two. By using a similar imaginative method, dialectical organization, Emerson and Blake are able to discover similar insights into human experience, similar not only in how they see things, but in what they see as well,[11] the topics of the next four chapters.

"The Eye altering alters all." Almost a throwaway line, it is the unlocking key in "The Mental Traveller." Here is the conceptual escape from the prison cycle of mental traveling, from the dull round, from dialectics itself. It is "the end of a golden string." If we wind it into our own ball, it will lead us not only to "Heaven's gate built in Jerusalem's wall." It will lead us simultaneously to "our own world" that Emerson admonishes us to build, in his peroration to *Nature,* since those two things are the same thing.

"The Eye altering alters all." Ralph Waldo Emerson discovered this line in 1863, in the two-volume edition of Gilchrist's *Life and Works of William Blake,* which he borrowed from the Boston Atheneum, from December 11 to 19 (*Journals and Notebooks* 15:219). He copied the line in his *WAR Journal* for December, 1863. He quoted it again, four years later, copying it a second time in his *LN Journal* of 1868 (*Journals* 16:90). And he quoted it still a third time, using it near the end of his essay, "Greatness" (*Complete Works* 8:319). Thus, thrice-quoted, it becomes the one line in Blake which Emerson most used. It is no surprise that Emerson was attracted to the line in 1863. "The Eye altering alters all." Quite independently of William Blake, Emerson had been saying exactly the same thing himself ever since 1836.

2

EYEBALLS, WINDOWS, AND THE WORLD'S BODY

෨෬

In the woods, we return to reason and faith. There I feel that nothing can befall me in life,—no disgrace, no calamity (leaving me my eyes), which nature cannot repair. Standing on the bare ground,—my head bathed by the blithe air and uplifted into infinite space,—all mean egotism vanishes. I become a transparent eyeball; I am nothing; I see all; the currents of the Universal Being circulate through me; I am part or parcel of God.

—Emerson

What it will be Questiond When the Sun rises do you not see a round Disk of fire somewhat like a Guinea O no no I see an Innumerable company of the Heavenly host crying Holy Holy Holy is the Lord God Almighty I question not my Corporeal or Vegetative Eye any more than I would Question a Window concerning a Sight I look thro it & not with it.

—Blake

IN THE SPRING OF 1825 Ralph Waldo Emerson was afflicted with a strange disorder affecting his eyesight. "Lost the use of my eye for study," was, as Rusk records, the "laconic autobiographical note that Waldo dated March, 1925, but certainly wrote much later" (111). At this time Emerson was supposed to be studying theology at Harvard to prepare himself for the ministry. Rusk speculates that it was "about this time" that the divinity student went to Andrews Norton, the professor of sacred literature, and "explained that his eyes would not allow him to take an active part" (Rusk 111).

Allen provides more details about this temporary disability:

> Actually, because of ill health, Emerson spent only a
> few weeks in 1825 in the Harvard Divinity School.
> First he suffered from a lame hip, and a month later
> from trouble with his eyes. . . . In an autobiographical
> note dated March 1825, perhaps written later, he
> recorded: "lost the use of my eye for study." Here he
> says one eye, but in another notation, probably writ-
> ten still later, "Being out of health, and my eyes
> refusing to read, I went to Newton, to my uncle
> Ladd's farm, to try the experiment of hard work for
> the benefit of my health."
>
> What was wrong with Emerson's eyes is a matter for
> conjecture. But in the spring Dr. Edward Reynolds in
> Boston successfully operated on one eye, and on the
> other in late summer or early autumn. Since the oper-
> ation completely restored Emerson's use of his eyes, it
> seems unlikely that the "affection" (Cabot's word) was
> either an *infection* or a psychosomatic symptom. But
> the condition was severe enough to stop Emerson
> from journalizing or writing letters for nearly a year.
> Naturally the interruption in his studies discouraged
> him and caused his ambition to sputter like an oil
> lamp with an untrimmed wick. (83–84)

Although it seems unlikely to Allen that this ocular disorder was psychosomatic, he finds it hard to explain an implication in a letter from
Emerson to his Aunt Mary: "'In the fall, I propose to be *approbated,*
to have the privilege, tho' not at present the purpose, of preaching
but at intervals.' Then this curious statement: 'I do not now find in
me any objections to this step.' The words convey reluctance—
certainly lack of enthusiasm" (Allen 89).

In 1832, preparing his "heretical" sermon on the Lord's Supper,
Emerson suffered from acute diarrhea. Before settling into his brief

career as a preacher, he needed to take a short trip to South Carolina and Florida for the sake of his lungs, a problem that never inhibited his subsequent, much longer, strenuous career as a lecturer. Whatever mixed feelings he may have had about entering the ministry, he successfully preached his first sermon on the text, "Pray Without Ceasing"; the sermon concluded, "We must beware, then, what we wish" (Allen 93). It is quite possible, given this pattern, that just as his lungs had rebelled at the prospect of preaching, and his intestines had rebelled at the idea of the Lord's Supper, his eyes may very well have betrayed his ambivalence about divinity as a committed life's study. By December 1832, he had finally resigned his Unitarian pulpit (Rusk 166). He never again had any serious problem with his sense of sight.[1]

Almost every biographical account of William Blake includes the mention of his first "vision." "When he was four, he saw God's head at the window, and the child—not surprisingly—screamed."[2] The usual context for this event supplied by Blake's biographers is the poet-painter's "visionary" experience. "For Blake, the world was already a place of visions" (Davis 14). Bronowski provides a refreshingly different context for the anecdote:

> While Frederick the Great marched and counter-marched like another Marlborough to hold France in Europe, Pitt took the hope of Indian empire from her at Plassey in 1757; won her Canadian empire at Quebec in 1759; and broke her sea power in two battles in the West Indies, in 1759 and 1761. Vast markets were opened to England: at the peace of 1763, she rated the untapped market of Canada higher than the spice islands of the West Indies. A world lay conquered for her trade; a greater Whig age seemed about to begin. The trade came, but the Whigs went. For in 1760 a Tory and a High Churchman, George III, had become by the Grace of God King, Defender of the Faith. In 1761, Pitt resigned. About this time, the child Blake saw his first vision of God, and screamed. (27)

This historical context may be less arbitrary and more perceptively Blakean than it might at first seem, given the mature Blake's typical identification of "God & his Priest & King" and his assertion that "God is only an Allegory of Kings & nothing Else" (*Poetry and Prose* 23, 669). At any rate, the child Blake's scream remains disconcerting: it is not an innocent babe's response to a benevolent Father.

It is a curious coincidence that both the young Emerson and the child Blake experienced visual phenomena having to do in some way with the divine. In their maturity both writers devoted a great deal of their creative energy to redefining the divine, and both writers obsessively use the image of the eye. This chapter will consider first their use of that image and secondly, what both see outside of it when they look *through not with it,* the two topics making a literary study of what philosophers would call epistemology and ontology.

Probably the most famous (and from some critical perspectives, then and now, the most infamous) passage in all of Emerson's prose is his description of himself in chapter 1 of *Nature* as a "transparent eyeball."[3] That central image, quoted in the head note to this chapter, deserves a closer look in its context. Emerson records an experience of being alone in the woods and feeling a profound rapport with the physical world around him, but "rapport" is an inadequate term here. The experience harmonizes modes of thought that are often at odds with each other: "In the woods, we return to reason and faith." Reason and faith, often (though not in Emerson or in Coleridge, his mentor here) contraries, are joined or married in this experience, which is one of profound consolation. "There I feel that nothing can befall me in life,—no disgrace, no calamity (leaving me my eyes), which nature cannot repair." The only fear is blindness; his eyesight is the mode and grounding of the consolation. In the experience mental constructs such as reason and faith disappear, and the human perceiver undergoes what seems like organic union with the physical world around him: "Standing on the bare ground,—my head bathed by the blithe air and uplifted into infinite space,—all mean egotism vanishes." The head, the organ of reason and reasoning, if not of faith, is cleansed by the elements, perceiving itself as one point in a space which is infinite. This realization causes egotism (which is small or petty or "mean," and a function of the "head") to disappear. With the vanishing of the cerebral, rational ego-functions, he becomes a pure perceptor. He is simply an organ of sight in what is the first metaphor of the passage: "I become a transparent eyeball." This figure is synecdoche, and, as a trope, is as traditional as Shakespeare's "Lend me your ears." The remainder of the passage is what startles: But this assertion "I am nothing; I see all," follows logically from the loss of egotism and the description of the experience as nothing more or less than seeing. Many of Emerson's readers, past and present, have had such aesthetic experiences either with nature or with art. (One recalls how Eliot expresses the same aesthetic with hearing in *The Four Quartets:* "music heard so deeply / That it is not heard at all, but you are the music / While the music lasts."[4]) But the very end of Emerson's passage is its most controversial part—"The currents of the Universal Being circulate through me; I am part or parcel of God." Rather than a glib note of impressionistic pantheism, what Emerson gives us here is the fulfillment of the terms of his metaphor. If figuratively in this experience he is only an eyeball, then the rest of nature that he feels connected with is the rest of the body of which that eyeball is one organ, hence the connectedness. Emerson's "Universal Being" (significantly "Being," not thing) is what Blake calls Albion, in a much more extended personification. Harold Bloom glosses the Emersonian passage in exactly this Blakean sense:

> Nature, in this passage as in the title of the little book, *Nature,* is rather perversely the wrong word, since Emerson does not mean "nature" in any accepted sense whatsoever. He means Man, and not a natural man or fallen Adam, but original man or unfallen Adam, which is to say America, in the transcendental

sense, just as Blake's Albion is the unfallen form of Man.[5]

It is essential that the "eyeball" in Emerson's metaphor is transparent. The actual human eyeball is, of course, not. What Emerson is expressing through the image of organic seeing is the honorific term, "vision," but it is crucial to Emerson's thought (as it is to Blake's) that he presents us with a literal eye as the literal term of his metaphor. He is not describing an "out of the body" experience, and the meaning in this passage is not that of Hamlet's "in my mind's eye, Horatio." It is not Emerson's mental eye that provides the experience, but his physical eye in a transformed condition.

Admittedly, this is a difficult passage because it expresses a difficult (to many readers paradoxical) concept. Perhaps the best possible gloss on Emerson's "transparent eyeball" can be found in a strikingly similar passage in Blake, from his "Vision of the Last Judgment," his personal description of his own large painting, now lost. The passage occurs at the very end of that "essay" (there are many "essays" in Blake, as there are many "poems" in Emerson). It begins with Blake having some satiric fun (a great deal of which is in Blake and very little in Emerson) at the expense of ordinary lowest-common-denominator modes of perception: doesn't the sun look like a gold coin? That simile itself reveals a necessarily bourgeois, materialistic bias. Blake's answer is a definitive "no."

> What it will be Questiond When the Sun rises do you
> not see a round Disk of fire somewhat like a Guinea O
> no no

What Blake sees instead of the coin is more, however, than most of us are prepared to bargain for:

> I see an Innumerable company of the Heavenly host
> crying Holy Holy Holy is the Lord God Almighty

He sees angels and hears prayers of adoration of the divine. Blake's metaphor is even more daring than Emerson's, insofar as synesthesia is more radical a disruption of prosaic logic than synecdoche. Blake ends the passage with an assertion and an affirmation that vindicate the physical organ of sight as physical:

> I question not my Corporeal or Vegetative Eye any more than I would Question a Window concerning a Sight

But he qualifies this physicality by using in the simile the same concept of transparency that Emerson employs: "I look thro it & not with it."

Emerson's "eyeball" is "transparent"; Blake's "Corporeal Eye" is like a "Window." Both images are transparent vehicles. Both Emerson and Blake look *through* their eyes in these passages, rather than *with* them. The transparency is crucial, because if the being enclosed (in a house with a window or in a body with an eye) can look through it to the outside, whatever is outside can also look in. Such seeing suggests at least a potential for a human/cosmic correspondence. Blake's passage, like Emerson's, is difficult and troublesome. Its best gloss may come from Northrop Frye:

> The Hallelujah-Chorus perception of the Sun makes it a far more real sun than the guinea-sun, because more imagination has gone into perceiving it. Why, then, should intelligent men reject its reality? Because they hope that in the guinea-sun they will find their least common denominator and arrive at a common agreement which will point to a reality about the sun independent of their perception of it. The guinea-sun is a sensation assimilated to a general, impersonal, abstract idea. Blake can see it if he wants to, but when he sees the angels, he is not seeing more "in" the sun but

more of it. He does not see it "emotionally": there is a greater emotional intensity in his perception, but it is not an emotional perception: such a thing is impossible, and to the extent that it is possible it would produce only a confused and maudlin blur—which is exactly what the guinea-sun of "common sense" is. He sees all that he can see of all that he wants to see; the perceivers of the guinea-sun see all that they want to see of all that they can see. (21)

It should perhaps be added to Frye's analysis here that Blake's passage emphasizes the personal quality of his special experience. "Do you not see?" is countered by an explicit, "No, not me. I see, etc." Similarly, Emerson is not presenting a normative experience in that particular passage in *Nature,* but an autobiographical epiphany; its source in his own experience can be traced to his journal entry for March 19, 1835 (*Journals and Notebooks* 5:18).

For the unpersuaded, skeptical reader, Frye goes on to make a quite different point about Blake's passage:

> It is no use saying to Blake that the company of angels he sees surrounding the sun are not "there." Not where? Not in a gaseous blast furnace across ninety million miles of nothing, perhaps; but the guinea-sun is not "there" either. To prove that he sees them Blake will not point to the sky but to, say, the fourteenth plate of the Job series illustrating the text: "When the morning stars sang together, and all the sons of God shouted for joy." *That* is where the angels appear, in a world formed and created by Blake's imagination and entered into by everyone who looks at the picture. (26)

In other words, Blake has validated his vision for us by evidencing its reality in his picture. In the same way, Emerson's "vision" of nature is objectified in the book *Nature,* which one modern commentator has suggestively described as a "miniature universe."[6] How close Emerson's view is to Blake's on the question of the guinea-glimpsers may be evidenced from another sentence in *Nature:* "Most persons do not see the sun. At least they have a very superficial seeing" (*Complete Works* 1:8).

Frye's mediating gloss may help us to look through Blake's window, but an immediate, direct aid to seeing through Emerson's eyeball is the body of which it is the most conspicuous organ, the text of the book *Nature* itself. The full context of the "eyeball" passage has not been sufficiently examined, in spite of the enormous amount of scholarship that has weighed down upon Emerson's first little book. Kenneth Burke's 1966 essay, "I, Eye, Aye—Emerson's Early Essay on 'Nature,'" is disappointing.[7] Its subtitle is "Thoughts on the Machinery of Transcendence," and it substitutes for close examination of the text a generalized and quite abstract discussion of the clichés of transcendence. Had Burke had more respect for the text, he might have discovered that the terms "transcendence," "transcend," "transcendental," or "transcendentalism" never appear in *Nature.* Burke is prevented from close examination by his glibly patronizing and condescending attitude toward Emerson's thought. An "enemy" might describe *Nature* as a "happiness pill," but Burke finds it "charming" (875); for Burke, Emerson's imagery "in general" is "starry-eyed" (885). Emerson is "tender-minded," and *Nature* gives us an example of "Emersonian unction" (889), whereby "something HERE is interpreted in terms of something THERE, something beyond itself" (894). No evidence supports the last observation; in fact, very little evidence of any sort informs Burke's overlooking overview.

A close look at the text, unlike Burke's distancing rhetoric, discovers very little "there" and a lot of "here." Let us put Emerson's "transparent eyeball" back into the socket of its context. Emerson uses the image of the eye twenty times in *Nature.* An examination of those references in the order of their appearance is both convenient and revealing. One occurs in the Introduction; five in chapter 1, "Nature," including the "transparent eyeball" passage; none, significantly, in

"Commodity"; seven, appropriately, in chapter 3, "Beauty"; one in "Language"; two in chapter 5, "Discipline"; two in chapter 6, "Idealism"; none (again, significantly) in chapter 7, "Spirit"; and two in the last chapter, "Prospects."

The dialectical method is very much at work in the structure of *Nature,* as Barry Wood has painstakingly observed (385–97). Confining our study of this text simply to the image of the eye, we can see a dialectical significance in the omission of the image from the two contrary or antipodal topics, "Commodity" and "Spirit," one consideration below the visionary sense of the image and the other above it. Between those absences the sense of the image oscillates in a wide-ranging interplay of meanings, from obviously literal to imaginatively metaphorical. This range of meanings of one term represents, in fact, a phenomenology of the single image and illuminates, in its one thread, the larger warp and woof, the structure of the whole text. It is Emerson's typical mode of thought, and the specifics reward close scrutiny.

The first mention of the eye in *Nature* forms part of Emerson's plea for originality of thought and of inquiry: "The foregoing generations beheld God and nature face to face: we, through their eyes. Why should not we also enjoy an original relation to the universe?" (*Complete Works* 1:3). This argument in Emerson will find its major expression in the "American Scholar" address of a year later. Here in *Nature* it is put in terms of a fresh look, of a new seeing. It also performs the rhetorical introductory function of persuading his readers to open their minds.

The four "eye" references in chapter 1, other than the central passage under discussion, instruct us positively and negatively in how to read that passage. "There is a property in the horizon which no man has but he whose eye can integrate all the parts, that is, the poet" (8). Here Emerson prepares the reader for an explicitly poetic or imaginative experience, one which is synthetic in the Coleridgian sense. In the next paragraph, Emerson indicates the negative alternative: "Most persons do not see the sun. At least they have a very superficial seeing. The sun illuminates only the eye of the man, but shines into the eye and heart of the child" (8). Here the adult eye is Wordsworth's eye of common day; the child's eye is closer to the poet's because its view includes emotion and value ("heart"). In the "transparent eyeball" passage, which occurs next, it should be noted that a literal sense of the term—"no calamity (leaving me my eyes)"— precedes the famous metaphor; literal sight is a precondition for poetic vision (10).

"Beauty" begins with eye references which are simply Romantic commonplaces, such as "the plastic power of the human eye" (15); the fact that visual pleasure "seems partly owing to the eye itself" (15); the thoughts, "as the eye is the best composer, so light is the first of painters" (15); and "individual forms are agreeable to the eye, as is proved by our endless imitations of some of them" (16). After these perhaps predictable reflections of Romantic aesthetic theory, the next ocular reference in "Beauty" is rather more intellectually challenging: "the health of the eye seems to demand a horizon" (16). It suggests that notion of correspondences between man and nature that runs as a thread (but only one of a pair of major threads) through the whole text. (The term "horizon" in Emerson is positive, suggesting expansion of perspective; in Blake it is negative, conveying a limit to perspective, as in the pun in the name Urizen.) Sometimes in the "Beauty" chapter of *Nature* "eye" is only the literal functional term, diminished in concrete reference by conventional phrasing, as in "to the attentive eye" (18), where the noun would have no specific substantive force, if it were not for nineteen other uses of it in the same essay. But the fact remains that the seven uses of "eye" in "Beauty" are conceptually disappointing; they express conventional, not visionary meanings.

One would not expect the word to appear in "Language," and it does so only in a metaphor that acquires its life from the more dynamic "transparent eyeball" passage under discussion. "A life in harmony with Nature, the love of truth and of virtue, will purge the eyes to understand her text" (35). Again, an otherwise moralistically vague metaphor acquires a peculiar vitality here by echoing the earlier "transparent eyeball" reference. Here Emerson also revives the medieval, Patristic notion of nature as God's "Book of the Creatures," the world as a second sacred scripture. Purgation reminds us of the vanishing of mean egotism, and the two passages considered together suggest that for Emerson the visionary or poetic is also intellectual and moral (a debatable correlation in Blake).

"Discipline" gives us "the eye of the leaf" (40), a beautiful metaphor for a botanical morphological datum, and one which subtly suggests that other parts of the universe than man are "eyed," that there are congruences in natural organs, and that, perhaps, when the fully human eyeball becomes transparent, the world may look back. It is in "Discipline," also, that Emerson gives us the metaphor we have been expecting all along, the one as old as Plato's use of it in the allegory of the cave at the beginning of the seventh book of the *Republic;* "the eye—the mind" (45). It should be noted that this metaphor is only one figure in a variety of tropes of the eye in this book, and that it does not usurp the meanings of the others. Further qualification of it is provided by its immediate context, a paragraph on "the human form, of which all other organizations appear to be degradations" (45). If that statement were not Blakean enough, Emerson goes on, "In fact, the eye,—the mind,—is always accompanied by these forms, male and female" (45).

But that paragraph is by no means the most Blakean passage in *Nature.* In "Idealism" we get what appears to be a cliché, "When the eye of reason opens" (49), but the sentence continues, opening itself into Emersonian originality, "to outline and surface are at once added grace and expression. These proceed from imagination and affection, and abate somewhat of the angular distinctness of objects" (49–50). The sentence is a miniature history of ideas; it takes one last quick look back at the eighteenth century, then plunges resolutely into the uncharted romantic thought of its own. "Idealism" gives us more than one such somersault or reversal; in what might be a piece of comic phenomenology (but no less phenomenological for its comedy), Emerson advises: "Turn the eyes upside down, by looking at the landscape through your legs, and how agreeable is the picture, though you have seen it any time these twenty years!" (51). This passage is sometimes ridiculed by critics who fail to perceive that its disruption of rhetorical tone is a perfect objective correlative to its meaning. At any rate, "Idealism" provides the least substantial meanings of "eye" in *Nature.* "God never jokes with us," says Emerson. But Emerson, like Blake, sometimes does. "Idealism" is followed by "Spirit." There are no eyes in "Spirit."

Emerson's concluding chapter, "Prospects" (a term with visual connotations) more than makes up for that lack. It returns us to the visionary context of the image in the "transparent eyeball" passage of the "Nature" of chapter 1; the structure of the book, like *Finnegans Wake,* is circular.[8] "The ruin or the blank that we see when we look at nature, is in our own eye" (73). This sentence diagnoses what we suffer when we fail to let our eyeballs become transparent. "The axis of vision is not coincident with the axis of things, and so they appear not transparent but opaque" (73). These assertions are from a paragraph on "the redemption of the soul." The last reference to the organ of sight in *Nature* occurs in its eloquent peroration, which imagines what can occur as such a redemption: "So shall we come to look at the world with new eyes" (75). The last word in *Nature* is "sight." "The kingdom of man over nature, . . ." (a major project in the major prophecies of William Blake) "he shall enter without more wonder than the blind man feels who is gradually restored to perfect sight" (77).

In *Nature* the "eye" has more than one meaning. The image in its permutations throughout the text reveals a miniature anatomy of significations that are phenomenological, dialectical, and seriously playful. Like Blake's visionary expression, Emerson's thought in *Nature* is playful because it is making art, and serious because it is prophetic, unveiling as it does a program for the possible redemption of the human condition in a vision of a humanized universe. The "transparent eyeball" looks out from that verbal context. "When we dead awaken," as Emerson might have said, our eyeballs, too, will become transparent. In Emerson, the "redemption of the soul" begins with a walk in the woods, to discover not a new reality but the newness of eternal reality through new eyes. "I am nothing; I see all." Yes. But also: "The eye altering alters all."

Moving from Emerson to Blake requires no wide turn. Frye's explication of the concluding lines of "A Vision of the Last Judgment" will provide an accurate understanding of Blake's text, but perhaps it will do so better if considered in the context of other references to the eye in Blake.

In several other places Blake reiterates his idea of authentic human perception as seeing "through," not "with" the eye. In "Auguries of Innocence," we find, "We are led to Believe a Lie / When we see not Thro the Eye" (*Poetry and Prose* 492). Incorporating the same window image he uses in "A Vision of the Last Judgment," he writes in "The Everlasting Gospel": "This Lifes dim Windows of the Soul / Distorts the Heavens from Pole to Pole / And leads you to Believe a Lie / When you see with not thro the Eye" (520). And the title plate of *Visions of the Daughters of Albion* includes as its motto a neat repudiation of eighteenth-century sentimentality, "The Eye sees more than the Heart knows" (45), where he certainly means by "Eye" more than the "Corporeal" or "Vegetative" organ.

Both Emerson and Blake play dialectically with the sense of sight, endowing it with two different levels of meaning. One level is ordinary perception which is Blake's state of Generation, the norm of fallen humanity, and Emerson's sense in "Most persons do not see the sun. At least they have a very superficial seeing" (*Complete Works* 1:8). The second or extraordinary level, for which both Emerson and Blake write as evangelists, is that of the synthesizing imagination—Blake's ability to see the sun as the choir of the angels and Emerson's "transparent eyeball" through which he sees all. Both see the function itself as relative to the condition (intellectual or psychological) of the perceiver. We have seen in the first chapter of this study how attracted the older Emerson was to Blake's line, "The Eye altering alters All."

Blake expresses the same idea in his annotations to Reynolds: "Every eye sees differently. As the Eye—Such the Object" (*Poetry and Prose* 645). Ordinary, limited vision is for Blake one result of the Fall. In *The Book of Urizen,* Blake's parody of Genesis, we find this description of the creation of the fallen organ of seeing:

> His nervous brain shot branches
> Round the branches of his heart.
> On high into two little orbs
> And fixed in two little caves
> Hiding carefully from the wind,
> His Eyes beheld the deep,
> And a third Age passed over:
> And a state of dismal woe. (*Poetry and Prose* 76)

This was written in 1794. In the striking conceptual consistency which some of his commentators have trouble *seeing,* he is still saying exactly the same thing in *Jerusalem* in 1804: "The Eye of Man, a little narrow orb, closd up & dark" (49:34, *Poetry and Prose* 198); and, in case we missed it there, "And as their eye & ear shrunk, the heavens shrunk away" (66:40, *Poetry and Prose* 219).

In a letter of October, 1800, from Felpham, to his friend Thomas Butts, Blake described in playful but serious fashion fluctuations in his vision when he experienced the novelty of the sea shore:

> To my Friend Butts I write
> My first Vision of Light
> On the yellow sands sitting . . . .
> My Eyes did Expand
> Into regions of air
> Away from all Care
> Into regions of fire
> Remote from Desire . . . .
> My Eyes more & more

> Like a Sea without shore
> Continue Expanding
> The Heavens commanding
> Till the Jewels of Light
> Heavenly Men beaming bright
> Appeard as One Man . . . .
> Such the Vision to me
> Appeard on the Sea (*Poetry and Prose* 712–13)

This correspondent elicited from Blake some of his most revealing observations on the subject of seeing versus vision. In another, later letter to Butts (22 March 1802), he includes some verses which describe the "thistle" he saw as an "old Man grey."

> For double the vision my Eyes do see
> And a double vision is always with me
> With my inward Eye 'tis an old Man grey
> With my outward a Thistle across my way
> (*Poetry and Prose* 721)

In the conclusion of this poem in this letter Blake gets explicit about his four levels of knowledge:

> Now I a fourfold vision see
> And a fourfold vision is given to me
> Tis fourfold in my supreme delight
> And three fold in soft Beulahs night
> And twofold Always. May God us keep
> From Single vision & Newtons sleep
> (*Poetry and Prose* 722)

Here then, in a more systematic schema, Blake has given us a straightforward exposition of his poetic epistemology. "Fourfold" is fully imaginative or Edenic vision; "Three fold" is the comforting perspective of sexual love in Beulah; "Twofold Always" is "always" because it is the ordinary, daily level of subject-object relations in Generation. The lowest possible level is limited to materialistic perception (a state Blake elsewhere calls Ulro).

Emerson, too, likes schema, or, rather, he likes to play with schema for serious rhetorical purposes; and while it is an oversimplification, it is not too inaccurate a one, to compare Emerson's use of the lower level of the Understanding and the higher level of the Reason (imported slightly from Kant but very largely via Coleridge) to Blake's four levels. The Understanding comprises Blake's bottom two (Generation and Ulro), and the Reason Blake's top two (Beulah and Eden), if one allows for some respectable New England expurgation of Beulah. One must also allow for possible confusions arising from the term "Reason": in Emerson it is a higher faculty; Blake uses the term to describe Deists, and "Bacon Newton & Locke," and "Idiot Questioners"; in Blake it is merely analytical or logical, and "low" because "Energy is the only life and is from the Body and Reason is the bound or outward circumference of Energy" (*Poetry and Prose* 34). "Energy," not "Reason" is "Eternal Delight."

Neither Emerson nor Blake ever suggests that the eye functioning in imaginative vision is the norm, either for others or for themselves. Emerson's ambivalence on the matter of his own capacity for inspiration is well documented: "I am God in nature; I am a weed by the wall," he writes in "Circles" (*Complete Works* 2:307). And Blake confesses with that candor which is one of his most endearing traits: "The Greeks represent Chronos or Time is a very Aged Man this is Fable but the Real Vision of Time in Eternal Youth I have however somewhat accommodated my Figure of Time to the Common opinion as I myself am also infected with it & my Vision is also infected & I see Time Aged alas too much so" (*Poetry and Prose* 563).

What Blake insists upon with unfailing consistency is the superiority of the imaginative mode of perception, superior in the sense that its being imaginative makes it fully human. "What Jesus came to Remove was the Heathen or Platonic Philosophy which blinds the

Eye of Imagination The Real Man" ("Annotations to Berkeley's *Siris*," *Poetry and Prose* 664).

There exists a very large body of critical and scholarly commentary on perception and imagination in Emerson. There exists at least an equally large body of similar commentary on these same topics in Blake. It is one of the aims of the present study to permit the texts of Emerson and Blake in juxtaposition to illuminate each other about perception and vision, as about other matters. Several pertinent critical comments support this intertextual explication.[9]

Tony Tanner in "Emerson: The Unconquered Eye and the Enchanted Circle," observes that much of Emerson's work "is occupied with attempts to define the appropriate angle of vision" (310). He continues:

> He felt that one of America's deepest needs was a "general education of the eye" . . . . If things appeared to lack unity, that was because of some disorder in the eye: a new eye would unify the world in a new way— salvation is visual . . . . Emerson wanted this eye to see the world from scratch . . . . But from the start we should alert ourselves to a doubleness which is inherent in almost everything Emerson says about man's visual relationship with nature . . . . To pick up his own words, the world is both opaque and transparent—it both resists and invites visual penetration. (310–11)

We shall see later that this "inviting" and "resisting" of "penetration" on the part of Nature is typical behavior of Blake's Vala, nature as whore. Tanner goes on to raise objections: "There are distinct problems of organization and evaluation inherent in Emerson's concept of vision," because "Emerson is endorsing an eye which refuses to distinguish and classify" (318). Like Damrosch on Blake, Tanner here seems to forget that he is discussing a literary artist, not a scientific or

philosophic system-maker. Nevertheless, Emerson's enduring value
for Tanner remains literary. "His prose often seems to create a still-
life of separately attended-to particulars. It conveys a sense of the
radiance of things seen" (319).

Barbara Packer is one of a very small number of scholars who
make explicit connections between Emerson and Blake. In "The Instructed Eye: Emerson's Cosmogony in 'Prospects'"—in addition to
observing in a note that Emerson's "preference for visual metaphors"
and his "insistence that vision was at least partially under the control
of the will" relate to his personal experience with problems of eyesight—she raises questions about the meaning of Emerson's phrase
"axis of vision" and his terms "transparent" and "opaque." She suggests that Emerson's "axis of vision" is "a formula which, properly
expanded, generates a unified and highly original myth of creation, fall, redemption, and apocalypse. The existence of a separate
object-world is, for Emerson as for Blake, the product of a Fall or
Dislocation, and the "axis of vision" formula is Emerson's laconic
story of that Fall: *Jerusalem* as it might have been written by Calvin
Coolidge" (209). Further, Packer offers two helpful explications
whose relevance will be discussed later in this study. First, "When
Emerson calls the world transparent . . . he is referring not to its appearance but to its intelligibility" (219); and second, "The Transparent
Eye-ball is a circle whose center is everywhere and its circumference
nowhere" (220), a paraphrase of Emerson's paraphrase of St. Augustine's description of God, which appears in the first paragraph of
"Circles."

Perhaps the most comprehensive view of the background of the
sight/vision metaphor as we find it in both Emerson and Blake is the
analysis by M. H. Abrams in *Natural Supernaturalism*. Blake's view
of vision, according to Abrams, is completely tied into Blake's account of the Fall: "From a flexible, 'expanded,' or imaginative mode
of vision—capable both of seeing the one as many and the many as
one, and all as human—man has lapsed into a fixed and 'narrowed'
mode of 'single vision' by means of the physical eye alone, which

sees reality as a multitude of isolated individuals in a dehumanized world" (341).

Abrams notes Blake's relating of ideas of sight and vision to concepts of liberty and servitude, whereby the triumphs of Urizen become correlative with a shrinking of human perception (364); he generalizes: "to the Romantic poet, all depends on [man's] mind as it engages with the world in the act of perceiving. Hence the extraordinary emphasis throughout this era on the eye and the object and the relation between them" (375). Abrams sees throughout the Romantic movement a shift in value from physical perception to imaginative insight. "The shift is from physical optics to what Carlyle in the title of one of his essays called 'Spiritual Optics'" (377). Finally, Abrams includes Emerson in his discussion of "perceptual transvaluations," quoting Emerson's journal entry for June 21, 1838, that "a fact is an Epiphany of God" (413).

What does the "transparent eyeball," the eye which is seen through, not with, observe? An answer that tells us frustratingly little is "Nature." The theme of this chapter is that that eye (always to be distinguished from the nontransparent or unimaginative eye) sees "nature" as the rest of the body of which it is one organ. What is essential to both Emerson's and Blake's theories of "vision" is the concept of a humanized universe.

Blake's originality consists in part in his ubiquitous rejection of both traditional (classical) mythology and orthodox Christianity. Damrosch is certainly accurate when he notes that "Blake wants to remythologize, not demythologize, in order to recover a truth that is not just a bag of debased coins" (12). Blake is equally heterodox, from both a Platonic and a Christian worldview, in his insistence that reality is human. As an artist (a poet, a painter), he expresses that view imaginatively, poetically in his own myth, and though the particular features of his mythic formulations changed throughout his career— from *The Marriage of Heaven and Hell* to *Jerusalem*—its central, radically humanistic core remains the same. The story changes every time he tells it, from work to work, and—disconcertingly enough—

within the same work *(The Four Zoas),* but it is always the story of the "giant form" Albion or Humanity, who underwent a Fall into the fragments of the human and the natural as we now know them, "natural" and "human" being dissociated in the fallen world. Since all of the poems necessarily express fragments of this myth (William Blake exists in time, not in eternity; writing and engraving are temporal and material; he is a worker in the fallen world), the reader can only reconstruct the central narrative by piecing the parts back together. Hence any reading of Blake is an effort to reorganize that human history. This "getting it together," which requires the imagination of the reader, becomes then a microcosmic effort of the larger synthesis which will put it "all" back together, ontologically. Each reader must do part of the work of Los.

This rather energetic "reader response" is not entirely idiosyncratic. The effort is really not much different from that required of the student of Greek mythology, when he pieces together the fragments about the Olympians from his reading of Homer, Hesiod, Pindar, the tragedians, Ovid, and later commentators. It is also like the effort at a unified view of Christianity undertaken by the orthodox Christian, who must put together the four Gospels (their number is significant), the Old Testament analogs to them (from a Christian point of view), and the commentaries and interpretations of the Church Fathers (who did exactly this kind of reading) to achieve a coherent "story" of Jesus as part of a larger coherent story that includes Creation, Fall, Redemption, and Apocalypse. Since *The Book of Urizen* or *Jerusalem* or *The French Revolution* are fragments of Blake's large story, we can see its meaning only by piecing them together. There will of course be inconsistencies, as there are, for example, between the Gospel of John and the book of Ecclesiastes. Blake is very consciously rewriting the Bible ("remythologizing"); he tells us in a number of places that that is what he is doing, and his titles, allusions, and rhetorical modes (principally the "prophetic") constantly remind us of that fact. His "story" is also the history of the universe, from Creation to Apocalypse. To discuss Blake's myth apart from the individual poems that express its parts is to engage in an artificial but necessary exercise if we are to understand his total vision. Any capsulization or summary incurs inevitable oversimplification in the interest of coherence. The major commentators on Blake have performed just that valuable but imperfect service. No synopsis of Blake will satisfy every reader. But in order to see Blake's worldview in relation to that of Emerson, some use of such a shortcut is necessary. Frye's is perhaps the most elegant and the most coherent, although his detractors have complained—with some justification—that it is too coherent, that he ignores too many fissures and ruptures in the poems.[10] One must respect the tender sensibilities of those for whom coherence is a liability, but Frye is useful for the purposes of this study.

> In Blake there are certain modifications of the orthodox account of the Fall. One is that as all reality is mental, the fall of man's mind involved a corresponding fall of the physical world. Another is, that as God is Man, Blake follows some of the Gnostics and Boehme in believing that the fall of man involved a fall in part of the divine nature. Not all, for then there would be no imagination left to this one; but part, because it is impossible to derive a bad world from a good God, without a great deal of unconvincing special pleading and an implicit denial of the central fact of Christianity, the identity of God and Man. The conclusion for Blake, and the key to much of his symbolism, is that the fall of man and the creation of the physical world were the same event. (41)

Frye further elucidates this "key":

> The fall of man involved a fall in part but not all of the divine nature. The particular "Giant form" or

> "Eternal" to which we belong has fallen, the aggregate of spirits we call mankind or humanity and Blake calls Albion (Adam in Blake has his regular place as the symbol of the physical body or the natural man). When Albion or mankind fell, the unity of man fell too, and although our imagination tells us we belong to some larger organism even if we cannot see it as God, in the meantime we are locked up in separated opaque scattered bodies. If the whole of mankind were once more integrated in a single spiritual body the universe as we see it would burst. (43–44)

Blake's central concept here is as radical a departure as possible both from orthodox Christian teaching about the transcendent Deity and from Newton and Locke's description of the physical universe. A third formulation from Frye may prove helpful:

> The most inclusive vision possible . . . is to see the universe as One Man, who to a Christian is Jesus. On nearer view Jesus is seen as a "Council of God" or group of "eternals" or Patriarchs, seen by ancient prophets as dwelling in a Golden Age of peace and happiness. On still nearer view these patriarchs, the memory of whom survives in the Bible under the accounts of Abraham, Isaac and Jacob, resolve themselves into vast numbers of individual men.
>
> One of these Eternals, named Albion, has fallen. Albion includes, presumably, all the humanity that we know in the world of time and space, though visualized as a single Titan or giant. The history of the world from its creation, which was part of his fall, to the last Judgment is his sleep. The yet unfallen part of God made seven attempts to awaken him, and in the seventh Jesus himself descended into the world of Generation and began his final redemption. (125)

The essential feature of Blake's myth, in other words, is cosmic personification.

One might summarize these summaries of Blake's myth in the following rough paraphrase: The Fall was the fall of the Ancient and Universal Man, Albion, one of the "Eternals" who abided within the "Eternal Council of God," a divine man with absolute wisdom, the circumference of every known thing outside of whom nothing in the universe existed. When he fell, his broken and scattered parts became the physical universe. It is through his greatly weakened energies and powers that earthly man, his miniature replica and therefore a god, is slowly struggling upward toward Albion's recreation, and simultaneously denying and destroying that recreation.

I have gone into some detail to provide a working outline or model of Blake's central myth because I am going to present the same myth one more time, but in this case not from the imagination of William Blake. Here is Ralph Waldo Emerson's version of the myth of Albion:

> I shall . . . conclude this essay [*Nature*] with some traditions of man and nature, which a certain poet sang to me; and which, as they have always been in the world, and perhaps reappear to every bard, may be both history and prophecy.
>
> The foundations of man are not in matter, but in spirit. But the element of spirit is eternity. To it, therefore, the longest series of events, the oldest chronologies are young and recent. In the cycle of *the universal man,* from whom all known individuals proceed, centuries are points, and all history is but the epoch of one degradation.
>
> . . . .
>
> A man is a god in ruins. When men are innocent, life shall be longer, and shall pass into the immortal as gently as we awake from dreams. Now, the world would be insane and rabid, if these disorganizations

should last for hundreds of years. It is kept in check by
death and infancy. Infancy is the perpetual Messiah,
which comes into the arms of fallen men, and pleads
with them to return to paradise.
    Man is the dwarf of himself. Once he was perme-
ated and dissolved by spirit. He filled nature with his
overflowing currents. Out from him sprang the sun
and moon; from man the sun, from woman the moon.
The laws of his mind, the periods of his actions ex-
ternized themselves into day and night, into the year
and the seasons. But, having made for himself this
huge *shell,* his waters retired; he no longer fills the veins
and veinlets; he is shrunk to a drop. He sees that the
structure still fits him, but fits him colossally. Say,
rather, once it fitted him, now it corresponds to him
from far and on high. He adores timidly his own work.
Now is man the follower of the sun, and woman the
follower of the moon. Yet sometimes he starts in his
slumber, and wonders at himself and his house, and
muses strangely at the resemblance betwixt him and it.
(*Complete Works* 1:70–72, emphasis added)

As Barbara Packer has observed of this passage from the concluding chapter of *Nature,* "The general shape of Emerson's cosmogony is
very close to Blake's, even down to details of phrasing" (*Emerson's Fall*
67). Harold Bloom's comparative analysis is bolder:

The eighth and final chapter [of *Nature*], "Prospects"... gives us Emerson at his most apocalyptic. The
prose-poem sung by the Orphic poet states magnifi-
cently a highly visionary account of Man's Fall, one that
verges on the Blakean heresy of identifying the Creation and the Fall. Yet here, too, at his most rapturous,
Emerson is not unconfused. Blake's version of the Fall
is properly a protest against all dualisms—Pauline,
Cartesian, Lockean. A unitary Man fell, and his fall

created dualistic man and dualistic nature. Emerson's Orphic poet is himself both dualist and monist, monist in his vision of what should be, but oddly dualist in what is. Yet if we set aside, arbitrarily, the statement that "the foundations of man are not in matter, but in spirit," we are left with the closest American equivalent to Blakean myth ever hazarded.[11]

In *Nature* what unites the "song" of the "Orphic Poet" in the last chapter to the description of the "transparent eyeball" in the first is the image of the cosmic man, the universe as human. "The currents of the Universal Being circulate through me; I am part or parcel of God." This visionary affirmation of the eyeball which sees in a "pre-fallen" condition is also a personification in which the blood of the cosmic living body supplies its organ of sight. Later, the Orphic Poet explains why that visionary moment can be only a moment. The "Being" in both passages is the same universal living body.

The parallels with Blake are indeed striking, especially when we bear in mind that Emerson had no acquaintance in 1836 or later with Blake's myth (nor, for all practical purposes, did any other readers until the twentieth century). But prophets validate each other—most dramatically when in different times and places they say the same thing. Here the correlations deserve a closer look than they usually get, even by such perceptive observers of the parallels as Packer and Bloom.

Emerson introduces the song of the Orphic Poet by describing its message as "traditions" which "have always been in the world," and which "may be both history and prophecy." *Nature* is Emerson's first published work. Blake writes in his first "canonical" (engraved) work, *All Religions are One:* "an universal Poetic Genius exists. . . . the Poetic Genius . . . is every where call'd the Spirit of Prophecy" (*Poetry and Prose* 1).

In the "song" itself "the universal man from whom all known individuals proceed" is clearly Blake's unfallen Albion. The man who is "a god in ruins" and "the dwarf of himself" is the Poet's description of those "known individuals" in their separate existences, or man in his fallen condition. "Infancy" as the "Messiah," innocence as the persuader of a return to paradise, is the central image running throughout Blake's *Songs of Innocence* ("I a child & thou a lamb, / We are called by his name" (*Poetry and Prose* 9). The cosmic dimensions of Emerson's "universal man" reflect the descriptions of Albion's parts in both the minor and major prophecies of Blake. The formation of the sun and moon from his body, the division into sexes, the genesis of time and space—all these as externalizations, an extraordinarily Blakean concept—all function in Blake's account of the Fall.

But perhaps the most striking parallels, beyond Emerson's "universal man" himself as Blake's Albion, are the two images of the "shell" and the "slumber." In Blake the "Mundane Shell" is the fallen perception of the physical universe, nature or the physical world as "otherness," as, when we look up into the dome of the sky, always present and always intangible, we seem to ourselves to be very small prisoners trapped inside a very large egg. The "slumber" of Emerson's "universal man" is the actual history of the world for Blake, "Albion's sleep of death," from which he can be awakened only by imaginative apocalypse. Further, when man "adores timidly his own work," he is in Blakean terms seeing his "Emanation" (everything the human being loves and creates) as external to himself, which may, for Blake, be the cause of the Fall.

Both Emerson and Blake wrote about "alienation" long before twentieth-century existentialists used the term. Unlike those abstract thinkers, the two Romanticists explain its genesis. Those strange and striking "resemblances" which Emerson's half-asleep man wonders at are here not the arbitrary "correspondences" that both Emerson and Blake found in Swedenborg, but in their mythic accounts these correspondences are the evidence that the scattered pieces have corresponding parts because they once belonged to the same body.

It is often assumed that the visionary, poetic, rhapsodic, "Orphic" voice disappears in Emerson's writing after his earliest essays. Ever since Stephen Whicher's overly influential *Freedom and Fate* convinced critics that the radical Emersonian "chariot of fire" depreciated around 1841 to an old conservative pickup hauling rhetorical clinkers and ashy clichés, the notion of a later diminished Emerson has held sway. Even Bloom, so perceptive about Emerson's affinities with radical romantic thought, seems to concur with the Whicher hypothesis, citing 1832 to 1841 as "Emerson's great period," although he allows for "a sudden but brief resurgence in 1846" (*Ringers in the Tower* 292). More recently, scholars such as Packer *(Emerson's Fall)* and Neufeldt *(The House of Emerson)* have worked persuasively against that trend, but a great deal more needs to be done in this direction, to pay less attention to Whicher's assumptions and more to the actual writings of the later Emerson. If that later work is examined closely, evidence can be found to contradict Whicher's notion of discontinuity in Emerson, the supposed split between the prophet of freedom and the "acquiescent" victim of fate. Such evidence can disclose threads and motifs (in dialectical opposition, it should be added, with their conceptual contraries) of the earlier "visionary" fabric. A case in point is the message of the Orphic Poet in *Nature*. It is simply not true that Emerson never sounded that particular note again. In fact, Emerson recalls the idea of the "universal man" in several later passages. These later references are not repetitions but variations on the theme (as Blake never simply repeats himself but plays variations on his mythic story). The "universal man" appears in slightly different rhetorical guises in at least three other Emersonian texts.

The first is admittedly still early; it occurs in the context of the "Man Thinking" passage in the "American Scholar" address of 1837. Both its closeness to and its difference from the "Universal Man" in *Nature* are of interest.

> It is one of those fables which out of an unknown antiquity convey an unlooked-for wisdom, that the gods,

in the beginning, divided Man into men, that he might be more helpful to himself; just as the hand was divided into fingers, the better to answer its end.

The old fable covers a doctrine ever new and sublime; that there is One Man,—present to all particular men only partially, or through one faculty; and that you must take the whole society to find the whole man. Man is not a farmer, or a professor, or an engineer, but he is all. Man is priest, and scholar, and statesman, and producer, and soldier. In the *divided* or social state these functions are parcelled out to individuals. . . . The fable implies that the individual, to possess himself, must sometimes return from his own labor to embrace all the other laborers. But, unfortunately, this original unit, this fountain of power, has been so distributed to multitudes, has been so minutely subdivided and peddled out, that it is spilled into drops, and cannot be gathered. The state of society is one in which the members have suffered amputation from the trunk, and strut about so many walking monsters,—a good finger, a neck, a stomach, an elbow, but never a man.

. . . .

In this distribution of functions the scholar is the delegated intellect. In the right state he is *Man Thinking*. In the degenerate state, when the victim of society, he tends to become a mere thinker. (*Complete Works* 1:82–84)

Although Edward Waldo Emerson glossed the source of this passage as Aristophanes' fable in Plato's *Symposium* (*Complete Works* 1:417), he ignored the literal term of that fable's metaphor, sexual division. From the perspective of the present study, Emerson's analog (though not source) would be again Blake's Albion, the "Ancient Man" or the "Eternal Man." What is curious about Emerson's passage is its turning upon itself. It begins with suggested optimism; human division is helpful to humanity. However, it quickly comes to see that same human division, in the present "divided" or "degenerate" state, as an evidence of the Fall; in fact, human division is seen as dismemberment. Blake's large myth simply dramatizes various aspects of that Fall into disunity—the divisions of Albion into the Zoas, their divisions from their Emanations, down to the present "divided" or "degenerate" social condition of war between nations and psychic splits in the self. What is significant in the Emersonian passage is the tracing of present disorganization of human culture, a fragmentation, back to a primal division of the "One Man."

A second variation of Emerson's "Universal Man" occurs significantly later, ten years after *Nature*. It is the passage on the "Central Man" in his Journal of 1846:

> We shall one day talk with the central man, and see again in the varying play of his features all the features which have characterised our darlings, & stamped themselves in fire on the heart: then, as the discourse rises out of the domestic & personal, & his countenance waxes grave & great, we shall fancy that we talk with Socrates, & behold his countenance: then the discourse changes, & the man, and we see the face & hear the tones of Shakspeare,—the body & the soul of Shakspeare living & speaking with us, only that Shakspeare seems below us. A change again, and the countenance of our companion is youthful & beardless, he talks of form & colour & the (boundless) riches of design; it is the face of the painter Raffaelle that confronts us with the visage of a girl, & the easy audacity of a creator. In a moment it was Michel Angelo; then Dante; afterwards it was the Saint Jesus, and the immensities of moral truth & power embosomed us. And so it appears that these great secular personalities were only expressions of his face chasing each other like the

rack of clouds. Then all will subside, & I find myself
alone. I dreamed & did not know my dreams. (*JMN*,
IX, 395)

It is certainly one of the most beautiful passages in all of Emerson's prose. With the mention of two of Blake's favorite painters,
Michelangelo and Raphael—as well as the greatest of medieval poets,
whose masterpiece Blake illustrated—Emerson here has again provided an evocation of the "universal man" of *Nature,* the "One Man"
of the "American Scholar," and his own version of Blake's Albion or
universal humanity as one personification.

Bloom is right to regard 1846 as another vintage year for Emerson. It is a year in which on more than one occasion his style becomes
rhapsodic, and in these modes he sometimes sounds uncannily like
Blake. Two pages earlier in the same journal from which the "Central
Man" passage was quoted above, Emerson writes: "Men quarrel with
your rhetoric. Society chokes with a trope, like a child with the croup.
They much prefer Mr Prose, & Mr Hoarse-as-Crows, to the danger-
ous conversation of Gabriel and the archangel Michael perverting all
rules, & bounding continually from earth to heaven (*Journals and
Notebooks* 9:395). The prophets sometimes become angry, and when
they do they seem to make the same allusions, and even the same
discoveries. Is it Blake inspiring Emerson here, polemical, satiric, self-
justifying, discovering the subversions of the angels "perverting all
rules"?

Whatever prompted Emerson in 1846 to bound "continually
from earth to heaven," that year was by no means the last time he
expressed a version of the "universal man." The "central man" in
1846 is a collective of imaginative geniuses (including Jesus) with
a fluctuating identity: now Socrates, now Shakespeare, then Raphael,
Michelangelo, Dante, Jesus. But the passage begins with a line
Emerson added later: "Walking one day in the fields I met a man."
And before he becomes Socrates and company, he has the features of
"our darlings," and at first the discourse is "domestic & personal."

Emerson is suggesting here a diversity-in-unity image which is frequent and important in Blake, and also one of his more difficult insights.

> Then those in Great Eternity met in the
> Council of God
> As one Man for contracting their Exalted Senses
> They behold Multitude or Expanding they
> behold as one
> As One man all the Universal family & that
> one Man
> They call Jesus the Christ & they in him &
> he in them
> Live in Perfect harmony in Eden the land of
> life
> Consulting as One Man above the Mountain
> of Snowdon Sublime (*Poetry and Prose* 310–11)

Blake expresses the same idea in "A Vision of the Last Judgment": "these various States I have seen in my Imagination when distant they appear as One Man but as you approach they appear Multitudes of Nations" (*Poetry and Prose* 556–57). What explains the fluctuation is a difference in perspective—fallen versus unfallen vision, imaginative versus corporeal perception. The letter to Thomas Butts, cited earlier, incorporates the human collective with a natural phenomenon, "the Jewels of Light / Heavenly Men beaming bright / Appeard as One Man" (*Poetry and Prose* 713). Emerson never goes so far as to include the sunlight in the image of the "Central Man," but the fluctuating identity, the many as one, the shifting apotheoses, the representative human faces that are the shifting appearances (like clouds) of the one human face, are certainly very Blakean.

"Representative" may suggest a key to Emerson's handling of the concept of the universal man. The "central man" passage is from the Journal of 1846. Emerson published *Representative Men* on January 1,

1850; the lectures which were the original versions of the chapters of the book were given in Boston in 1845–46 (*Complete Works* 4:297–98). Several of the "faces" of the "central man" reappear as portraits in the essays of the book. Jesus is absent, but Swedenborg as "The Mystic" may be taking his place; Socrates reappears in some detail in "Plato"; Shakespeare, himself, is there. The painters and Dante are replaced by Montaigne, Napoleon, and Goethe; and the skeptic, the man of action, and the writer recall the mood of the end of the "central man" passage— "I find myself alone"—which will also furnish the terminal motif of "Illusions" ten years later. What holds these six "biographical" sketches together? Emerson's introduction, "Uses of Great Men," will not satisfactorily answer that question. What, indeed, do they "represent"?

Critical Heroism wants to suggest, over the embarrassed objections of scholarly Prudence, that Emerson's *Representative Men* are his *six* Zoas. Like the faces in the dream of the "Central Man," these nonbiographical biographies suggest six fragments of total human wholeness, that each represents one aspect of the central man.[12]

If one turns from that "Central Man" passage and looks at the six sketches in *Representative Men,* it becomes obvious that no one of them, not Plato, nor Swedenborg, nor Napoleon, nor Montaigne, nor Goethe, nor even Shakespeare is "Man Thinking" as described in "The American Scholar." This deficiency in each figure explains why each chapter of the book includes a very negative criticism; these are "partial portraits," to borrow Gertrude Stein's suggestive phrase. Having read the whole book, the reader puts together in his own mind these six "representatives" and may then conceive of what Emerson means by a "central man." Each figure represents one fragmented face.

Putting them thus together reveals not only a more accurate image of Emerson's "Man Thinking," but a sharp difference between Emerson's "central man" and Blake's integrated, composite Albion. Even as six Zoas, Emerson's representatives leave out a lot of what is essential in Blake's image of human wholeness. Napoleon,

Montaigne, and Goethe bear similarities to Blake's Urizen (reason), while Swedenborg, Plato, and Shakespeare may approximate his Los (imagination). The human faculties conspicuously absent (if I may oversimplify here) are sensation (Tharmas) and sexual emotion (Luvah). This composite would be characteristic of Emerson; just as Blake's four Zoas are a highly personal projection of Blake himself. The absence of passion and sensation here lend some support to Joel Porte's negative criticism of Emerson, that he was "intellectually and emotionally predisposed to leave sense experience alone" ("Nature as Symbol" 459). Of course Emerson's "Zoas" are at a conceptual and metaphorical remove from Blake's; they are all historical figures while Blake's are personifications of psychic impulses and forces. Nevertheless, reading Emerson's subjects as something like Blake's "giant forms," as allegorized, larger-than-life representatives of human characteristics, rescues them from possible charges as failed biographies or bastard literary critiques. They may in fact work in that mysterious form, the Emersonian "essay," much as the actual historical characters do in Blake's poems, such as George Washington in *America* or Louis XVI in "The French Revolution," where biographical verisimilitude is far from the point and no sensitive reader demands or even expects it.

Deducing a "central man" from Emerson's *Representative Men* is admittedly speculative. But explicit textual evidence of a still later avatar appears in Emerson's work, this particular incarnation one that only an American writer could write or think. It occurs in "Abraham Lincoln," the speech Emerson gave in Concord on April 19, 1865, at the memorial service for the assassinated president. We are thirty years past the "rhapsodies" of 1836. Emerson is thirty years older. A heart-breaking Civil War has further, and horribly, externalized human division. Here is Emerson, on Lincoln, in 1865.

Lincoln was a "quite native, aboriginal man" (*Complete Works* 9:330). He was a "plain man of the people" (332). However, the phrase "man of the people" in Emerson's context becomes not an abstraction or cliché, but a metaphor with a literal force, an Apocalyptic revelation. "The poor negro said of him, on an impressive occasion, 'Massa Linkum am eberywhere'" (332). Further,

> He is the true history of the American people in his time. Step by step he walked before them; slow with their slowness, quickening his march by theirs, the true representative of this continent; an entirely public man; father of his country, the pulse of twenty millions throbbing in his heart, the thought of their minds articulated by his tongue. (335)

In this passage, Lincoln is Jesus, "walk[ing] before them," living, suffering, and dying for the American people; Lincoln is Albion, "the true representative of this continent." And, as both, and with the people's pulse in his heart and their thought on his tongue, he is the "Universal Man" of *Nature,* the "One Man" of the "American Scholar," the "Central Man" of 1846.

The visionary eye of Emerson or Blake, the "transparent eyeball," the eye looked "through" not "with," sees the world or nature as a living human form, the rest of the body of which that eye is one organ. It sees the universe as human, and that cosmic humanity appears in history in different avatars or individual incarnations, as Jesus or John Milton in Blake, as the Orphic Poet or Lincoln in Emerson. It can be seen as a "multitude"; it can be seen as "one man." This perspective is exclusively visionary.

But the visionary moment is just that, a moment. The rest of the time Emerson, as well as Blake, operates on the level of "Generation." In dialectical terms, the visionary and nonvisionary modes can be seen as basic polarities operating within the work of both writers. Emerson keeps moving back and forth between Blake's "unfallen" and "fallen" worlds. And so does Blake. Only the very last lines of *The Four Zoas, Milton,* and *Jerusalem* are apocalyptic. The Orphic Poet appears as the rhapsodist, not Emerson the public lecturer or publishing essayist. These visionary moments, however, determine the character of the rest of Emerson's and Blake's work; they create the distinctive shape of their thought.

This dialectical play between the visionary and nonvisionary in the work of both writers may at least partially resolve the critical debate about whether they are monists or dualists. They are monist when expressing the voice of the "universal man." They are dualist when dramatizing (Blake) or diagnosing (Emerson) the symptoms of his fall. As Harold Bloom put it in the passage quoted earlier in this chapter, "A unitary man fell, and his fall created dualistic man and dualistic nature" (*Ringers* 224). Blake's and Emerson's vision of a personified ontological unity gives point and depth to their critiques of the partial perspectives of the ordinary human condition— "a finger, a neck, a stomach, an elbow, but never a man," as Emerson says (*Complete Works* 1:83). Further, these two writers can be usefully and revealingly connected in this context: Blake's "metaphysical" myth illuminates Emerson's "mythic" metaphysics. Emerson's abstractions do not float so freely in our minds if we recall the Blakean underlying personification which anchors them on the literal level. Blake's dramatic, prophetic epics seem less arbitrarily self-indulgent when related to Emerson's "cultural" (social and ethical) concerns.

Such a visionary perspective (even if only sporadic) creates a paradoxically practical stance in regard to "the world." Different as they were in circumstances—Emerson eminently public, Blake tragically private—their biographers convincingly show how practical both were in facing the daily problems of their lives. In both men this practicality is the uncompromising individualism, almost the solipsism, of a visionary. What save them from solipsism is the writer's mission, the need to communicate a message to an audience. Both the solitary engraver and the public lecturer were teachers.

Near the very end of *Nature,* Emerson's Orphic Poet returns to exhort the reader:

> Every spirit builds itself a house, and beyond its house
> a world, and beyond its world a heaven. Know then

that the world exists for you. For you is the phenomenon perfect. What we are, that only can we see. All that Adam had, all that Ceaser could, you have and can do. Adam called his house, heaven and earth; Ceasar called his house, Rome; you perhaps call yours, a cobbler's trade; a hundred acres of ploughed land; or a scholar's garret. Yet line for line and point for point your dominion is as great as theirs, though without fine names. Build therefore your own world. (*Complete Works* 1:76)

Blake, in *Milton*, offers the same value:

> The Sky is an immortal Tent built by the
> Sons of Los
> And every Space that a Man views around
> his dwelling-place:
> Standing on his own roof, or in his garden
> on a mount
> Of twenty-five cubits in height, such a
> space is his Universe;
> And on its verge the Sun rises & sets. the
> Clouds bow
> To meet the flat Earth & the Sea in such an
> ordered Space:
> The Starry heavens reach no further but here
> bend and set
> On all sides & the two Poles turn on their
> valves of gold:
> And if he move his dwelling-place, his heavens
> also move. (*Poetry and Prose* 127)

As for the brute fact of the "otherness" of objective reality as seen through ordinary, fallen perception, that is the topic of the next chapter. Neither Emerson nor Blake can be read as a Kantian idealist; neither rejects the existence of objective reality; neither relegates it to mere "phenomena." Although Emerson in the "idealism" chapter of *Nature* flirts with such metaphysics in the "noble doubt" about "whether nature outwardly exists" he rather quickly reveals himself to be the pragmatic American by asking, "What difference does it make?" (*Complete Works* 1:47).[13] He goes on, "whether nature enjoy a substantial existence without, or is only in the apocalypse of the mind, it is alike useful and venerable to me" (48). And he further protests in the same chapter, "I do not wish to fling stones at my beautiful mother, nor soil my gentle nest" (59).

"What difference does it make?" has most practical philosophical applications. Emerson's position, like Blake's, is not that objective reality does not exist, but that it is simply not very important that it does so. Here the visionary moment corrects the overall perspective. At the very end of *Nature* the Orphic Poet prophesies what will happen in the building of one's own world: "A correspondent revolution in things will attend the influx of the spirit. So fast will disagreeable appearances, swine, spiders, snakes, pests, madhouses, prisons, enemies, vanish; they are temporary and shall no more be seen. The sordor and filths of nature, the sun shall dry up, and the wind exhale" (*Complete Works* 1:76).

Blake expresses the same sentiments. He does not deny that disagreeable facts exist (*The Four Zoas* includes a multitude of them), but asserts that it does not matter that they do:

> Error is Created Truth is Eternal Error or Creation will
> be Burned Up & then & not till then Truth or Eter-
> nity will appear It is Burnt up the Moment Men cease
> to behold it I assert for My self that I do not behold
> the Outward Creation & that to me it is hindrance &
> not Action it is as the Dirt upon my feet No part of
> Me. (*Poetry and Prose* 565)

This last simile brilliantly reveals Blake's perception of reality. The dirt upon Blake's feet is *real*, but he accurately sees the "Outward

Creation" for what and where it is; the dirt is upon his feet, not in his eyes.

What Emerson and Blake both express in these passages is not a denial of the existence of objective reality, but a radical reevaluation of it. Blake's dirt is real (he was, after all, a gardener); spiders and prisons exist in Massachusetts. They simply appear as insignificant for the person who has experienced total imaginative vision. The body of the Universal Man would include an anus as well as an eye, but in a state of health there is no good reason for Albion to thrust his attention up his rectum.

The humanized universe would have been an irrational fantasy to an eighteenth-century Newtonian. It is no longer so to the scientific mind of the twentieth century. Science has caught up with Blake (and Emerson) as cosmological prophets. If some of the "humanist" commentators on Blake seem to be observing him through the glasses of Newton, Bacon, and Locke, capturing only a dismembered Blake, it seems at the same time that a physicist like Bronowski can be quite comfortable viewing a whole Blake. Neither Emerson nor Blake rejected the physical universe; they merely rejected the picture of it made by Newton and Locke. Our own picture of that physical universe is much closer to the Blakean than to the Newtonian paradigm, more Emersonian than Lockean. "Nature is not fixed but fluid," according to Emerson (*Complete Works* 1:76), describing Blake's "eternal world that ever groweth" (*Poetry and Prose* 60). The phenomenologist Hannah Arendt, a thinker who has never been accused of indulging in flights of fancy, summarizes the way in which twentieth-century astrophysicists have come to concur with Emerson and Blake, have come to recognize that a "humanized universe" is considerably more than a poetic conceit:

> The modern astrophysical world view, which began with Galileo, and its challenge to the adequacy of the senses to reveal reality, have left us a universe of whose qualities we know no more than the way they affect

> our measuring instruments, and—in the words of
> Eddington—"the former have as much resemblance to
> the latter as a telephone number to a subscriber." In-
> stead of objective qualities, in other words, we find
> instruments, and instead of nature or the universe—
> in the words of Heisenberg—man encounters only
> himself. (261)

Both Emerson and Blake have told us that the scientist must also be a visionary if he is to see anything at all. But the visionary moment passes, and the rest of the time we look through fallen senses at the evidence of the Fall—the other, darker tail side of the dialectical coin whose head is vision; Vala instead of Albion; fate or illusion in place of the free exercise of the self. The Fall is the topic of the next chapter. This chapter, where it has quoted the visionary utterances of Emerson and Blake, has been about Creation.

[3]

Circles, Wheels, and Cycles

The eye is the first circle; the horizon which it forms is the second; and throughout nature this primary figure is repeated without end.

—Emerson

The same dull round even of a univer[s]e would soon become a mill with complicated wheels.

—Blake

"AH! SUN-FLOWER" is one of Blake's *Songs of Experience;* it has no companion piece in *Innocence.*

Ah Sun-flower! weary of time,
Who countest the steps of the Sun;
Seeking after that sweet golden clime
Where the travellers journey is done.

Where the Youth pined away with desire,
And the pale Virgin shrouded in snow:
Arise from their graves and aspire,
Where my Sun-flower wishes to go. (*Poetry and Prose* 25)

There is no counterpart in *Innocence* because this poem, often cited as one of the most beautiful in the English language, expresses a perception of the fallen world which no innocent persona would be capable of. That perception is ghastly, an argument for total despair. It is not the only song in *Experience* to sound that note: "The Sick Rose" and "London," in two very different ways, convey the same message. "Ah! Sun-flower" envisions human existence in terms of endless futility and frustration. It suggests the mood at the end of *King Lear*. It is Blake's version of Sartre's *No Exit*.

Given the enormous amount of commentary and interpretation devoted to Blake's work, it is both surprising and disappointing that the poems are so seldom analyzed simply as poems. "Ah! Sun-flower" rewards such an examination. Blake uses an anapestic rhythm (frequent in *Innocence* and *Experience)*, here structured in trimeters. Such a rhythm might suggest a lilt as it does in "The Echoing Green" of *Innocence*, but here it is—to post-Romantic ears, at any rate—more a macabre waltz, the dance Byron was to satirize a generation later. This waltz is a Lisztian "Mephisto Waltz," a "Dance of Death," and, given the age of the human protagonists, a *Kindertotenlied*.

The nonhuman protagonist is the sunflower, the most dramatic of the heliotropic plants because of its enormous and sunlike head. The first stanza describes its life as an endlessly frustrated attempt at the impossible; it follows the course of the sun throughout the day in an effort to unite with the sun in its "sweet golden clime." There is a pun on "clime"; the "climb" of the sunflower seeks the region of the sun, but the pun reminds us that the sun, too, is climbing, and perhaps as "weary of time" as the sunflower, so that the notion of the place where the traveller's "journey is done" is patently false, an error. The geometric image which the stanza draws is that of an endlessly repeated arc, one segment of a circle. We have seen in "The Mental Traveller" that the circle is an image of frustration for Blake; even more frustrating would be a repeated portion of a circle. In the first stanza nothing gets anywhere; there is no arrival because there is no possibility of arrival, either for the rooted plant or the star in its fixed orbit.

The second stanza metaphorically parallels the first (everything in the poem is structured in parallels). Just as the sun and the sunflower, whose head reflects the image of the sun, frustrate each other, the boy who neurotically dies from excessive sexual passion and the virgin who perishes as a result of her sexual frigidity are perfectly matched to torment each other endlessly. This pattern is endless because it is repeated over and over again in fallen human history. The two past participles, "pined" and "shrouded," in lines five and six (some readers miss the syntactical status of the first) are laid out in parallel positions like a pair of coffins. The Youth's and the Virgin's rising "from their graves" is metaphoric, not literal; personal, individual immortality is at best dubious in Blake (as it is in Emerson, despite his late essay, "Immortality"). Their metaphoric resurrection has the same sense Blake gave it when he added to his signature in an autograph book, "born 28 Nov. 1757 in London & has died several times since" (*Poetry and Prose* 316). In other words, this resurrection is psychological, and every other detail of the poem suggests that the two are doomed to repeat their hideous, mutually destructive mistake over and over again. What they want, wish for, aspire to (they are not free floating any more than their metaphoric equivalent the sunflower is) is that false, erroneous "absolute," a "there" where journeys are over, and no such "there" exists in this poem, for the sunflower, for the young couple, or, in fact, for the sun. Such a "there" exists nowhere else in Blake either. In fact, Blake once described this concept as "Satan"—"The Son of Morn in weary Nights decline / The lost Travellers Dream under the Hill" (*Poetry and Prose* 269).

The young couple "aspire" just as the sunflower "wishes" (the two words are synonyms), and the last line brings us back to where we were in the first line. "And all is done as I have told," might have been the conclusion of this poem as well as of "The Mental Traveller." What the sunflower wants is to get beyond his botanical condition; the young couple, analogously, desire to get beyond their human condition, making the same mistake: they "aspire, / Where" he wants to be. There is no escape from the trap of "aspiration." The problem is that for Blake nothing exists outside of the human condition. The young couple in "Ah! Sun-flower" make the same error as Thel, in *The Book of Thel*, but Blake is dramatizing Thel's error from a reversed perspective. This young couple have failed to marry the contraries which are each other, can make no progression and want to get "out" of human life. Thel foresees the problem (sexuality is bound up with mortality) and refuses to get "in." "Ah! Sun-flower" presents us with a death-in-life as a result of the failure of imaginative vision, and this death-in-life has the poetic image of an arc of a circle, one of Blake's many figures of the "Satanic wheels."

Blake's "Sun-flower" has not enjoyed consistently sunny weather in the pages of the critics, some of whom betray an urge to prune and graft. E. D. Hirsch, Jr., finds it "perhaps Blake's most beautiful lyric poem," but he also finds it, bewilderingly enough, "fundamentally a poem of Innocence" (54). It is "poised in perfect balance between the desire of the Youth for the Virgin and the desire of the moth for the star" (55). The cliché moth is Hirsch's; there is no moth in Blake's poem, nor any analogous image of one (the sunflower does not flit around). But Hirsch gets considerably more "creative" at the expense of the text. The poem "displays" a "double emphasis on fulfillment [sic] both in the natural world and in Eternity. Unlike any other poem of *Experience,* it pays serious homage to the 'Holy Word' both as a concept and as part of biblical tradition (John was Blake's favorite Gospel) (209). There are no allusions to the Gospel of John in the poem. In this rather stunning example of invalidity in interpretation, Hirsch fails to substantiate any of these "findings" or support them in any way (from textual evidence or otherwise). Though he does not get specific enough about the poem to reveal the fact, his bizarre reading may have resulted from a misapprehension of the meaning of "aspire" in line 7. The OED gives as a *third* possible meaning of the verb, "to rise, mount up," used in that sense by Dr. Johnson in 1738. Dr. Johnson was *not* one of Blake's favorite authors.[1] But such a reading demolishes most of the coherence of the poem, destroys the metaphoric as well as syntactical parallel of the Sun-flower's "wishing" with the frustrated pair's "aspiring," and invents a happy ending for the poem's angst of Experience.

Less eccentric readings of the poem serve it more justly. Like Schorer, who praises the poem for its "compressed and lovely lucidity" (49), Gleckner grants that "Ah! Sun-flower" is a "universally admired poem" (*Piper and Bard* 78). But he goes on to give a detailed, sensitive reading of it:

Its main symbol is traditional, the flower rooted in the earth but turning its blossom toward the heavens and the moving sun. All well and good. But the earth in Blake's world is experience; in it the youth and the virgin pine away in desire because their enjoyment is prohibited, not by the earth, but by the laws and restrictions of earthly morality. In a sense, then, the earth is Blake's church, the priests of the raven of dawn who bind with briars joy and desire. Similarly, the sun is not God in the traditional sense, nor is it heaven; it is Eden, the higher innocence suffused with the spiritual warmth of love, the realm in which energy is eternal delight and an improvement in sensual enjoyment is one's pass through the gates. The sunflower and the young couple are thus in the grave of experience, the same grave from which Thel fled. The death implied is spiritual, not physical; the youth and maid are physically alive, but in Blake's eyes they are fundamentally, imaginatively dead. Without some such reference to Blake's modifications of traditional symbols in this poem, it becomes little more than a trite analogy for aspirations of immortality. (79)

As perceptive a reading as Gleckner's, but one keeping more distance from the text itself, is that of Thomas R. Frosch:

Blake is never willing in any way to renounce the here-and-now, or to surrender his conviction that the body will be risen in the world . . . . Similarly, imagination for Blake does not exist beyond form and matter, for desire without a distinct materialization is synonymous with unfulfillment, and the energy that seeks its liberation in specific acts becomes destructive and, in the end, self-consuming, unless it finds them. This is the story of "Ah! Sun-flower" . . . in which the traveller, whose vision cannot take him beyond a vague

yearning, can only look forward to the end of his
seeking and desiring—or death. (26)

Frosch also sees the poem as one of Blake's frequent dramatizations
of the frustration of energy: "Incapable of adequate release, energy
is deflected in the unsatisfying form of the voyage through space to
'that sweet golden clime / Where the travellers journey is done' . . . or
it is discharged into pre-molded patterns of an oppressive regularity,
such as the natural cycle" (30–31).

If we set aside Hirsch's interpretation, we can discern a substantially consistent critical view of the theme of "Ah! Sun-flower" as a
profound poetic statement about human frustration (not fulfillment).
It has not been sufficiently observed, however, that the action of the
poem involves four "persons," in two pairs of dialectical opposition:
the sun is to the sunflower as the virgin is to the youth; fulfillment is
frustrated in the one case because the object of desire is too cold, in
the other because it is too hot, and both objects are too distant,—
the sun, spatially; the virgin, emotionally. The error on the part of
the two active aspirants, however, consists in precisely that defining
of the object of desire as the "other." If fulfillment is thought of as
outside the self, what happens is repetition of the original Fall: Albion
sees Jerusalem as outside himself, and disintegration begins. Just
as, then, the Four Zoas—Urizen, Los, Tharmas, and Luvah—become
separate warring parties or parts of Albion, so in this short lyric, the
youth, the virgin, the sunflower, and the sun are seen as divided from
each other rather than parts of one cosmic whole; the poem expresses
fallen perception, not unfallen vision.

But its interest for this chapter is in its geometric image, the arc
that the action of the sunflower keeps making, that fragment of a
circle which is in itself an image of frustration. The circle is not an
image of perfection in Blake, but of futility; one broken part of a
circle seems even more negative. Even the arc of the horizon is for
Blake the image of the "Mundane Shell," a perception (however false,
in Blake's view) of limitation. In Emerson, perhaps the closest con-

ceptual analog to Blake's "Ah! Sun-flower" is "Circles," from the first series of essays of 1841. One critic who has already noted that analogy is Thomas Weiskel:

> In "Circles," Emerson speaks of man's "continual effort
> to raise himself above himself, to work a pitch above
> his last height," and he finds his image for such cease-
> less sublimating in the "generation of circles, wheel
> without wheel." The soul moves outward, bursting
> over each concentric orbit of limitation. But since the
> soul's self-transcendence is without term, the genera-
> tion of circles itself succumbs to the circularity of
> succession: this is "the circular or compensatory char-
> acter of every human action . . . the moral fact of
> the Unattainable . . . at once the inspirer and con-
> demner of every success." It is true that in "Compen-
> sation," Emerson excepts the soul—unjustifiably, it
> seems to me—from the universal "tax" or "penalty"
> of compensation. But the debt returns to be partially
> paid in "Circles," in the relativity of ceaseless superses-
> sion . . . . Readers of Blake will be tempted to recognize
> in Emerson's "generation of circles, wheel without
> wheel" . . . Blake's central imagery of fallen limitation,
> the circle of destiny or the mills of Satan. Emerson pro-
> pounds an exuberance without a determinate object,
> so that the prolific soul of "Circles" seems more so-
> lipsistic than creative, and it is always subject to time.
> And repetition, however large the scope of its acts, is
> tantamount to disaster for Blake. (117–18)

In "Circles," analogs to Blake's thought certainly do become apparent, but while "Ah! Sun-flower" achieves its perfect lyric form by
confining itself to a purely dramatic depiction of the fallen condition,
Emerson's "Circles" is itself a dialectical work—it is at once an evocation of human aspiration and a disturbing critique of it. "Circles"

is, as it were, "Ah! Sun-flower" seen from both a fallen and unfallen perspective, alternatively, throughout.

Its first sentence, one of the epigraphs to this chapter, if examined carefully provides a clue to the unfallen or visionary perception: "The eye is the first circle; the horizon *which it forms* is the second; and throughout nature this primary figure is repeated without end" (*Complete Works* 2:301, emphasis added). What is crucially important here is the awareness that it is the human eye which forms the horizon; in so doing the eye cannot be said to be bounded or restricted by the horizon. In this sense the circular figure is "primary"; it is so because it is human, rather than "natural." This is a level of perception, as Blake shows us, that the fallen sunflower and the fallen youth simply do not have; they perceive and respond as victims of their world, not makers of it, which is why they must go on repeating their "natural" mistake.

Emerson, however, seems to forget for a time the implications of his first sentence, a forgetting which begins in the second: "It is the highest emblem in the cipher of the world." This sentence suggests that the symbol is mysteriously superior to its maker, the human imagination. The two terms, "emblem" and "cipher," will themselves take us round and round in a semantic circle of their own. An emblem is a symbolic image of something else; that something else here is a "cipher," which is both a riddle or code and a zero (another circle). These first two sentences, in fact, create an epistemological dilemma which the rest of Emerson's essay will try to fight its way out of: is the circle human and humanly meaningful, or "natural" and therefore mysterious, enigmatic? The third sentence paraphrases St. Augustine on God, suggesting the latter (enigmatic) rather than the former (human) meaning. But the essay now situates itself, in its own point of view, within a spiral or cycle of relativities. "Our life is an apprenticeship to the truth that around every circle another can be drawn; that there is no end in nature, but every end is a beginning." By the end of the first paragraph we have lost the confidence suggested by the horizon-forming human eye. By the end of this paragraph, in fact, we are in the middle of a central ambiguity about whether "man" is inside the circle or the circle is circumscribed by Man. If man is inside the circle, we are locked again into the world of "Ah! Sun-flower"; if the circle is created by and thus "within" Man, we are in the world of Emerson's "transparent eyeball," of his Orphic Poet, and of Blake's level of prophetic vision. The rest of this essay is, to paraphrase Blake on Urizen, "Emerson exploring his dens." By the end of the essay he may have found a way out. If so, that way of breaking the circle will lead us, eventually, to "Jerusalem," but only by way of *The Marriage of Heaven and Hell*.

The single long sentence of the second paragraph could serve *in part* as a very accurate paraphrase of "Ah! Sun-flower": "This fact, as far as it symbolizes the moral fact of the Unattainable, the flying Perfect, around which the hands of man can never meet, at once the inspirer and condemner of every success, may conveniently serve us to connect many illustrations of human power in every department" (301). The phrases—"the Unattainable," the "flying Perfect," the "inspirer and condemner of every success"—place us in the context of Blake's sun as seen by his sunflower. "Human power" suggests that Emerson wants to contemplate the success, not the condemnation of success, in human endeavor, though the rest of the essay will play tug-of-war with that dichotomy. But clearly "human power" is the opposite of the conclusion reached by Blake in his lyric, which epitomizes powerlessness. The dualism is built into Emerson's rhetoric here, demanding his typical dialectical development.

The essay quickly becomes a study of relativities, the first those of culture and history. "Permanence is a word of degrees. Every thing is medial. Moons are no more bounds to spiritual power than bat-balls" (303). The first two of these sentences are relativist and determinist; the third, however, is humanist and asserts a freedom over the relativities.

"Spiritual power" is what opens the next circle, the next paragraph. More than one observer has likened the structure of this essay to its subject, a series of concentric circles.[2] Emerson here is at his least logical or expository in the traditional rhetorical sense. One paragraph simply opens up from the one before it, without necessarily logical links. "The key to every man is his thought." This assertion clearly restates "spiritual power" in human terms, but before the reader can assume too rational or intellectual a definition of "spiritual" or "thought," Emerson goes on to indicate how "existential" these terms are to him: "The life of man is a self-evolving circle, which, from a ring imperceptibly small, rushes on all sides outwards to new and larger circles, and that without end. The extent to which this generation of circles, wheel without wheel, will go, depends on the force or truth of the individual soul" (304). If "force or truth of the individual soul" means the visionary dimension, then Emerson is speaking once again in terms sympathetic to Blake's thought. However, a curious coincidence has occurred; Emerson uses the phrase "wheel without wheel" which Blake often uses, and, in *The Four Zoas* and *Jerusalem,* the phrase has distinctly negative connotations, sometimes contrasted with "wheels within wheels" in the same works, indicative of human freedom and harmony. Again, the question seems to be raised by Emerson's text, is man inside the circles, or are the circles inside Man?

As if he guesses our perplexity, perhaps our anxiety, Emerson hurries to console us: "the heart refuses to be imprisoned" (304). He goes further, and seems to make a definitive statement on the side of human power and human freedom. "There is no outside, no inclosing wall, no circumference to us" (304). It could be a major text for existential meditations; it is certainly in harmony with the most visionary moments in Blake (and in himself). And to cap that visionary tone, he adds, "Men walk as prophecies of the next age" (305).

But then the rhetorical pendulum swings back again, revealing reflections on impermanence, radical impermanence, an instability in consciousness itself, and then comes Emerson's assertion of the authority of moods, an unsettling force in consciousness which questions this day's words by the standard of another day, a questioning so deep as to challenge the identity, and psychic continuity, of the author. No present day "deconstructionist" theoretician could go further in radical skepticism, but no one of them could have written Emerson's sentence, "I am God in nature; I am a weed by the wall" (307). This sentence is perhaps the quintessence of Emerson's idiosyncratic dialectical balance.

The "weed by the wall" is Blake's sunflower; the "God in nature" (not, significantly, somewhere "out" of nature) is the poetic vision that sees the relationship of sunflower and sun and virgin and youth.

After that single sentence which captures so perfectly an existential dichotomy, Emerson is reduced to cataloging more relativities. "The sweet of nature is love; yet if I have a friend I am tormented by my imperfections" (307). But, on the other hand, "The only sin is limitation" (308). (Uncomfortably enough for most readers, "love" seems, indeed, to be one of the limitations, a problem to be discussed later in this chapter.) The relativities continue in a list which seems more and more random or perhaps moody: relativities in thought or philosophy, in society, in law, in Christianity, in idealism itself, in conversation, in literature, and even in "the natural world," which "may be conceived as a system of concentric circles" (313). Even Emerson's beloved moral virtues are shown to be relative, including prudence and justice. "There is no virtue which is final; all are initial" (316). And in a tone which begins to sound like Blake's in *The Marriage of Heaven and Hell*, Emerson goes even further: "The virtues of society are vices of the saint" (316–17). And, still much in the mood of Blake's *Marriage*, Emerson goes so far as to say, "It is the highest power of divine moments that they abolish our contritions also. I accuse myself of sloth and unprofitableness day by day; but when these waves of God flow into me I no longer reckon lost time" (317). Emerson is here clearly back in the visionary experience; the persona might be the Orphic Poet himself. In this context occurs a peculiarly Blakean insight: "these moments confer a sort of omnipresence and omnipotence which asks nothing of duration, but sees that the energy of the mind is commensurate with the work to be done, without time" (317). Blake puts the same idea this way: "Eternity is in love with the productions of time" (*Poetry and Prose* 36). But a key word, perhaps the breakthrough word in Emerson's passage, is the highly charged Blakean term, "energy."

It is at this point that Emerson's essay "Circles" performs its most unusual rhetorical trick. It is as if Emerson thinks he may have gone too far. He invents a heckler in his audience: "And thus, O circular philosopher, I hear some reader exclaim, you have arrived at a fine Pyrrhonism, at an equivalence and indifferency of all actions" (317). The objection mocks sarcastically what, in fact, Blake seriously suggests in the *Marriage:* "our crimes may be lively stones out of which we shall construct the temple of the true God!" (317).

Astonishingly, Emerson does not disavow the implication. He merely defends his dialectical method: "I am not careful to justify myself" (317). But then comes the "Warning Label":

> But lest I should mislead any when I have my own head and obey my whims, let me remind the reader that I am only an experimenter. Do not set the least value on what I do, or the least discredit on what I do not, as if I pretended to settle anything as true or false. I unsettle all things. No facts to me are sacred; none are profane; I simply experiment, an endless seeker with no Past at my back. (318)

But once again Emerson's rhetorical pendulum swings in the opposite direction. From the almost anarchic position of "whims" and of "unsettling," he retreats to assert "some principle of fixture or stability in the soul" (318) from which we are able to perceive the "incessant movement" and "progression." Although "the eternal generation of circles proceeds," there exists also an "eternal generator" which "abides" (318). That "eternal generator" is a "central life" which is "superior to creation, superior to knowledge and thought, and contains all its circles" (318). Again, this concept seems both ontological and personified, perhaps another variation on the "Universal Man."

In response to that "central life," Emerson registers a complaint against "all forms of old age: . . . rest, conservatism, appropriation, inertia" (319). These "forms of old age" can and should be rejected. "We grizzle every day. I see no need of it" (319). This "old age" can be resisted, for "in nature every moment is new." Here he returns to the notion of unsettling: "People wish to be settled; only so far as they are unsettled is there any hope for them" (320).

The conclusion of the essay pulls together a number of the images from the later section, images of *energy*. The "new position of the advancing man" includes "all the energies of the past," but is "an exhalation of the morning." We do not know the meanings of the simplest words "except when we love and aspire" (320). Our "insatiable desire" is "to forget ourselves, to be surprised out of our propriety" or "to draw a new circle." This phrase, the end of the first sentence of the last paragraph, comes thuddingly, a disappointment. We have not, then, broken out of the pattern of circularity after all. Or have we? The last paragraph invokes "enthusiasm" and "abandonment . . . dreams and drunkenness, the use of opium and alcohol" as substitutes for "oracular genius." Similar substitutes occur in "gaming and war," which exercise men's "wild passions . . . to ape in some manner these flames and generosities of the heart" (322). This ending, with its tonality of diminuendo, its playing with extremely negative images (intoxication, addiction, war), and its "unsettling" nonresolution, must be one of the strangest conclusions in all of Emerson.

If one reviews the apparent discords in "Circles," particularly in its last few pages, from the defiant, "I unsettle all things," to the very end, one may detect a very interesting phenomenon: a writer's attempt to break out of the conceptual circles he himself has created. Rather than an essay in the traditional sense, it might be better to view "Circles" as a poetic mini-drama, as a sort of simultaneous combination of Aeschylus and Shelley on the theme of Prometheus. The structure of this essay, as the above analysis has tried to show, is a series of *agons,* conflicts of Emerson with himself, acted out in conceptual diction.³ The struggle is total: it means and costs everything which can be at stake for Emerson in 1841. Its outcome is necessarily ambiguous, since defeat would mean a kind of intellectual suicide. It is an example of "Man Thinking," but pushing the consciousness of his own act of thinking to its farthest psychological limits. Given the enormous difficulty of the task, it is a wonder that this essay is not more chaotic than it is. Blake once put the same problem this way, in a couplet, "To God":

> If you have formd a Circle to go into
> Go into it yourself & see how you would do
> (*Poetry and Prose* 516)

Emerson is indeed playing God in "Circles" (which is perhaps why the invented heckler startles), but that is not its most grave danger; he also plays the "weed by the wall." One way of explicating the dialectical difficulties of this essay is to apply to it as an exegetical tool a text of Blake's, namely, *The Marriage of Heaven and Hell.*

Whether or not Satan is the hero of *Paradise Lost* (and it was Shelley who made that suggestion, not Blake), "the Devil" is certainly a hero in Blake's *Marriage of Heaven and Hell,* and on the fourth plate of that early but engraved work, "The voice of the Devil" delivers a little lecture:

> All Bibles or sacred codes. have been the
> causes of the following Errors.
> 1. That Man has two real existing principles
> Viz: a Body & a Soul.
> 2. That Energy. calld Evil. is alone from
> the Body, & that Reason. calld Good. is
> alone from the Soul.
> 3. That God will torment Man in Eternity for
> following his Energies.

But the following Contraries to these are True
1. Man has no Body distinct from his soul for
that calld Body is a portion of the Soul discernd
by the five Senses. the chief inlets of Soul
in this age.
2. Energy is the only life and is from the Body
and Reason is the *bound or outward circumference*
of Energy.
3. Energy is Eternal Delight. (*Poetry and Prose* 34,
emphasis added)

"Reason is the bound or outward circumference of Energy."
Typically, Blake sees the figure of the circle as restriction, not freedom. And, just as Urizen, the rationalist tyrant, is both the *horizon*
and *your reason,* "Reason" here is not only in dialectical opposition
with "Energy," Reason is the fence or wall which keeps energy in
check. Given the metaphor of the circle, reason is its circumference,
its outward encircling but limiting line; energy is at the center of that
circle. This concept, which Blake never afterwards abandons (though
the meanings of "energy" change), neatly subverts both the Platonic
and Pauline soul-body hierarchy.

If we apply this concept to the structure of Emerson's "Circles,"
we may have a way of understanding its internal push and pull, a rationale for its "agons." Emerson's reason keeps drawing the circles as
circumferences; Emerson's energy keeps breaking out of them, asserting itself, in spite of all the essay's intellectualism, as the "only life"
and "Eternal Delight." This pattern becomes more noticeable as the
essay proceeds and is most explicit in its concluding paragraphs.

Thus we begin with the horizon-forming eye which is imaginative energy functioning. But once the imagination creates its work, it
mistakenly sees it as outside of itself, as an "emblem" or "cipher,"
which are "reasonable" symbols. Deceived into accepting the rational
forms as separate existences, the human imagination begins to see that
pattern everywhere. Insofar as it is seen to be external, it is of course

humanly "unattainable," the "flying Perfect," or, an *abstraction* responded to *as if it were real.* This definitely "fallen" perception leads to the disillusioning meditations on the relativities. And at this point Emerson must oppose to those mental constructs "spiritual power" or "thought," but they, too, seem to be subsumed, to be mere concepts. So he is forced to invoke "the life of a man" as a *self-evolving* circle, autonomy restored not by rational thought but by "life" (energy). Further assertions are made in defense of that life, as "the heart" and as the "us" of which there is no "outside" or "circumference." If the circumference is Blake's "reason," then clearly Emerson is postulating a more primary *existence* that underlies that *essence.* But the dialectical movement back and forth catches him in its stressful pattern, and "I am God in nature; I am a weed by the wall" is a confession of that fact. However, in this statement, we should now note that the weed is by the *wall,* at the external limit, at the circumference; one's self perceived as "God in nature" is the energetic, creative center. But the sentence in its perfectly balanced syntax proffers both values as equal—a dialectical balance which could be self-destructive, the two halves of the sentence cancelling each other out, leaving nothing, a void, a cipher as semicolon, a circle as pure negativity, nonexistence.

It is here that the imaginary critic intrudes, most appropriately, for Emerson is as close to perfect solipsism at this point as he ever gets. The "heckling" produces a psychologically recognizable "responding" answering, talking-back, and that response, to a voice "outside" the speaker's solipsistic voice, is a reassertion of energy. The self-justifying answer here advocates the unsettling of all things, clearly a value of anarchic energy over restrictive reason.

In terms of the essay's final swing in the direction of energy, rather than of reason, we can now see the attack on "old age"; we can understand in a new way the "eternal generator." The "exhalation of the morning" which includes "all the energies of the past" becomes more relevant. And even the past reaction of rationalistic conceptualizing, the phrase "draw a new circle," is overwhelmed by "insatiable desire," by "forget[ing] ourselves," by "enthusiasm," and by "abandon-

CIRCLES, WHEELS, AND CYCLES

ment." Finally, it is clearly as forces of energy that the last paragraph heaps up those images of irrationality: "dreams and drunkenness, the use of opium and alcohol . . . gaming and war" as substitutes for "oracular genius." They exercise men's "wild passions." They "ape . . . flames and generosities of the heart." That "heart," the last word in the essay, is *not* a circle. Emerson's early essay "Circles" can be read then as a debate with himself, as a "mental warfare" between the Orc and the Urizen within him. As in Blake's early, minor prophecies, Orc is the stronger of the two. The essay ends with the "heart" because the rational circle has been broken.

Almost all of the major critics of Emerson devote some attention to "Circles"; It functions rather like Blake's "Mental Traveller," enforcing a hypnotic spell on commentators which no single commentary seems able to release. Stephen Whicher, in *Freedom and Fate,* finds "Circles" to be one of the early warning signs of the coming breakdown in Emerson's powers, perhaps a first astigmatism in the "transparent eyeball." It is for him "the most unsettled and unsettling of the *Essays, First Series*" (94). He sees in it a wavering of Emerson's optimistic faith—"The restlessness of this essay infects even his conception of the Soul itself" (96), and that "infirmity of faith" is "Emerson's deepest disillusionment" (97). In short, Whicher uses "Circles" as support for his own thesis: "Time and experience are teaching Emerson to respect their dominion. His transcendentalism is steadily giving way to a basic empiricism—one which, though it includes and stresses man's peculiar experience of the Soul, nevertheless pragmatically recognizes the priority of experience over 'Reality'" (97). Just as the term "transcendentalism" is a facile label which fails to describe the particulars of Emerson's thought in "Circles" (or elsewhere), the word "soul" in Whicher's usage is a glib catch-all abstraction which fails to explore the ambiguities of the word in the essay itself.

Sherman Paul subsumes discussion of the essay under his own thesis, so that in *Emerson's Angle of Vision* he talks about "the circle" as "the basic figure" in "Emerson's geometry of morals" (98). A "geometry of morals" is a strange way of describing Emerson's highly literary essays; if that description were accurate, how then would one describe the style and structure of Spinoza's *Ethics?* But Paul's "angle" is very wide, and he seeks to include in it a great deal of intellectual history:

> By joining the static and mechanistic circle of New-
> tonian astronomy (his debt to eighteenth-century
> science) with the dynamic science of Ideas or dialectic
> of Coleridge, Emerson made his circle an organic
> symbol capable of representing both the unfolding
> mind and the ascending natural chain of being. His
> circle united his two desires: the desire for fixity or
> centrality in the universe of the spirit, and the desire
> for change and growth and freedom in the organic
> universe of prudence. (101)

Paul, then, wants it both ways: he sees the dualism, the dichotomy, in Emerson's structure of thought here, but does not see any dialectical resolution of the polarities. In the cluster of allusions to intellectual history, the idiosyncratic Ralph Waldo Emerson gets lost.

Paul's book was published in 1952; Whicher's in 1953. More recent studies try to get further inside either the text or the mind of its author. Leonard Neufeldt in *The House of Emerson* (1982) does much more sophisticated rhetorical analysis than either Paul or Whicher, but he seems to be writing from the viewpoint of the imaginary heckler in the essay. He assumes that a great deal of the "Pyrrhonism" in "Circles" adequately explains how the essay works as a whole. "Circles" is a "sophisticated justification of circular philosophy" (214), in which, however, "the reference to 'central life' is perhaps the most significant transitional point" (217–18).

> "Circles" is limited to but not limited by a single per-
> sona as teacher-student, who joins the reader in
> learning even though he is doing much of the teach-
> ing, and who repeatedly appears to have adjourned the

essay only to draw another circle, enlarge the prospect, and so more closely approach or act out the central life. (218)

Clearly, Neufeldt, too, wants to have it both ways: "Circles" as surrender to the circles and "Circles" as approaching or acting out "the central life." All options remain open; this reading sees a lot but decides very little.

A more recent study is David Van Leer's *Emerson's Epistemology: The Argument of the Essays*. Published in 1986, it is a Kantian reading of Emerson, and brings formidable analytical skills, appropriate to formal philosophical texts, to bear upon the "unsettling" essayist. For Van Leer, "'Circles' is finally not about how humans feel, or even how images work, but about what concepts are buried in other concepts" (113). Perhaps this is not so much a "Kantian" reading of Emerson as a reading of Emerson *as Kant*. Here we have the "eyeball" per se, totally disconnected from its body.[4]

Finally, Barbara Packer, in her *Emerson's Fall* (1982) shows herself philosophically acute but is not, like Van Leer, murdering to dissect. Some of the conclusions of this present study of "Circles," though arrived at independently, echo her own. She works with the advantage of perceiving Blakean analogies which for her, too, illuminate the text of "Circles."

> [Emerson] has arrived, in fact, at something very like what Blake scholars call the Orc cycle—a vision of human history that sees it as a ceaseless dialectic generated by the opposing powers of order and energy. Emerson's version of this story is given its fullest expression in one of his shortest and most explosive essays, "Circles." (133)

Commenting on the last sentence of the first paragraph of "Circles"— "Our life is an apprenticeship to the truth that around every circle another can be drawn; that there is no end in nature, but every end is a beginning; that there is always another dawn risen on mid-noon, and under every deep a lower deep opens," Packer observes:

> The final clauses of the sentence splice together Adam's joyous description of Raphael's approach with Satan's lament on Mt. Niphates; they constitute a sort of *Marriage of Heaven and Hell* on the level of the sentence. And, like Blake's little book, "Circles" deliberately confounds traditional ethical categories. (134)

There is nothing like a nudge from William Blake to get an inquiry back into the human world. Helping herself to Blake to illuminate Emerson's text, Packer reaches the same conclusions as I do concerning "Circles," including a reading of its ending as supportive of "energy" rather than "reason." "We can infer that the central principle, however fixed or stable, is neither rigid nor motionless; its stability is alive with all the energy of desire" (136).

It is satisfying to see a critic of Packer's sensitivity and depth describe an Emersonian concept as "alive with all the energy of desire." The language is certainly Blakean, but it is also, for a modern reader, Freudian, which leads to a consideration of perhaps the most dramatic circle that can be imaged in words, the cycle of human sexuality.

Sexual imagery is ubiquitous in Blake, from *The Book of Thel* to *Jerusalem*. Erotic language constitutes one of Blake's major rhetorical modes, perhaps the major rhetorical mode for the expression of his philosophical dialectic, as we have already noticed in the introduction of this study. In Emerson's writing, it can be said without exaggeration that overt sexual imagery simply does not exist, a fact which should make Emerson, rather than Blake, a candidate for Freudian explication, perhaps as analysis of modes of "repression." Recent Emersonian criticism has, in fact, been endeavoring to fill that felt need.

Evelyn Barish, among other uses of Freud in her 1989 *Emerson: The Roots of Prophecy,* cites "Mourning and Melancholia" as supporting theory for her explanation of Emerson's response to the early loss of his father (28). In *The Transparent: Sexual Politics in the Language of Emerson* (1981), Freud's theory of the Oedipus Complex functions as a basic foundation for Eric Cheyfitz's analysis of Emerson's concealing/revealing diction in *Nature.* Mark Edmundson in *Towards Reading Freud: Self-Creation in Milton, Wordsworth, Emerson, and Sigmund Freud* discovers important conceptual analogs in Emerson and Freud, especially in their views on loss and grief. All three of the above critics mine Freudian texts for insights in areas where they find Freud indispensable for explicating Emerson. Such a nexus is inevitable: there is simply no more accurate theoretical explication for Emerson's practice when his language, presciently pre-Freudian, uncovers sexual archetypes in his myth of the Fall.

"Freud read Emerson indirectly, through Nietzsche" (Edmundson 139). But the texts of Emerson, of Nietzsche, and of Freud can also be read as responses to archetypes. The following pages invoke as explicator of Emerson a Freud who is not a pragmatic clinician but a Romantic visionary, if I may borrow Edmundson's illuminating distinction that lends itself so well to the themes of this study. He is also the Freud whom Bruno Bettelheim shows us: a humanist philosopher of spiritual concerns. And he is the Freud of Auden's great elegy, "no more a person / Now but a whole climate of opinion."[5]

Emerson and Freud sometimes wear the same mythic mask, that of Oedipus. Both seekers confront the Sphinx who is both Nature and the human mind. Both thinkers liberate us with their answers to her riddle. Both fathers hear the "Ancient Voices of Children" echo from forgotten graves a song about the primal mystery.[6]

In "The Marriage of Heaven and Hell: Emerson's Alternative to Blake," Erik Thurin analyzes what he takes to be Emerson's "androgyny," both in his rhetorical persona and in his concept of human love (223). Commenting on Emerson's "heaven of invention," Thurin observes, "By no coincidence, Emerson makes lavish use of the circle to describe this spiritual milieu. A closed circuit—'puss and her tail,' as he puts it in 'Experience'—is a good image of the 'solitary performance' of the soul which has attained its 'due sphericity' (circularity)" (223). If this elucidation leaves Emerson's meanings obscure, so does Thurin's exposition of the relationship between Emerson and Blake, except for his rather obvious linkage, "In a sense the essay Emerson calls 'Experience' is to him what 'Songs of Experience' is to Blake" (225). Thurin finds Emerson less of a "devil's advocate" than Blake (226), a debatable point, and then hurries on to a comparison of Emerson and Goethe (229). For the thesis of his book as a whole, Thurin sees Emerson associating the "feminine principle with earth and the masculine principle with heaven" (x), an unoriginal observation. In attempting a very large "philosophical" focus, Thurin has mostly evaded a discussion of sexuality itself as it appears in Emerson. The book displays a lot of rather cloudy "metaphysics," but exposes very little sex.

More interesting in his approach, more substantial in his critical contributions, and much more recent is Alan Hodder's *Emerson's Rhetoric of Revelation: Nature, the Reader, and the Apocalypse Within*. This study offers more than its title implies, more than just an analysis of the textual and subtextual allusions to the book of Revelation in *Nature*. On the idea of the "Divine Marriage," Hodder observes:

> Throughout *Nature,* in fact throughout much of his writing, Emerson reinvokes the image of the divine marriage as a way of imaginatively overcoming the separation between Nature and Spirit . . . . The image is of Biblical origin, but in *Nature* Emerson develops it into a kind of allegory or running parable for the life of Man. In ignorance Man looks up to Nature as a child to his mother; but as he grows in self-consciousness his attitude changes, and increasingly he finds in Nature his spouse and mate, until, recognizing in her

nothing but his own imperial nature, he places her at
his feet and lords it over her. (27–28)

Hodder explains the above progression in *Nature* by references to its
opening, "embosomed for a season in nature," with its suggestion of
the sucking infant. Then, in "Beauty," "the second stage . . . begins
when Man's natural Mother appears to him as his spouse." And in
"Discipline," "the original relationship has begun to reverse itself"
(28–29). Hodder's exposition is intriguing, but in these passages, with
his own eyes fixed on biblical parallels, he seems not to notice that he
is describing as "Divine Marriage" incest and incestuous sadism.

Eric Cheyfitz is not so chaste in his critical perceptions. In *The
Trans-parent: Sexual Politics in the Language of Emerson,* he discusses
the same Emersonian relationship, that between Man and Nature, but
his emphasis is candidly sexual. Glossing the passage in "Discipline,"
from *Nature,* in which Emerson writes, "A rule of one art, or a law of
one organization, holds true throughout nature. So intimate is this
Unity, that, it is easily seen, it lies under the undermost garment of
nature, and betrays its source in Universal Spirit" (*Complete Works*
1:49). Cheyfitz observes:

> Put in the crudest terms—terms that Emerson might
> appreciate, given his suggestive figures and his attrac-
> tion for and use of common speech—the manly
> "whole" that the reader seeks to contemplate is sug-
> gested as a womanly "hole," an abyss that "lies under
> the undermost garment" of the mother and lies to the
> reader about the fatherly "rest or Identity" it repre-
> sents, luring the reader, seeking certain ground, into a
> perpetual fall of uncertainty. The figure of the w/hole
> (and this may be the appropriate way for us to visual-
> ize it, since it is neither simply a "whole" or a "hole")
> suggests the Emersonian figure of the circle . . . with
> which, in its form as the eye, we have been continually

concerned in this essay and are concerned at this moment, since the Emerson of *Nature* is encouraging us to "see" the mother's apparitional organ. (165–66)

Cheyfitz then goes on to relate the passage in *Nature* to two early sentences in "Circles": "the eye is the first circle" and "our life is an apprenticeship to the truth that . . . . under every deep a lower deep opens." Their relationship suggests support for a major idea of his book:

> In the passages from *Nature* and "Circles" that we are observing . . . it is not a figure of the father's sexuality that appears to dominate the mother's, but a figure of the mother's that appears to undermine the father's, implicating it in a simultaneous rise and fall, a circular, or revolutionary, ascent to "dawn" that is also a descent into the "deep." Implicated in the mother's apparitional organ, the father is sent wandering, up and down . . . . It is difficult to tell in the scene of seduction from *Nature* that we are looking at who is the seducer and who is the seduced, whether it is the mother who tempts the child to peer under her "undermost garment" or whether it is the child who teases the mother into letting him look. Whatever the case, it is the manly, or aristocratic, whole, the FATHER, who appears at this moment to be the victim of the seduction, the victim of a double vision that, looking at "the lap of immense intelligence which createth us," necessarily sees the figure of a mixed wo/manly organ and with this vision commits parricide. (166)

Two of the three critics quoted above, Thurin and Cheyfitz, writing on sexuality in Emerson, make reference to his figure of the circle. Two of the three, Hodder and Cheyfitz, read *Nature* in terms of incest; one, Cheyfitz, in terms of incest and parricide. The latter images exist in a recognizably Freudian landscape, but I would like to turn to Blake, before I turn to Freud, to help explain the circularity of sex in Emerson.

The combination of incest and parricide suggests, of course, the mythic archetype of Oedipus. When a critic such as Cheyfitz finds the Oedipal motif in Emerson's *Nature*, he is necessarily reading that motif in an allegorical, highly conceptual way. Blake, in contrast to Emerson, treats the Oedipal paradigm frequently in direct and literal terms. It occurs in the minor prophecies, and in a number of places in *The Four Zoas*, but perhaps its most succinct expression in Blake is in his short lyric, "Infant Sorrow." Blake engraved two stanzas of this poem for inclusion in *Songs of Experience:*

> My mother groand! my father wept.
> Into the dangerous world I leapt:
> Helpless, naked, piping loud;
> Like a fiend hid in a cloud.
>
> Struggling in my fathers hands:
> Striving against my swadling bands
> Bound and weary I thought best
> To sulk upon my mothers breast. (*Poetry and Prose* 28)

This engraved version is already quite Freudian enough: the child is pure libidinous energy, and as his libido is restricted, by his father and by the imposed "swadling bands" which bind his genitals, he learns to practice what Freud calls repression, by his sulking. But the sulking occurs at his mother's breast, and he remains "like a fiend hid in a cloud."

The manuscript draft in Blake's notebook continues for seven more stanzas, "heavily revised," according to Erdman, who offers this reconstruction of the first manuscript reading:

And I grew day after day
Till upon the ground I stray
And I grew night after night
Seeking only for delight

And I saw before me shine
Clusters of the wandring vine
And beyond a mirtle tree
Stretchd its blossoms out to me

But a Priest with holy look
In his hand a holy book
Pronounced curses on his head
Who the fruit or blossoms shed

I beheld the Priest by night
He embraced my mirtle bright
I beheld the Priest by day
Where beneath my vine he lay

Like a serpent in the night
He embraced my mirtle bright
Like a serpent in the day
Underneath my vine he lay

So I smote him & his gore
Staind the roots my mirtle bore
But the time of youth is fled
And grey hairs are on my head
(*Poetry and Prose* 797)

One of Blake's variants in the manuscript for the line, "But a Priest with holy look" was "My father then with holy look": (*Poetry and Prose* 799). If one makes the metaphoric leap (comprehensible both in Blakean terms and those of traditional nature myths) of identifying the mirtle or vine with the mother, and reads either the "Priest" as "father" or simply Blake's alternative literal father, there is here a working out, on a small scale, of the whole Oedipal motif. Its project, significantly, is successful: the jealous father-priest is murdered; the mirtle-mother is enjoyed. But, also significant for the context of this chapter, that resolution itself succumbs to circularity. Once the Oedipal Project is achieved, and the son succeeds in sexually acting out the role of his father, he does indeed become his own father: "the time of youth is fled / And grey hairs are on my head." He also produces the replication of himself. Since the mirtle has borne roots, stained in fact by the shed blood of the father, it is clear that the cycle will be repeated—the speaker, become his own father, begets his son (himself) upon his mother, and that son will, in turn, live up to his genetic inheritance and slay that father in turn. He has his father's "blood" in him. A successful Oedipal Project is a nightmare because, on one level, it is a closed circle.

Here it might be best to step back (or forward) and review the Freudian motif in Freud's own terms. He has provided a number of formularizations of the concept. The following one is from *The Ego and the Id* of 1923:

> In its simplified form the case of the male child may be described as follows. At a very early age the little boy develops an object-cathexis of his *mother,* which originally related to the mother's breast and is the earliest instance of an object-choice on the anaclitic model; his *father* the boy deals with by identifying himself with him. For a time these two relationships exist side by side, until the sexual wishes in regard to the mother become more intense and the father is perceived as an obstacle to them; this gives rise to the Oedipus complex. The identification with the father then takes on a hostile coloring and changes into a wish to get rid of the father in order to take his place with the mother. Henceforward the relation to the father is ambivalent; it seems as if the ambivalence inherent in the identification from the beginning had become manifest. An ambivalent attitude to the father

and an object-relation of a purely affectionate kind to
the mother make up the content of the simple positive
Oedipus complex in the boy.[7]

What is extremely interesting about Blake's "Infant Sorrow," from
the Freudian point of view, is that the first two stanzas, engraved and
published, present only repression of the Oedipal drive; the remain-
ing unpublished stanzas in Blake's notebook work out not its repression but its successful completion, if not resolution. Blake's first two
stanzas show civilization; the rest of the poem dramatizes its discontents. As fantasy-fulfillment, the poem is extraordinary, even for Blake.

But what has this Oedipal Project to do with Ralph Waldo
Emerson? Cheyfitz is certainly on a valuably suggestive track in his
observations quoted earlier, but I want to suggest that he does not go
far enough in his interpretive speculations. If we look at the basic
outline of Blake's myth, and then use that outline to illuminate the
analogous conceptual terms in the work of Emerson, it becomes possible to see that in the work of both Emerson and Blake the Oedipal
Project is realized conceptually. In other words, Emerson as well as
Blake dramatizes the murder of the Father (Jehovah, Nobodaddy) for
the express purpose of repossession of or reunion with the Mother
(Nature or Vala).

It was Stephen Whicher who first described Emerson's *Nature* as
"an effort to assimilate nature into himself, to reduce the NOT ME to
the ME" (52), a valuable insight gratefully acknowledged by Cheyfitz
(31). Now, the most primary model of the human being assimilating
and transforming the NOT ME into the ME is quite obviously the
child at his mother's breast; he is engaged in the act of eating the
mother, and the mother, at the earliest stage of the infant's development, is essentially all of the NOT ME that he can perceive. The
mother is the totality of "nature" in the child's world.

If we combine Whicher's quite profound insight into *Nature*
with the discoveries made by Freud about the Oedipus complex, we
have a way of relating Emerson's "sublimation" or conceptualization

of the sexuality in *Nature* to Blake's overt fantasy-fulfillment. Of course the "eating of the mother" on the part of the child would have to be pre-Oedipal in terms of an actual child's development, but this study is not on the behavior of children, but about the psychological insights of maturely developed artistic myths. Lest the reader be uneasy about identifying one of the meanings of *Nature* as an "eating of the mother," however, it might be helpful to substantiate evidence from Emerson's own unconscious mind which would be supportive of such a wish on his part. Now the only records that exist of the workings of Emerson's unconscious are his recordings of his dreams in his journals, and although he wrote down his dream-memories very infrequently (and often disappointingly for the purposes of this study), there is one such record which can serve as very clear-cut and explicit substantiation of the point under discussion: "I dreamed that I floated at will in the great Ether, and I saw this world floating also not far off, but diminished to the size of an apple. Then an angel took it in his hand and brought it to me and said, 'This thou must eat.' And I ate the world."[8] Emerson's dream is a Blake poem. It is enormously, almost endlessly, suggestive. It makes itself available to Freudian analysis, but also to Blakean analysis, and, ultimately and most importantly, to Emersonian analysis.

The "oceanic" free floating in the "ether" is the libidinous activity of the id freed in sleep. It is the mental environment of pure wish-fulfillment. It is Blake's Beulah. And it is a common dream image for orgasm. The diminishment of the world to an apple is perhaps the quintessential ambition of Emerson's philosophical ego: all of "nature" simple and perceptible as a "bat-ball." But this dream has allusions, for the dreamer was a student of Scripture. The world-as-apple is also the world-as-apple-of-knowledge, the forbidden apple of Genesis, and the clue to that dream allusion is the presence in the dream of the angel. Here the angel's role is reversed; not the forbidding, biblical "Covering Cherub" who bars out our original parents, here he is the id's advocate, the permissive provocateur, a sensual, energetic Blakean "devil," a persuasive Miltonic Satan. Here the

Scriptural "thou shalt not eat" is reversed to "this thou must eat" in an ironic echo of Christ's words in that "Lord's Supper" that so troubled Emerson's conscience, "Take, eat: this is my body" (Mark 14:22). The eating of the body of the divine redeemer is conflated with redemptive ingestion of nature. The world as knowledge is Emerson's apple, and his deepest inspiration, his personal angel, his poet, his whim, commands him to devour it. But the apple is not only the apple of knowledge, it is also the apple of the world; it is Nature, the Great Mother, and she becomes in the dream totally consumable, totally consumed. The mother becomes ingested and part of the child; nature, the NOT ME, becomes the ME; nature *becomes* Emerson.

The dream records incest by ingestion. The same idea finds expression in *Nature* itself: "The lover of nature is he whose inward and outward senses are truly adjusted to each other; who has retained the spirit of infancy even into the era of manhood. His intercourse with heaven and earth becomes part of his daily food" (*Complete Works* 1:9). But where, in this Oedipal paradigm, is the Father? The total absence of the Father in the dream is as significant as the reduction of Eve (or Nature) to apple. Outside of the dream, in Emerson's conscious, creative work, the Father will be murdered, but only *after* the Mother is enjoyed, in a reversal of the chronological order of the two acts that constitute the Oedipal Project. Emerson enjoys union with the "Mother" in *Nature;* he murders the "Father" in "The American Scholar" and the "Divinity School" address.

Biographical fact might seem an impertinence here, but it throws a small suggestive light if not read too narrowly. Emerson's own father died when Waldo was eight. As a distinguished public man, a Unitarian minister highly placed in Boston society, and a believer in and enforcer of strict familial habits (Rusk 26–28), William Emerson could have appeared to his son only as a rather distant authority figure. Allen records that William Emerson wrote to a friend, "Ralph doesn't read very well yet," a week before the boy's third birthday (4). Both Allen and Rusk make something (though neither enough) of the incident of the curative baths enforced by the father:

> Some forty years later Ralph could not forget the
> severity of a father "who twice or thrice put me in
> mortal terror by forcing me into the salt water off
> some wharf or bathing house, and . . . the fright with
> which, after some of this salt experience, I heard his
> voice one day, (as Adam that of the Lord God in the
> garden,) summoning us to a new bath, and I vainly
> endeavoring to hide myself." (Rusk 23)

The voice of his father was that of "the Lord God in the garden."
The Garden, Nature the Mother, could only be enjoyed if the Father,
Jehovah, were removed from it. His biological father dies when he is
eight, and the parricide of God the Father is exactly what Emerson,
as the new American Adam, does in fact achieve as a writer. It is
analogous to Blake's poetic "destruction" of the error, "Nobodaddy,"
his Jehovah. But Emerson first enjoys union with the mother in 1836
(Nature); only then does he murder the father. But he murders the
Father twice. In 1837 in "The American Scholar," he murders the
father of European intellectual tradition. The Father of organized in-
stitutional Christianity is killed in the Divinity School "Address" in
1838. Having thus achieved the Oedipal Project, Emerson must then
deal with his fate, that of becoming his own father, in all its conse-
quent circularity.

The parallel with Blake is close enough to be instructive. Evi-
dently, Blake had no *unusual* problems with his father. Davis follows
Gilchrist in observing, "Blake seems to have found his father lenient
and affectionate and his mother tender and loving" (13). But when as
a child he talked at home about seeing angels, it was only his mother's
plea that prevented his father from thrashing him (Davis 14). Whatever the biographical father-son relationship may have been, the father
figure in Blake's poetry is universally negative. From the father who
"sells" his little boy in "The Chimney Sweeper" of *Innocence,* to the
father-priests in "The Garden of Love" of *Experience,* who "in black

gowns, were walking their rounds / And binding with briars, my joys and desires," to the tyrannical Urizen of the minor prophecies who binds and crucifies the rebel youth Orc, all are variations of "Nobodaddy," Blake's Joycean portmanteau name for God-the-Father or Jehovah. For Blake he is *nobody* because he has *no body* and therefore can be *nobody's Daddy,* a monstrous fiction and *no Daddy* at all. In "To Nobodaddy," Blake questions, "Why art thou silent & invisible / Father of jealousy." He asks, "Why darkness & obscurity / in all thy words & laws." And he supplies a Freudian answer: "Is it because Secresy / gains females loud applause" (*Poetry and Prose* 471).

Cheyfitz analyzes the Oedipal situation in Emerson's *Nature* differently than I do. He finds the father-figure present in Emerson's term "Spirit." Commenting on the desire of the speaker (for Cheyfitz the "child-hero") for "an original relation to the universe" (*Complete Works* 1:3), he observes:

> The hero's search for the original sense of nature is a search for an unmediated vision of what Emerson calls "my beautiful mother" . . . a vision unclouded by intervening, or approximate, terms, by other eyes. And when this vision is achieved, when nature is "beheld . . . face to face," at that precise moment the hero will also see God directly; for the original sense of the "mother," Emerson tells us in *Nature,* is the FATHER. He is her cause and meaning; she, but an effect, a representation of this meaning . . . "a great shadow pointing always to the sun behind us." (3–4)

That "shadow" has other possible interpretations, ones leading away from Cheyfitz's reading into the world of Blake's "fallen perception." Even if we accept Cheyfitz's terms here, they suggest a radical dualism in *Nature* that the visionary passages, discussed in the previous chapter, certainly contradict. Undoubtedly, the shadow exists. Yet the transparent eye-ball saw no shadows. Is the dualism found in *Nature* then the product of fallen perception rather than unfallen vision, both dialectically operating in the little book as a whole?

Blake has a name for that shadow. He calls her (Nature is always feminine) "Vala." "Vala" is another portmanteau name, like "Nobodaddy" or "Urizen." Nature as Vala is how the NOT ME is perceived in the fallen world through fallen senses. Vala is indeed a shadow. She is an illusion. Vala is a *veil.* Since all reality is human for Blake, perception of the other-than-human as *other,* the NOT ME, must be an error. Vala is also a *vale,* a ravine, a valley, a vagina. Vala is both veil and vale, and as Blake's version of both Emerson's "shadow" and his "Sphinx," she is the veiled vagina, nature as seductress-whore, the cosmos as tease.

The Oedipal Project of Emerson's *Nature* is to repossess Nature, to eat the Mother, to turn Nature into *Nature.* The project is successful—hence Emerson's dualism when as the child he is contemplating the mother, his monism when he is acting as the visionary father in union with her. The project is successful, which is why it is Emerson's first book, not his last: it begets the ensuing cycle of its conceptual brothers-sons, all the other books that follow from it.

Emerson gives us a Freudian catalog in *Nature.* In its "Introduction" the "phenomena" that are "now" thought of as "not only unexplained but inexplicable" are "language, sleep, madness, dreams, beasts, sex" (*Complete Works* 1:4). *Nature* discusses "Language" and conceptually acts out sex. Blake often explores the other four, but one of my aims is to show how Blake's sexual dramatizations illuminate Emerson's language.

The Fall is, psychologically, the experience of disillusionment, the fall into experience itself. In the fallen perception of the fallen world, there is no way out. Human experience is perceived in endless closed circles; man is trapped within his wheels—conceptual, industrial, or sexual. The "tyranny of sex" is essentially its cyclic quality. Reproductive genitality cannot lead to redemption or apocalypse, to the total freedom of vision, since reproduction is itself a dead end, a closed circle: the sexes reproduce the sexes, who reproduce the sexes, who reproduce the sexes. Freud's pessimism is based largely on a commitment to a so-called "reality principle" which asserts the ubiquity of genital dominance:

> Whether one has killed one's father or has abstained from doing so is not really the decisive thing. One is bound to feel guilty in either case, for the sense of guilt is an expression of the conflict due to ambivalence, of the eternal struggle between Eros and the instinct of destruction or death. This conflict is set going as soon as men are faced with the task of living together. So long as the community assumes no other form than that of the family, the conflict is bound to express itself in the Oedipus complex, to establish the conscience and to create the first sense of guilt.[9]

"Love" is *not* the answer to the problem of the human condition, either in Emerson or in Blake.[10] The Victorian sentiment, "Love is enough," would be equally rejected by both these writers. If there is a way out of the fallen world, it is not through human sexuality; Blake, as well as Emerson, would have scorned D. H. Lawrence's mystique of sex—Blake because it is a mystique, Emerson because it is based on mere sex. For Emerson, as for Blake, neither redemption nor apocalypse is attainable through sexuality, which is simply one of the primal divisions of the Fall, created by the Fall. The awareness of the fact of the Fall is what grounds all of the nonvisionary moments in Emerson and Blake, and their nonvisionary passages far outnumber their visionary ones. Both are far from being sentimentalists, and their astonishing optimism—to be discussed later in this study—is based upon other foundations than that of sex. This chapter has been about fallen perception. In it the words of Emerson and Blake necessarily sound the note of disillusionment. That disillusionment may find expression in the vehicle of the metaphor of sex or in its philosophical tenor. Thus Blake can put that awareness into a couplet:

"Grown old in Love from Seven till Seven times Seven / I oft have wished for Hell for Ease from Heaven" (*Poetry and Prose* 516). The same awareness finds expression in one of Emerson's saddest insights, appropriately enough in "Experience": "It is very unhappy, but too late to be helped, the discovery we have made that we exist. That discovery is called the Fall of Man" (*Complete Works* 3:75).

[4]

JESUS LOST AND JESUS REGAINED

∞⟨⟩

I am not a God afar off, I am a brother and friend.
—Blake

I will love him as a glorified friend.
—Emerson

CREATION IS VISIONARY for Emerson: "I am nothing; I see all" (*Complete Works* 1:10). It is the same for Blake: "If the doors of perception were cleansed every thing would appear to man as it is: infinite" (*Poetry and Prose* 39). Creation dissolves the distinction between time and eternity. For Emerson, such "a moment is a concentrated eternity" (Whicher 98); just as for Blake the inspired motive is to "Hold Infinity in the palm of your hand / And Eternity is an hour" (*Poetry and Prose* 493). But the visionary moment is precisely that, momentary, and, except in those moments, the human condition is perceived as the Fall, which Emerson, as we saw at the end of the last chapter, identifies with self-consciousness: "The discovery we have made that we exist . . . is called the Fall of Man" (*Complete Works* 3:75). Self-consciousness is awareness of the self as a *separate* entity. Blake identifies the Fall with *separateness* (including the perception of nature or the NOT ME as other-than-human) or division or alienation—Albion, sick and half-asleep, rejects the words of Jesus quoted in the epigraph to this chapter and mistakenly insists, "We are not One: we are Many, thou most simulative" (*Poetry and Prose* 146).

As long as the fallen world is perceived in its own fallen terms, as a "dull round" within a "Mundane Shell," as an endless repetition of "Circles," there is no way out. But Emerson, like Blake, is a writer who asserts a predominantly optimistic faith. Redemption is the third archetype in the myth of the human cosmos, and Emerson embraces it, as does Blake. The problem, for both, is that the dead myth of redemption which they inherited from their Christian culture had to be transformed before it could be resurrected. Redemption must be redefined, remythologized. The Redeemer must himself be imaginatively redeemed. This chapter concerns the Emersonian (and Blakean) revision (which is re-vision) of Jesus.

Early in their careers neither Emerson nor Blake hesitates to identify *himself* as Jesus, but this figure is already thoroughly revised. This "Jesus" is not the redeemer as prophet, but the prophet as redeemer. Emerson's most explicit identification of himself with this Jesus comes at the very end of the Divinity School "Address":

> I look for the new Teacher that shall follow so far those shining laws that he shall see them come full circle; shall see their rounding complete grace; shall see the world to be the mirror of the soul; shall see the identity of the law of gravitation with purity of heart; and shall show that the Ought, that Duty, is one thing with Science, with Beauty, and with joy. (*Complete Works* 1:151)

This conclusion is one of Emerson's most challenging (and most radical) perorations. One should note, first, that "Teacher" is capitalized; Emerson is clearly describing a Messiah. His audience is the senior class in divinity at Harvard in 1838. They knew, as he was acutely aware, that he had resigned his own pulpit in 1832. He is coming to them, therefore, as the announcer of a new "Gospel," one freed, as he had freed himself, from the traditional trappings of even the orthodoxy of Unitarianism. At first glance, then, the persona of that final paragraph would seem to be John the Baptist, announcing the coming of the "new Teacher." But between 1832, Emerson's resignation of his pastorate of the Second Church of Boston, and the delivery of this address in the summer of 1838, had appeared Emerson's little book,

Nature. It is in Emerson's own words in *Nature* that "Those shining laws . . . come full circle." It is explicitly in *Nature* that we find a "demonstration" of "the World" as "the mirror of the soul," as well as other correspondences between "nature" and "spirit" which could include even "gravitation" and "purity of heart," and "Duty" with "Joy." In other words, the gospel Emerson is prophesying here has already been announced, by himself. The "Teacher" he is here looking for has already arrived; it is himself. In the peroration of the Divinity School "Address" Emerson metamorphoses himself from the prophet John the Baptist, announcing the coming of Jesus, to the prophet Jesus himself. Further, there is no need for a voice from heaven validating this new Jesus in the words, "Thou art my beloved Son; in thee I am well pleased" (Luke 3:22) because that heavenly "Father" has already been murdered by the whole thrust of the argument of the address. The new "redeemer" validates himself, as he does also in *Nature* and in "The American Scholar." The new Jesus is a self-created Son.[1]

Blake at least as boldly claims for himself messianic authority. In the early but engraved work, *The Marriage of Heaven and Hell,* Blake announces: "As a new heaven is begun, and it is now thirty-three years since its advent: the Eternal Hell revives. And lo! Swedenborg is the Angel sitting at the tomb; his writings are the linen clothes folded up. Now is the dominion of Edom, & the return of Adam into Paradise" (*Poetry and Prose* 34). Blake's initial attraction to Swedenborg was quickly followed by serious and permanent disillusionment with him (a pattern that can be traced in a very close parallel in Emerson's essay on Swedenborg in *Representative Men* [*Complete Works* 4:93–146]).[2] But the figure of Swedenborg as the angel at Christ's tomb is of much less interest than the implied figure of Blake—who is not "in the picture" because he has already gotten up and left, the Swedenborgian influence (the grave clothes as Swedenborg's writings) discarded and abandoned. Blake is here the resurrected Jesus.

Blake was born in 1757. *The Marriage of Heaven and Hell* was begun in 1790 (*Poetry and Prose* 801). Swedenborg's *Last Judgment* was begun in 1757. Bloom's commentary clarifies Blake's satiric point: "So

it came about that Blake, at the Christological age of thirty-three, revised the Eternal Hell of imaginative desire within himself and rose
from nature's tomb, leaving Swedenborg sitting there, with [Sweden-
borg's] *Divine Providence* the castoff clothing of death" (*Poetry and
Prose* 897). Blake, writing *Marriage of Heaven and Hell* at age thirty-
three, is the resurrected Jesus. Emerson, delivering the Divinity
School "Address" at age thirty-five, is the self-baptized Jesus at the beginning of his career. It is clear that neither Emerson nor Blake suffers
from any inferiority complex or false humility in his rhetorical projection of himself as "redeemer." This revision of the figure of Jesus
for their own authorial purposes, however, involves a necessary revision of "scripture" itself. Both Blake and Emerson recognize that
necessity. Near the end of *The Marriage,* Blake writes:

> This Angel [not Swedenborg but an angelic character
> in one of the "Memorable Fancies" in the work] who is
> now become a Devil, is my particular friend: we often
> read the Bible together in its infernal or diabolical
> sense which the world shall have if they behave well.
> I have also: the Bible of Hell: which the world shall
> have whether they will or no. (*Poetry and Prose* 44)

Emerson agrees, and not just in his early work. At the end of his essay
on Goethe, in *Representative Men* (1850), he observes, "We too must
write Bibles, to unite again the heavens and the earthly world" (*Complete Works* 4:290). Of course he had himself been doing just that
since 1836, as had Blake, quite self-consciously, ever since the "tractates" on religion of 1788. His major poems continue this work, and
hence his use of "biblical" titles such as *The Book of Ahania* or *The
Book of Los,* and certainly the engraved works constitute Blake's
"Bible" up to the final *Jerusalem* in 1804.

It is now necessary to take a closer look at this revised "Jesus"
whom Emerson and Blake can identify themselves with. He is not
the inherited corpse of orthodoxy, but, for both writers, an original,

imaginative concept. I shall look at the Emersonian and the Blakean "Jesus" as he appears in a selection of "representative" texts, passages that develop a revised archetype of Redemption.

Emerson begins his revision of the figure of Jesus very early in his career, at a crucial point of transition in it. It might be more accurate to say that this moment is the end of his abortive first career and the official beginning of his second, real vocation. The sermon, "The Lord's Supper," records his resignation as pastor of the Second Church in Boston, on September 9, 1832. Emerson's farewell address to Unitarian orthodoxy marks the end, at least officially (though he preached at times in the next few years), of his functioning as a clergyman and simultaneously the anticipation of his eventual professional switch from pulpit to lecture podium. It is because he can no longer administer in conscience the ritual of the Lord's Supper that he resigns his ministry. What that ritual symbolizes for him is closely bound up with what "The Lord" means to him; clearly, and without intellectual or ethical compromise, Emerson tells his congregation then and us now that Jesus is not, for him, a "Lord."

In the first half of the sermon Emerson performs a formal and rigidly logical demonstration supporting his conviction that there is no inherent authority in the Scriptural texts to support the practice of the "Lord's Supper" as a required rite. His exposition is so logical here as to be quite uncharacteristic of his mature style.[3] He uses certain principles of scriptural exegesis which had been practiced by his former professor, Andrews Norton, but, as John Michael points out (*Emerson and Skepticism* 9–21), Emerson uses these modes here very much against Norton's views. Part of the critical strategy is the use of extrinsic instead of intrinsic evidence, the language, as Norton had pointed out, being intrinsically ambiguous (Michael 13–14). So Emerson places the "Last Supper" in its cultural, historical context, and his resulting concept of Jesus is thoroughly humanized: "I see natural feeling and beauty in the use of such language ['This do in remembrance of me'] from Jesus, a friend to his friends" (*Complete Works* II:7). Emerson's own language, "A friend to his friends," removes even the slightest suggestion of the supernatural from the event, which is presented as a social occasion. We have here, in this early characterization by Emerson, a thoroughly (and merely) *human* Jesus.

Emerson then clarifies precisely the theological distinction he is making. He warns against "a painful confusion of thought between the worship due to God and the commemoration due to Christ" (17). That distinction is at the base of his objection to the ritual: "I fear it is the effect of this ordinance to clothe Jesus with an authority which he never claimed and which distracts the mind of the worshipper" (17). The distinction is explicit and clear—between God and Jesus. Emerson makes his idea of the nondivine Jesus even more explicit near the end of the sermon, in the section in which, as Edward Waldo Emerson noted, "he speaks from within—the way native to him" (551): "The Almighty God was pleased to qualify and send forth a man to teach men that they must serve him with the heart . . . . This man lived and died true to this purpose" (22). It is in this context, then, that of a desupernaturalized, fully human but merely human (not divine) Jesus that Emerson can say, "I will love him as a glorified friend" (20).

That was in 1832. *Nature* in 1836 makes only three references to Jesus, none of them suggesting divinity: "The visible heavens and earth sympathize with Jesus"; "prophet and priest, David, Isaiah, Jesus, have drawn deeply from this source [Nature]";[4] "Such examples ['of the action of man upon nature with his entire force'] are, the traditions of miracles in the earliest antiquity of all nations; the history of Jesus Christ; the achievement of a principle" (*Complete Works* 1:22, 41, 73). In "The American Scholar" of 1837 there are no references to Jesus at all.

By 1838 then and the Divinity School "Address," we can detect an evolved, more idiosyncratically Emersonian concept of Jesus. In 1832, in "The Lord's Supper," Jesus was a kind of ambassador sent from God to the rest of mankind: "The Almighty God was pleased to qualify and send forth a man to teach men" (*Complete Works* 11:22). But that transcendent Deity, that commissioning Father-figure, has disappeared into the "Spirit" of *Nature*. That Father-figure has been removed, is being removed, in "The American Scholar" and in the Divinity School "Address" itself. Emerson revises further his concept of the status of Jesus, who is demoted from an orthodox point of view but promoted in purely Emersonian terms. No longer an emissary from some ontologically distant "God," Jesus is now a *representative* of the divine by being a *participant* in a divinity now defined in exclusively human terms.

"If a man is at heart just, then in so far is he God; the safety of God, the immortality of God, the majesty of God do enter into that man with justice" (*Complete Works* 1:122). Here divinity is coexistent with human virtue, a "rapid intrinsic energy," and "By it a man is made the Providence to himself" (122–23). It is from this point of view that Emerson can denounce the orthodox definition of Jesus:

> When a man comes, all books are legible, all things transparent, all religions are forms. He is religious. Man is the wonderworker. He is seen amid miracles. All men bless and curse. He saith yea and nay, only. The stationariness of religion; the assumption that the age of inspiration is past, that the Bible is closed; the fear of degrading the character of Jesus by representing him as a man;—indicate with sufficient clearness the falsehood of our theology. It is the office of a true teacher to show us that God is, not was; that He speaketh, not spake. The true Christianity,—a faith like Christ's in the infinitude of man,—is lost. None believeth in the soul of man, but only in some man or person old and departed. (144)

Emerson's theological revisionism here has become quite extraordinary, in fact, revolutionary. In the above passages Jesus is divine *because* he is human. Jesus is no longer the object of faith; he is an example of having faith, and his faith has for its object "the infinitude of man." A humanist revisionism of Christianity can go no further. Or can it?

In the same address, Christian orthodoxy is described as an "eastern monarchy of a Christianity." Emerson tells his audience that such an ideology has been built from "indolence and fear." And in this antidemocratic, oriental tyranny, "the friend of man is made the injurer of man" (130). Edward Waldo Emerson's note to this passage records that Elizabeth Peabody urged Emerson "at least to put a capital F to the 'friend of man,' but Mr. Emerson answered, 'If I did so, they would all go to sleep'" (*Complete Works* 1:427). That "they" did not "go to sleep" is more than evidenced by the well-documented history of the furor that the Divinity School "Address" aroused.

But the concept of Jesus as "friend of man" is by no means the most radical aspect of Emerson's new definition. The "life and dialogues of Christ" (133) make him a Jewish Socrates, it is true. But Emerson makes a still more radical departure from orthodoxy, one which will bring him close to the iconoclasm of Blake:

> The divine *bards* are the friends of my virtue, of my intellect, of my strength. They admonish me that the gleams which flash across my mind are not mine, but God's; that they had the like, and were not disobedient to the heavenly vision. So I love them. Noble provocations go out from them, inviting me to resist evil; to subdue the world; and to Be. And thus, by his holy thoughts, Jesus serves us, and thus only. (132; emphasis added)

Emerson's Jesus as a "divine bard," an inspired poet, echoes the central concept of Jesus in Blake. But for Blake a "divine bard" must also be a prophet. And so he is for Emerson as well in the most dramatic and definitive statement on Jesus that Emerson makes in the "Address":

> Jesus Christ belonged to the true race of prophets. He saw with open eye the mystery of the soul. Drawn by its severe harmony, ravished with its beauty, he lived in

it, and had his being there. Alone in all history he estimated the greatness of man. He saw that God incarnates himself in man, and evermore goes forth anew to take possession of his world. He said, in this jubilee of sublime emotion, 'I am divine. Through me, God acts; through me, speaks. Would you see God, see me; or see thee, when thou also thinkest as I now think.' But what a distortion did his doctrine and memory suffer in the same, in the next, and the following ages! There is no doctrine of the Reason which will bear to be taught by the Understanding. The understanding caught this high chant from the poet's lips, and said, in the next age, 'This was Jehovah come down out of heaven. I will kill you, if you say he was a man.' The idioms of his language and the figures of his rhetoric have usurped the place of his truth; and churches are not built on his principles, but on his tropes. Christianity became a Mythus, as the poetic teaching of Greece and of Egypt, before. He spoke of miracles; for he felt that man's life was a miracle, and all that man doth, and he knew that this daily miracle shines as the character ascends. But the word Miracle, as pronounced by Christian churches, gives a false impression; it is Monster. It is not one with the blowing clover and the falling rain. (128–29)

This study aims to show that Blake's thought is less idiosyncratic, and Emerson's more radical, than they are usually thought to be, by demonstrating important congruences between these authors. Here, too, Blakean texts offer analogies to Emerson's on this critical matter of the *human as divine* with its focus on the representative divine humanity of Jesus.

In Blake's earliest engraved works, the two tractates on religion, the name of Jesus Christ does not appear, but the Emersonian concept of divinity in humanity is already expressed in the quasi-Platonic concept of the "Poetic Genius." Blake writes, "the Poetic Genius is the true Man" and "the Poetic Genius is every where call'd the Spirit of Prophecy." Further, "The Jewish & Christian Testaments are An original derivation from the Poetic Genius" (*Poetry and Prose* 1). Blake comes very close here to Emerson's interpretation of Scripture, that Jesus is a "divine bard" and a "prophet." It should be noted that Blake describes the "Jewish & Christian Testaments" as *An* "original derivation from the Poetic Genius," not *the* original derivation; here he anticipates Emerson's use of Scriptures from Hindu and other cultures. Blake's grounding of religious revelation is as thoroughly humanistic as Emerson's: "The true Man is the source he being the Poetic Genius" (*Poetry and Prose* 2). This passage closely resembles Emerson's "When a man comes . . . all religions are forms. He is religious. Man is the wonderworker" (*Complete Works* 1:144).

Here the poets present the possibility of human redemption—but in exclusively human terms. The theme of Redemption grounds the optimism of both Emerson and Blake, and their most optimistic statements may be better understood by relating them to each other. Thus it is in this context that Emerson proclaims at the beginning of *Nature:* "Undoubtedly we have no questions to ask which are unanswerable" (*Complete Works* 1:3), a sentence which our own century has had trouble with. It may be better understood in Blake's version: "If any could desire what he is incapable of possessing, despair would be his eternal lot. The desire of Man being Infinite the possession is Infinite & himself infinite" (*Poetry and Prose* 2–3). Both writers make the point that all questions are necessarily human questions and therefore have human answers. But this epistemological position has an ontological rationale. Blake says, in a statement which could quite easily be mistaken for a sentence of Emerson in any number of contexts, "He who sees the Infinite in all things sees God" (*Poetry and Prose* 3). And Blake concludes the second tractate with a redefinition of the doctrine of the Incarnation: "Therefore / God becomes as we are, / that we may be as he / is" (*Poetry and Prose* 3). These words are

Blake's version of Emerson's paraphrase of Jesus: "Would you see God, see me; or see thee, when thou thinkest as I now think" (*Complete Works* 1:128).

For Emerson, as we have seen, Jesus is a "glorified friend," a "divine bard," and a "prophet." Blake certainly agrees, but the rhetoric of *The Marriage of Heaven and Hell* which wittily, satirically, and self-consciously subverts Christian orthodoxy, takes him farther from the conventional figure of Jesus than Emerson (with a few striking exceptions) is willing to go. Although for Blake, "All deities reside in the human breast" (*Poetry and Prose* 38), and "The worship of God is. Honouring his gifts in other men each according to his genius. and loving the greatest men best . . . for there is no other God" (*Poetry and Prose* 43), sentiments which are Emersonian enough, Blake in *The Marriage* reveals a major difference from Emerson in his concept of the relationship between Christian morality and the figure of Jesus. Much of Emerson's later writing seems in part an effort to preserve Christian ethical teaching as a cultural value, removed from any "supernatural" authority for it inherent in the founder. Blake, on the other hand, so identifies Jesus with the energy of creative imagination that he sees the founder of Christianity in opposition to orthodox Christian morality.

In the dialogue between the distraught angel and the serene devil in *The Marriage,* the angel angrily asks, "Has not Jesus Christ given his sanction to the law of ten commandments?" (*Poetry and Prose* 43). Blake's answer, in the mouth of the "devil," is a resounding "No!":

> If Jesus Christ is the greatest man, you ought to love him in the greatest degree; now hear how he has given his sanction to the law of ten commandments: did he not mock at the sabbath, and so mock the sabbaths God? murder those who were murdered because of him? turn away the law from the woman taken in adultery? steal the labor of others to support him? bear false witness when he omitted making a defence before

Pilate? covet when he pray'd for his disciples, and
when he bid them shake off the dust of their feet
against such as refused to lodge them? I tell you, no
virtue can exist without breaking these ten commandments: Jesus was all virtue, and acted from impulse:
not from rules. (*Poetry and Prose* 43)

Emerson almost never takes such a position on Christian ethics—
almost never. Recall the passages on the relativity of the virtues in
"Circles": "The only sin is limitation"; "There is no virtue which is
final; all are initial"; "The virtues of society are vices of the saint"; and
even, "No evil is pure, nor hell itself without its extreme satisfactions"
(*Complete Works* 2:308, 316, 316–17, 318). Outside of "Circles," however, Emerson seldom goes so far. He is, in the area of ethics,
considerably less of a revolutionary than Blake. Consequently,
although they agree on Jesus as the "friend," the "bard," and the
"prophet," for Blake that bardic prophecy of Jesus is ethically and
politically revolutionary; for Emerson, it is not.

There remains, however, substantial agreement between the
revised figures of Jesus in Emerson and in Blake. Not the least important factor in this congruence is their mutual removal of the "Father,"
or Jehovah. It is necessary to kill this father in order to free this son; in
other words, the nonhuman deity must be negated so that the fully
human divine figure can be imaginatively available in his full humanity. But this particular father is not easily murdered, and both Blake's
and Emerson's rhetoric reveal the seriousness of the problem. Blake
writes, "Know that after Christs death, he became Jehovah" (*Poetry
and Prose* 35), which may be a difficult line until glossed with Emerson's equally dramatic, "This was Jehovah come down out of heaven.
I will kill you, if you say he was a man" (*Complete Works* 1:129). Both
assertions are savagely ironic, and both indicate the power of the orthodoxy these two writers have set themselves to oppose. Orthodoxy,
tradition, convention—the Past *is* "The Father." Both Emerson and
Blake assume a rhetorical stance as a fatherless son; the Jesus whom

they positively invoke is also a son without a father, a "brother," a "friend." Blake tends to be explicit about the Father-Son dichotomy; Emerson "murders" the Father by, first, an attack on the cultural repositories of paternal influence (the church in the Divinity School "Address" and the "school" in "The American Scholar"), and then by total omission of his existence from his subsequent works.[5] Blake, typically, confronts the problem head-on: "Thinking as I do that the Creator of this World is a very Cruel Being & being a Worshipper of Christ I cannot help saying the Son O how unlike the Father First God Almighty comes with a Thump on the Head Then Jesus Christ comes with a balm to heal it" (*Poetry and Prose* 565).

What unites the Blakean and Emersonian figures of Jesus is the fact of their humanity. In "The Everlasting Gospel," which details the same rebellion against the moral virtues on the part of Jesus (in this a late work) as Blake had argued in the early *Marriage,* Blake says, "Thou art a Man God is no more / Thy own humanity learn to adore" (*Poetry and Prose* 520). Blake's variations on the concept never abandon it. "So spake the Family Divine as One Man even Jesus" (*Milton* 21:58; *Poetry and Prose* 116). He is "one Man Jesus the Savior" (*Milton* 42:11; *Poetry and Prose* 143). He is "Human Divine, Jesus the Saviour" (*Jerusalem* 36:47; *Poetry and Prose* 182). "There is no other / God, than that God who is the intellectual fountain of Humanity" (*Jerusalem* 91:9–10; *Poetry and Prose* 251). "Every / Particular is a Man; a Divine Member of the Divine Jesus" (*Jerusalem* 91:29–30; *Poetry and Prose* 251). The variations on this concept in Blake's later works can indeed be difficult, even bewildering, but they are always variations on the core idea of the identity of the human and the divine. Jesus is Blake's most effective symbol of that identification.

The difficulties inherent in understanding Blake's concept of Jesus, especially in the later prophetic books, occur because of that archetypal figure's complex connections with Blake's total myth, a symbolic burden that Emerson never had to carry. Since all reality is human for Blake, the identification of Jesus as cosmic-divine-human

appears as one of multiple manifestations of that idea. Sometimes
Blake thinks of Jesus as Albion. "All things have proceeded from a
divine Man, the body of Jesus, and will be reabsorbed into him"
(Frye 386), and the poet's work is to activate that concept in his
reader's mind. "The true Jesus is the present vision of Jesus, the uniting of the divine and human in our own minds, and it is only the
active Jesus, the teacher and healer and storyteller, who can be recre-
ated" (Frye 387). At other times Blake identifies Jesus with Los, as the
artist-prophet; as Orc, the youthful revolutionary who undergoes
crucifixions in the minor prophecies; or as Luvah in the later ones, a
figure of passion, suffering, and violent death. These avatars in other
words are interchangeable because of the central thesis of the myth.
Thus the identities of Jesus in the poems change much in the
manner of the faces in Emerson's dream of the "Central Man." But
the concept, as distinct from its specific figurative representation, remains the same: "man or humanity, who is Jesus the Saviour" ("A
Descriptive Catalogue," *Poetry and Prose* 536).

The concept of the divine humanity of Jesus occurs throughout
Blake's work, in the early tractates (given later contexts, the "Poetic
Genius" can be thought of as Jesus), and the satiric *Marriage,* as well
as in the late major prophecies, *Milton* and *Jerusalem.* This figure is
also often present in the poems even when not named; when to use
the name would violate poetic or dramatic verisimilitude. It is in
these latter contexts, where Blake's "Giant Forms" do not appear, that
the Emersonian values of Blake's Jesus may be more clearly discerned.
Particularly the figure of the "friend," as distinct from prophet or
bard, acts and speaks in *Innocence* and in *Experience.* A poem which
demonstrates the human values of such a religious vision is "The
Chimney Sweeper" from *Songs of Innocence.*

> When my mother died I was very young,
> And my father sold me while yet my tongue,
> Could scarcely cry weep weep weep weep
> So your chimneys I sweep & in soot I sleep.

Theres little Tom Dacre, who cried when
    his head
That curl'd like a lambs back, was shav'd,
    so I said.
Hush Tom never mind it, for when you head's
    bare,
You know that the soot cannot spoil your
    white hair.

And so he was quiet, & that very night
As Tom was a sleeping he had such a sight,
That thousands of sweepers Dick, Joe, Ned
    & Jack
Were all of them lock'd up in coffins of black.

And by came an Angel who had a bright key,
And he open'd the coffins & set them all free.
Then down a green plain leaping laughing
    they run
And wash in a river and shine in the Sun.

Then naked & white, all their bags left behind,
They rise upon clouds, and sport in the wind.
And the Angel told Tom if he'd be a good boy,
He'd have God for his father & never want joy.

And so Tom awoke and we rose in the dark
And got with our bags and our brushes to work.
Tho' the morning was cold, Tom was happy & warm,
So if all do their duty, they need not fear harm.
(*Poetry and Prose* 10)

The effect of Blake's "The Chimney Sweeper" is pathos, to arouse in the reader the feeling of pity for the speaker of the poem and for his fellow sweeps.[6] He achieves this effect by dramatic irony, in that the chimney sweeper neither asks for pity nor does he himself in the action of this poem require it. The irony is created by the reader's understanding more of the boy's situation than the innocent child does himself. It thus works like the dramatic irony generated when Othello praises Iago's fidelity or when Oedipus seeks to discover the murderer of Laius. The narrator of this dramatic monologue speaks in all innocence; his situation, however, is not innocent, though he is in no way responsible for it. If the reader feels a secondary effect, or aftereffect, anger or indignation, it is probably in response to what is only implied in the poem; or to historical knowledge of the social and economic system which permitted this cruel form of child labor; or perhaps to this poem's companion piece, the "Chimney Sweeper" from *Songs of Experience,* where another boy in the same plight, or the same boy—older, experienced—names villains and explicitly assigns blame. "They [his father and mother] think they have done me no injury: / And are gone to praise God & his Priest & King / Who make up a heaven of our misery." But that is the voice of experience speaking; the earlier poem voices only innocence.

It is by means of this irony that Blake makes the innocent "Chimney Sweeper" the more effective poem of the pair. Our pity for the speaker is increased by the fact that he in no way invites it. He is matter-of-fact about his plight: his mother died when he was very young, his father sold him, he sleeps in soot, he must labor to sweep—in a direct address to the reader—"your chimneys." All the rest of the poem, except for the last stanza, focuses on another boy, and it is in the speaker's selfless concern for his companion, his forgetting of his own plight, that we are most moved by him and by his pitiful situation.

The plot of this poem is the action of consoling a suffering coworker. The need for that consolation is the inciting action (stanza two), and when it is achieved the poem concludes. Blake is extremely economical in imitating this action; the whole poem is only six quatrains. After a first stanza of exposition, in which the speaker explains his situation, his (and our) attention shifts to another chimney sweeper, "little Tom Dacre." Tom cries when his head is shaved, "so" (the causal conjunction is crucially important) the speaker consoles him. It does not matter that the literal meaning of the consolation is absurd: if you're now shaved bald, you won't need to worry about soot in your hair. What does matter is that the consolation works; it is efficacious moral action. Again conjunctions function economically but essentially to depict this action: "And so he was quiet." Because Tom stops crying, becomes quiet, he sleeps and has the beautiful dream. It does not matter that the beautiful dream is a fantasy or (for Blake) a lie. Both Tom and the speaker are innocent. Tom's mental state has been changed by the dream. "Tho' the morning was cold, Tom was happy & warm." By this act of consolation the speaker has brought Tom from a state of suffering to a state of ease. This imaginative, efficacious moral action, a positive use of spiritual energy, would be for Blake the "vision" of the fully human condition, not the child's fantasy contained in the dream. Tom has been brought from a state of mental misery to one of contentment, although the sweepers' situation has not changed and still deserves our pity.

What is most moving about the character of the speaker is that he is not so hardened by or submissive to his situation that he lacks sympathy for his fellow sweep. He is able to take the imaginative, moral initiative to perform the act of consolation, which works, although what he says in the consolation is childish, or foolish, or innocent. The speaker is of course the real angel in the poem, in contrast to the fantasy figure of the angel in the dream. The speaker focuses spiritual energy in a positive direction by acting to improve the human condition, which in this poem is Tom Dacre's state of mind. The speaker is powerless over the social and economic situation in which he and Tom Dacre are trapped. He is not powerless, however, to effect a real human difference within it. It is a very real difference (not a fiction in a dream): "Tho' the morning was cold, Tom was happy & warm."

Blake alters diction and rhythm very subtly to achieve his effect.[7] It is important to note that the most factually true statements are in a slightly irregular and therefore disguised anapestic rhythm (the exposition of the first quatrain and the important action of the second). When the poem moves away from the factually true, the anapests become more explicit, even exaggerated, childishly sing-song, notably in the dream sequence and in the poem's last line, which sounds false (though true to the speaker's childishly innocent voice and character), because it is false. If all these boys do their duty, they not only *should* fear harm, they *will* be harmed; their work is literally killing them. When a real moral good is achieved in the poem, it is through the speaker's transcendence of duty. It was not his duty to console Tom. His duty consists in sweeping chimneys.

The diction also changes, from the beginning exposition, the first two lines of which sound like a factual report (because they are a factual report), through the fantasy images of the dream sequence, to the empty abstractions of the innocently repeated cliché of the last line ("duty" and "harm"). Also, the diction of this poem ironically plays with itself, doubles back upon itself, echoes and transforms meanings. If the coffins in the dream are metaphorically chimneys, then the chimneys outside the dream are also coffins. In other words, Tom dreams about coffins because he's confined in chimneys day after day, but those chimneys are these boys' coffins; they often die in them and have to be pulled out dead from them. If the boys' lives are coffined in the chimneys, their only escape is death. This identification of images makes the angel's key in the dream highly ambiguous. It suggests that the sweeps' only freedom from their slave labor is death, and if Tom's consolation in the dream (as distinct from the waking consolation he gets from the speaker) is the freedom offered by death, then the dream functions as an analogy of the advice the speaker gives to Tom: being rendered bald as the "cure" for sooty hair is analogous to death as a "cure" for a life of suffering. Blake's satire exposes not just the evil of child labor. It goes much further and exposes a fallacy central to orthodox Christianity, namely, that human *life* is redeemed *after death,* the theological equivalent of your-hair-won't-be-dirty-when-you-no-longer-have-any-hair. Not for Blake. Further, when the Angel in the dream promises Tom that, given the ambiguously stated condition, he'd "have God for his father," a less innocent Tom might have been alarmed rather than consoled. Fathers in this poem, as everywhere else in Blake, are bad news (and mothers are no help, either). The reader, unlike Tom, remembers the speaker's "father" in line 2, who "sold" his son. So much for fathers. This "God the Father" is clearly the fictitious monster, Nobodaddy.

It would be uncharacteristic of Blake's art if he were to leave the reader merely with the emotional response of pity, an emotion he often distrusts ("Pity divides the soul"). The conclusion of "The Chimney Sweeper" from *Innocence* works as realistic observation of some harsh facts of socioeconomic life: "we rose in the dark / And got with our bags and our brushes to work." Nothing has changed. Yes and no. It also works as equally realistic observation of *spiritual metamorphosis:* "Tho' the morning was cold, Tom was happy & warm." Everything has changed. Who is this anonymous sweep, this speaker of the poem who has brought about a mental revolution?

The last two lines of the poem consolidate its whole ironic strategy. They move in opposite conceptual directions, united by the same dramatic voice. The speaker, in the next to last line, innocently witnesses the fact of the imaginative transformation he has himself brought about. In the last line, still the innocent child, he falls back into parroting the empty moralistic cliché he has heard from adults, an Establishment lie. Eternity has been innocently experienced within the fallen world of time.

Rising in the dark to go back to work is presented as fact. But Tom is "happy & warm," and that is also and equally presented as fact. Tom is happy and warm in spite of misery and cold. A miracle has occurred. The speaker of the poem, then, is a miracle worker, and he has used imagination to achieve this miracle.[8] He is one voice (although an innocent one) of the "Eternal Divine Imagination." He also reminds us of the voice that cries out to Albion: "I am not a God afar off, I am a brother and friend" (*Jerusalem* 4:18; *Poetry and Prose* 146). The speaker of "The Chimney Sweeper" of *Songs of Innocence* is Blake's Jesus.[9]

A very accurate paraphrase of the religious significance of Blake's innocent "Chimney Sweeper" can be found in a sentence of Emerson from a late essay, "Worship," in *The Conduct of Life* (1860): "The happiness of one cannot consist with the misery of any other" (*Complete Works* 6:230–31). Emerson never reverted to orthodoxy, nor did Blake. Edward Waldo Emerson, Ralph Waldo's son and first editor, may be presumed to speak with some authority on this matter:

> Soon after Mr. Emerson had completed his three-score and ten years, a young clergyman in a Western State, whose growth had been helped by his writings, was troubled at an authoritative statement, which he had heard, that Emerson had been led by the preaching of a popular Orthodox divine in Boston to see the error of his ways and teachings, "had accepted Jesus as his Saviour, The Bible as inspired, and had formally joined the Church." Mr. Emerson smiled, but did not think it worth while to deny these assertions, yet allowed his son to answer the letter of inquiry as to whether he had suffered a late conversion. This sentence from Saadi, which he enjoyed, and quotes in *Representative Men,* would have been a simple and appropriate answer: "It was rumored abroad that I was penitent, but what had I to do with repentance?" (*Complete Works* 8:416)

Blake smiles too, and often. A close parallel to Edward Waldo Emerson's anecdote about his father, quoted above, is one of Henry Crabb Robinson's reminiscences about the elderly Blake. During the winter of 1825 (Blake would have been sixty-eight), walking home from a dinner party with him, Robinson asked Blake "about the divinity of Jesus. '*He is the only God,*' said Blake, but then he added, 'And so am I and so are you'" (Davis 158–59). It would be hard to find a more Emersonian idea, outside of the words of Emerson himself.

Whicher's view of an "acquiescent" older Emerson (and Emerson gets old fast for Whicher) is now being increasingly challenged by more recent critics.[10] Damrosch and Hirsch have offered us a purged, tamed, and "converted" Blake (someone should tell Crabb Robinson), but the best rebuttal against academic conservatism's dismay at poetic radicalism (a permanent problem) is the poet's texts themselves.[11] As Frosch points out, "to maintain a concept of the late Blake as turning away from the body, one must simply ignore" such late works as "The Everlasting Gospel" (Frosch 160). And Frosch finds "the Jesus of the last epic [*Jerusalem*], while identified in his aspect of savior with Los, is still in his crucifixion and resurrection a manifestation of Luvah [sexual energy]" (160). Thus the Jesus of the last engraved major poem is still a character in Blake's humanistic myth. There is simply no evidence to suggest that Blake ever departed from the central conviction he expressed in "Auguries of Innocence":

> God Appears & God is Light
> To those poor Souls who dwell in Night
> But does a Human Form Display
> To those who Dwell in Realms of Day.
> (*Poetry and Prose* 493)

Emerson, too, is uncompromising in his permanent break with orthodoxy. In the Divinity School "Address," he wrote, "Now do not degrade the life and dialogues of Christ . . . by insulation and peculiarity. Let them lie as they befell, alive and warm, part of human life and of the landscape and of the cheerful day." And he adds, "The need was never greater of new revelation than now" (*Complete Works* 1:133, 135). In "Character," from the *Essays: Second Series* of 1844, he uses this historical exemplum:

> The ages have exulted in the manners of a youth who
> owed nothing to fortune, and who was hanged at the
> Tyburn of his nation, who, by the pure quality of his
> nature, shed an epic splendor around the facts of his
> death which has transfigured every particular into an

universal symbol for the eyes of mankind. (*Complete Works* 3:114)

It is the symbol, much more than the historicity, that interests Emerson. "Jesus is not dead; he is very well alive: nor John, nor Paul, nor Mahomet, nor Aristotle; at times we believe we have seen them all, and could easily tell the names under which they go" ("Nominalist and Realist," *Complete Works* 3:244). But in the same essay he is careful to distinguish symbolic value from historic fact: "Our exaggeration of all fine characters arises from the fact that we identify each in turn with the soul. But there are no such men as we fable; no Jesus, nor Pericles, nor Caesar, nor Angelo, nor Washington, such as we have made" (227). A more important statement of the same distinction occurs in the much more important essay, "Experience":

> People forget that it is the eye which makes the horizon, and the rounding man's eye which makes this or that man a type or representative of humanity, with the name of hero or saint. Jesus, the "providential man," is a good man on whom many people are agreed that these optical laws shall take effect. By love on one part and by forbearance to press objection on the other part, it is for a time settled that we will look at him in the centre of the horizon, and ascribe to him the properties that will attach to any man so seen. (*Complete Works* 3:76–77)

It is a precise formulation of Emerson's concept of Jesus; he is a "type" or "representative" of "hero" or "saint," but he is also, in Emerson's characteristic, most significantly charged terms, "in the centre of the horizon." The later writings show no change in view. In "Worship," in *The Conduct of Life* (1860), he says: "The dogma and mystic offices of Christ being dropped, and he standing on his genius as a moral teacher, it is impossible to maintain the old emphasis of his personality; and it recedes, as all persons must, before the sublimity of the moral laws" (*Complete Works* 6:209).

Jesus appears in, of all places, "Clubs," in *Society and Solitude* (1870), where he shares a paragraph, very clubbily indeed, with Martin Luther and Samuel Johnson. "Jesus spent his life in discoursing with humble people on life and duty, in giving wise answers, showing that he saw at a larger angle of vision, and at least silencing those who were not generous enough to accept his thoughts" (*Complete Works* 7:236). The passage gives us perhaps a fantasy-image of Emerson himself, but it also employs, again, the loaded Emersonian diction, "angle of vision." In humanizing Jesus, Emerson is never derogating him.

Letters and Social Aims appeared in 1875, but the dating of its individual essays is difficult. Edward Waldo Emerson finds that the basis for "Immortality" was a lecture from 1861, but it may have been used in his father's very late university lecture series in 1870 or 1871 (*Complete Works* 8:434).[12] In it Emerson remarks, "Jesus explained nothing, but the influence of him took people out of time, and they felt eternal" (347).

The miscellaneous material in *Lectures and Biographical Sketches* (*Complete Works*, vol. 10) is even harder to date. Edward Waldo suggests that parts of "The Preacher" come from 1867 to 1879; it was first published in January, 1880. In it either the old or very old Emerson says, "An era in human history is the life of Jesus; and the immense influence for good leaves all the perversion and superstition almost harmless" (228). "Character," from the same volume (not to be confused with "Character" in *Essays: Second Series),* the editor dates from 1864–65 (531). In it comes a statement that sounds less like the Emerson of 1864 and more like the Emerson of 1838: "The excellence of Jesus, and of every true teacher, is, that he affirms the Divinity in him and in us,—not thrusts himself between it and us" (*Complete Works* 10:97). Jesus "affirms the Divinity in him and in us" It is the echo of Blake's remark to Crabb Robinson, "He is the only God. And so am

I. And so are you." Emerson had said in 1854, "To interpret Christ it needs Christ in the heart" ("The Fugitive Slave Law," *Complete Works* 11:234). He ended a speech in 1869 with "the history of Jesus is the history of every man, written large" (*Complete Works* 9:491). But perhaps one should not leave this phase of the topic without recalling Emerson's quotation of Voltaire on the subject of Jesus. Its transitional sentence is arresting. "Every hero becomes a bore at last. Perhaps Voltaire was not bad-hearted, yet he said of the good Jesus, even, 'I pray you, let me never hear that man's name again'" ("Uses of Great Men," *Representative Men, Complete Works* 4:27).

Emerson took the line, "The history of Jesus is the history of every man, written large," quoted above from his speech at the Second Annual Meeting of the Free Religious Association at Tremont Temple, May 28, 1869 (*Complete Works* 9:483) from an earlier recording of it in his journal of 1840: "The history of Jesus is only the history of every man written large. The names he bestows on Jesus belong to himself,—Mediator, Redeemer, Saviour" (*Journals* 5:478). Robert E. Burkholder, after pointing out that the "atheist" Abner Kneeland's "attack on Universalism . . . sums up Emerson's complaints about Unitarianism as enumerated in the Divinity School Address" and noting that "Kneeland was jailed and Emerson was not," goes on to make a very valuable distinction: "[Emerson] did not compromise his truth, only state it in a way that would make it less offensive."[13] This distinction—that Emerson's truth or message or vision remains uncompromised, but that its expression gets rhetorically modified under the pressures of dealing with an audience—can be usefully applied to many other Emersonian texts. Here the example of Blake will contrast, for Blake, ignored and neglected, enjoyed by that very isolation a unique freedom to express himself uninhibited by any actual audience response. It would be interesting then to see if there are any substantial differences between the public statements Emerson made about Jesus (as exemplified in the various essays and lectures quoted above) and the more private musings and speculations of his journals. One says "more private" rather than "private," because the rhetorical problems of the journals have yet to be explored, among them, the question of whether or not Emerson is writing for an "audience" even here.[14] One need not take the extreme position of John Michael, namely, that not "anxiety of influence" but anxiety about audience was Emerson's dominant and often crippling obsession throughout his career, an *idée fixe* for Waldo in Michael's study that makes Ahab's interest in the whale seem casual by comparison.[15] Yet a problem about Emerson's relation to his audience or audiences does exist, and Evelyn Barish is most perceptive when she describes the *Journals and Miscellaneous Notebooks* themselves as "both an unparalleled opportunity and a dilemma . . . . What is most important is often hard to perceive amid an often radiant chaos."[16] Certainly *JMN* does not read like a personal, private diary. But is there in Emerson's journal pages more candor about how he felt about the figure of Jesus?

So far we have observed that Blake consistently humanizes Jesus as an incarnation of the human imagination, whether as the rebel anti-Decalogue figure of the *Marriage* (replacing a law figure, Jehovah, with a love figure, "the Son how unlike the father") or in the later works as the consoling friend to Albion, a function of the moral imagination that is exemplified also by his early figure as "The Chimney Sweeper." In Emerson one can detect a subtle shift, chronologically, from the figure of Jesus in the Divinity School "Address" and other earlier passages, as "Friend," "Prophet," and "Bard," to the later figure of the "teacher" of moral truth and spiritual wisdom. The figure remains human but is treated less personally. Was Emerson aware of a shift? Was he accommodating his vision to his audience? Was he aware that either his earlier or his later versions of Jesus could pose a problem for his audience? The journals should give us a look behind the lecture platform.

For this purpose it will be necessary to ignore most of the huge number of references to "Jesus" or "Christ" in the journals, many of which occur in transcribed quotations from other authors, in paraphrases of prayers or other religious sources, or as conventional historical exempla. We are looking for a more personally Emersonian Jesus. The most useful allusions occur, predictably enough, in the years just before and just after the Divinity School "Address"; but there are some significant ones in the 1840s, and, though their number dramatically declines in Emerson's later years (a fact significant in itself), a few significant references to Christ appear as late as the 1860s.

In 1835 Emerson mentions "the religious Revolution effected by Jesus Christ" (*Journals and Notebooks* 5:5), stressing the contribution of Jesus as a break with tradition and convention, not as an expression of it. He is a "god," but a human, not a transcendental deity: "When the gods come among men they are not known. Jesus was not. Socrates & Shakspear were not" (12). As teacher, he is compared to Plato in his pedagogic methodology: "Fable avoids the difficulty [explanation], is at once exoteric and esoteric, & is clapped by both sides. Plato & Jesus used it" (31). So far we have sentiments correlative to the publicly expressed ones in the "Address." But there are also more candid revelations:

> You affirm that the moral development contains all the
> intellectual & that Jesus was the perfect man. I bow in
> reverence unfeigned before that benign man. I . . .
> know more, hope more, am more because he has lived.
> But if you tell me that in your opinion he has fulfilled
> all the conditions of man's existence, carried out to the
> utmost at least by implication, all man's powers, I sus-
> pend my assent. I do not see in him cheerfulness; I do
> not see in him the love of Natural Science; I see in him
> no kindness for Art; I see in him nothing of Socrates,
> of Laplace, of Shakespeare. The perfect man should re-
> mind us of all great men. Do you ask me if I would
> rather resemble Jesus than any other man? If I should
> say Yes, I should suspect myself of superstition. (71–72)

Those sentiments Emerson did not share publicly at Harvard's Divinity Hall in 1838.

More predictable and recognizable responses follow. "Jesus Christ was a minister of the pure Reason" (273) is also from 1835. But, probably in 1836 (one guesses here on the basis of context, exact dating being impossible), Emerson reveals a more personal insight: "Jesus simply affirmed, never argued" (*Journals and Notebooks* 6:183). This admired method throws considerable light on Emerson's own characteristic rhetoric in the *Essays,* as well as his failure to respond to his critics. In 1836 we get a mature Emersonian concept in "The All is in Man. Ask no idle questions concerning the nature or deed of Christ. See thou do it not. He is thy fellow worshipper and all power belongeth unto God" (*Journals and Notebooks* 5:230–31). In 1837 we have Jesus as both a present-day lecturer (and possibly reformer) and as an original affirmer of the self: "If Jesus came now into the world, he would say—You, YOU! He said to his age, I" (362). By 1838 we are really into the context of the Divinity School "Address": "The Belief in Christianity that now prevails is the Unbelief of Men. They will have Christ for a lord & not for a brother. Christ preache[d]s the greatness of Man but we hear only the greatness of Christ" (459). The manuscript's indecision about the tense of Christ's preaching is interesting. "God is; not was." But *did* Christ preach or *does* he preach? Also from 1838 comes an unusually personal note: "See how easily these old worships of Moses, of Socrates, of Zoroaster, of Jesus, domesticate themselves in my mind. It will be admitted I have great susceptibility to such. Will it not be as easy to say they are other Waldos?" (465). "Other Waldos" reflects the same metaphoric impulse that I have suggested as occurring at the end of the "Address": Emerson himself is the messianic "Teacher." But here, with the names of "Jesus" and "Waldo," the identification is much more psychologically revealing.

There is a lot of early, undated material in the *Lecture Notebooks: 1835–1862,* but again context is a guide to approximate chronology, and a number of jottings suggest the year of the "Address," 1838.

"Jesus taught sentiments & stood on instincts" (*Journals and Notebooks* 7:9) reminds us of Blake's Jesus in the *Marriage,* who "acted from impulse, not from rules." "The hope of mankind must rest in the sometime appearance of a true Messiah who shall complete the Epos of moral nature & write out those laws for the charmed world to read & to obey" (11) reminds us of the messianic "Teacher" whom the end of the "Address" invokes, and also distinguishes this "true Messiah" from the historical Jesus. "Jesus was a man & taught alone in history the greatness of man" (11) paraphrases a passage in the "Address." So does "Jesus was a teacher of the Soul: men have not received the Soul but Jesus" (12). And the brief note, "Jesus a poet" (13), suggests another major term in that speech, as well as an analogy with Blake. Other relevant passages become increasingly harder to pin down chronologically, such as "We think so meanly of man that 'tis thought a profanity to call Jesus one" (256); "Christ preaches the greatness of man but we the greatness of Xt [Christ]" (410, 459); "Jesus never preaches personal immortality" (558); and the much more autobiographically revealing, "Not wholesome to *say* I love not Xt [Christ]" (473). A few of these statements may be considerably later than 1838.

The dating is clearly 1838, however, for "Happy pilgrim of nature . . . . By a single wise man he knew Jesus & Plato, Shakspear & the angels" (*Journals and Notebooks* 7:26); "Another wood-thought was that since the parrot world will be swift to renounce the name of Christ in amends to its pride for having raised it so high, it behooves the lover of God to love that lover of God" (35); "The great facts of history are four or five names[,] Homer—Phidias—Jesus—Shakspeare" (147). And on the sixth of January, 1838, almost six months after the delivery of the "Address," we find:

> It seemed to me at church today that the communion service as it is now & here celebrated is a document of the dulness of the race. Then presently when I thought of the divine soul of my Nazarene whose name is used

here & considered how these my neighbors the bend-
ing deacons with their cups & plates would have
straightened themselves to sturdiness if the proposi-
tion came before them to honor thus a known
fellowman[,] I was constrained to feel the force of
Genius that hallowing once those Hebrew lips should
propagate its influence thus far & not be quite utterly
lost in these ultimate shoals & shores of our Concord
Congregation. (163–64)

Here are reminiscences of the "Lord's Supper" sermon mixed with
echoes of the Divinity School "Address" in a tone which is critical but
benevolent.

The furor that resulted from the "Address" causes a noticeable
change in journal entries a year or two later. The change begins subtly
enough. "How strange that Jesus should stand at the head of history,
the first character of the world without doubt, but the unlikeliest of
all men, one would say, to take such a rank in such a world" (249).
This is from 1839, as is, "Cannot Montaigne & Shakspeare consist
with Plato & Jesus?" (253), and, more impatiently, "Divine as the life
of Jesus is[,] what an outrage . . . to represent it as tantamount of the
Universe!" (254). More interesting as a personal concept of Christ is
this passage, also from 1839:

We have nothing to do with Jesus in our progress,
nothing to do with any past soul. The only way in
which the life of Jesus or other holy person helps us is
this[,] that as we advance without reference to persons
on a new, unknown, sublime path, we at each new
ascent verify the experiences of Jesus & such souls as
have obeyed God before. We take up into our proper
life at that moment his act & word & do not copy
Jesus but really are Jesus, just as Jesus in that moment
of his life was us. Say rather, it was neither him nor us,

but a man at this & at that time saw the truth & was transformed into its likeness. (255)

Here Jesus seems to be both devalued and revalued, but an important aspect now is a sort of deification of the individual self. This self-transformation makes redemption itself a totally human phenomenon.

The year 1839 includes a number of observations similar to "Jesus & Shakspeare were two men of genius" (285). But in 1840 we begin to see significant changes. "The effect of Jesus on men, after an immense deduction is made for false reception of all kinds, is an impure theocracy" (334). Here Emerson stresses the distortion of the "Poet's" song by his audience, and perhaps reflects his own feelings about the negative public reception of the 1838 "Address." At any rate, it is at this point in the journals that Emerson begins to pay more explicit attention to his audience, and he raises explicitly the problem of how to communicate his heterodoxy:

> In all my lectures, I have taught one doctrine, namely, the infinitude of the private man. This, the people accept readily enough, & even with loud commendation, as long as I call the lecture, Art; or Politics; or Literature; or the Household; but the moment I call it Religion,—they are shocked, though it be only the application of the same truth which they receive everywhere else, to a new class of facts (*Journals and Notebooks* 7:342)

This passage sounds clearly the note of frustration. Here we are behind the lecture platform, getting a candid glimpse into the difficulties this lecturer faced. But this tone of frustration becomes much more extreme, more dramatic, perhaps even shocking, in a passage that for obvious reasons certainly never received public exposure, either in lecture or essay:

Strange how hard it is for cultivated men to free themselves from the optical illusion by which a great man appears an institution. They know & have observed in particular instances that the demonstration of a strong will[,] of a vast thought[,] at once arrested the eyes & magnetized the wills of men, so that society & events became secondaries & satellites of a man; and the genesis of that man's thought is not now explored (in) after the laws of thought, but externally in his parent-age, in his country, climate, college, election by his fellow citizens, & the like,—as we know is the tenor of vulgar biography. And yet though familiar with this fact the moment Jesus is mentioned, they forget their knowledge, & accept the apparatus of prophecy, miracle, positive supernatural indication by name & place, & claim on his part to extraordinary outward relations;—all these, which are the prismatic hues & lights which play around any wonderful genius, they regard as of an adamantine reality, and in the selectest society where Beauty, Goodness, & the Soul are named, these men talk of 'preaching Christ,' & of 'Christ's being the ideal of Man', &c. &c. so that I told them it might become my duty to spit in the face of Christ as a sacred act of duty to the Soul, an act which that beautiful pilgrim in nature would well enough appreciate. (*Journals and Notebooks* 7:347–48)

One should invite back Kenneth Burke to analyze the above passage in his terms of Emerson's "tender-minded . . . starry-eyed . . . charm" and "unction." And since for Whicher Emerson's period of "acquiescence" begins in 1841, it must be dismaying to find Emerson so fiercely unready to acquiesce in 1840. What we have here is a very dramatic devaluation of the status of the historical Jesus, expressed in a tone which betrays a great deal of personal frustration, even anger, on Emerson's part, some of which must be triggered by the failure of his own "word" to be "received" by the "world." This reaction comes two years after the Divinity School "Address." One notes even the breakdown of syntax beginning with the "so that I told them" clause in the last long sentence. Another factor may be disconcerting here: in this highly charged, personally revealing expostulation, one of the earlier values of Jesus for Emerson seems to have been lost: Jesus as "friend."

But there can be, for Emerson, no compromise with orthodoxy, no return to the faith of the fathers, no resurrection of the father by the self-created son. The later journal entries confirm that fact. By this point in his own development, Emerson would have agreed with Blake's harsh sincerity: "The Modern Church Crucifies Christ with the Head Downwards" (*Poetry and Prose* 564).

In 1841 Jesus, for Emerson, still finds himself in the company of representative men or great souls. "Only a few are the fixed stars which have no parallax, or none for us; Plato & Jesus & Shakspeare" (*Journals and Notebooks* 8:127). In 1843, "There is nothing in history to parallel the influence of Jesus Christ" (9:7). Also in 1843, planning a "Pantheon course of lectures" which will later become *Representative Men*, Emerson lists "Plato, Montaigne, Shakspeare [sic], Swedenborg, [Napoleon], Goethe," and "Bonaparte" and observes, "Jesus should properly be one head, but it requires great power of intellect & of sentiment to subdue the biases of the mind of the age, and render historic justice to the world's chief saint" (8:139). Thus it is "the biases of the mind of the age," the prejudices of his audience, which prevented Emerson from including Jesus in his *Representative Men*.

But in 1845 he begins to detect a change in public opinion. "All that concerns the resurrection of the body of Christ &[,] & in short all the miraculous history[,] the youth of today has no ears for" (8:335). If this is not Emerson's wish-fulfillment fantasy at this time, then he must have realized that his lecture audience was not "the youth of today." What does remain of orthodoxy, at any rate, seems to persist as a problem: "In any popular view of Christianity it must be said to have failed. Jesus came to save the world, but it is . . . as bad as ever" (364). This is in 1846. Also in that year, 1846, Emerson records his "dream" of the "Central Man," quoted in an earlier chapter of this study; in which the changing face of that "Central Man," after being Socrates, Shakespeare, Raphael, Michelangelo, and Dante, becomes "the Saint Jesus" (8:395), which apparition indicates at least how serious for Emerson was the omission of this figure from *Representative Men*.

As late as 1864 Emerson was still explaining the absence of Jesus from *Representative Men:* "When I wrote 'Representative Men,' I felt that Jesus was the 'Rep. Man' whom I ought to sketch: but the task required great gifts,—steadiest insight & perfect temper; else, the consciousness of want of sympathy in the audience would make one petulant or sore, in spite of himself" (*Journals and Notebooks* 15:224). Again, the reason for the omission has to do with self-consciousness about the audience. The "prophet" is adapting his vision, his message, to the limitations of his readers. But Emerson's highly personal vision of the "redeemer" and of redemption remains: "It is no matter what Christ did or suffered, or Moses, or John, but of great import how you stand to your tribunal" (471).

What emerges from a reading of Emerson's references to Jesus in his journals is a gradual shift in emphasis, not a change of concept. Jesus remains a charismatic figure, but the rationale of the charisma undergoes a transformation. The early emphasis on the uniqueness of Jesus as a "revolutionary" thinker in religion shifts to a regard for him as *representative* of humanity in the way that Emerson's other culture heroes (Shakespeare, Plato, Montaigne) represent the race. A traumatic turning point in the journal jottings focuses on the practical rhetorical problem of the omission of Jesus from *Representative Men*. Emerson is troubled by that omission both at the time of the lectures and subsequent book and troubled by it long afterward. We see evidence of the seriousness of the rhetorical problem: in private, Emerson's concept of Jesus is even more heterodox than his public

depiction of that figure to an audience. Privately, this particular personification of the "Central Man" begins to lose its centrality for
Emerson. He does not remind us of "all men." And, as a "sacred act
of duty to the Soul," Emerson confides to his journal (but to no
public audience) that it might become his "duty to spit in [his] face."
Curiously, there is a dichotomy here between "Soul" and "Jesus," in
which the value of the former is simply greater than the value of the
latter, a distinction which Emerson assumes this "other Waldo" would
understand and appreciate. Jesus, then, is *a* great soul, not *the* great
soul. In Emerson's mature thought, Jesus redeems us by exemplifying
our humanity, by returning us to ourselves. In a curious way, Jesus becomes an avatar of Emerson's own mythologized "self." But this
emphasis does not forego, it reaffirms redemption. We must save ourselves (partly at least through self-awareness), but the teachings of
Jesus are relevant openings into that awareness. In his moral and
spiritual wisdom, Emerson's Jesus is intended to have the same effect
on us, Emerson's readers, as Rilke's sculptured torso of an archaic
Apollo: "*Du muss dein leben ändern* (you must change your life)." But
it is *we* who change our lives, not Jesus, just as Ralph Emerson created
Waldo Emerson.

Many of the critics tend to avoid this important thread in the
tapestry of Emerson's thought, or at least they betray some uneasiness about it.[17] Alan Hodder has observed: "From the standpoint of
church history, Emerson is generally regarded as a radical, if not revolutionary, figure. He is situated, not without justification, at the far
left of Protestantism, if not off the spectrum of Christian denomina-
tions altogether" (143). It must be a difficult admission, occurring as
it does late in a study of biblical parallels and influences. Hodder
finds the above view "valid with respect to Christian doctrine" but
"an oversimplification with regard to Christian piety," and he is still
able to find "that in important ways Emerson was a deeply conservative religious thinker" (143). Edward Waldo Emerson, in his note
quoted earlier, would seem not to agree with that view of his father,
and a number of the above passages gleaned from the journals suggest

an even more radical, more heterodox Emerson than has been usually assumed.

Neufeldt thinks that "when Emerson returned from Europe in 1833 he had pretty much abandoned revealed theology" (179), a dating of Emerson's heterodoxy that is close to mine, coming as it does between the "Lord's Supper" sermon and the Divinity School "Address."

In a fascinating and very recent study, Evelyn Barish concurs with Neufeldt about Emerson's break with orthodoxy, but dates that break as earlier by a year: "Emerson was not very different as a Unitarian until his rejection in 1832 of Christology."[18] Barish finds significant early evidence of Emerson's radical theology in an 1827 sermon:

> Preaching on "Christ Crucified," Emerson stressed not Christ's birth, life, or purported miracles, but his influence. The sermon adduced the "affecting" and powerful influence of the "being" whose character "has taken such strong hold of the mind as to divide the opinions of men as to his nature & office . . . [leaving] foundation for the opinion that he was a portion of the Deity & in the opinions least reverent that he was first of men." (204–05)

Sherman Paul confirms my conclusions drawn from extracts from the journals: "As an ethical teacher Emerson considered Jesus beyond comparison, but he did not think him a complete man" (167). Richard Poirier has also noticed the "derisive undertone" in Emerson's comments on Jesus in "Experience":

> Time and again his approbations for a figure like Jesus are preyed upon by his critical aloofness about the process by which "genius" gets appropriated to and recognized within cultural hierarchies. Though Jesus is

not put into a list with several others, which is Emerson's usual way of modifying his enthusiasm for anyone in particular, the claim that he is the "providential man" is accompanied by the curious suggestion that "the type of humanity" who is hero or saint is actually the beneficiary of "the *name* hero or saint," and that Jesus got that "name" thanks not to indisputable merit, but because "many people [were] agreed that these optical laws shall take effect." (173–74)

On the same passage in "Experience," Van Leer expresses Poirier's uneasiness in presumably more "philosophical" terms: "Treating Jesus 'as if' divine is not merely a prescinding from questions about categories for which we have no objective standards. It ascribes to him a neutrality that, like the horizon, is entirely phenomenal" (179). "Neutrality" does not emerge from the evidence brought forward by the present study.[19]

The evidence suggests that indeed Emerson broke early with Unitarian orthodoxy, and, further, that he continued throughout his life to move farther and farther away from it. In his mature writings and in his later years, he expresses what in 1827 he called "opinions least reverent" such as the idea that Christ was "first of men," a position he qualifies by moving Jesus around in a personal pantheon of great or "representative" men. But most striking is the discovery that Jesus as "a portion of the Deity" has been subsumed within another "portion of the Deity" announced in unqualified terms as early as 1836. "I am part or parcel of god" (*Complete Works* 1:19).

The evidence shows not contradiction but consistency in Emerson's view of Jesus. I have focused on "Jesus" as a figure, a trope, an image. The metamorphoses of that image in Emerson's writings (both public and private) retain its integrity as a figure of redemption. But the image has become "Emersonized" in a totally characteristic way. Just as, in Whicher's view, *Nature* was Emerson's effort to transform the NOT ME into the ME, Emerson gradually but consistently transforms "Jesus" into a function of Emerson's own personal "self." He does not connect the Christ-figure at all to that "Over-Soul" he almost never mentions anyway.[20] Instead, the "Teacher," the bard, the prophet, the great man, becomes another "Waldo." This discovery becomes extremely significant in a mythic context, revealing a certain integrity in Emerson's thinking on Jesus throughout his life. If Emerson transforms "Jesus" into "Emerson," in much the same way he metamorphoses the NOT ME into the ME in *Nature,* the sermon on the "Lord's Supper" can be related to all of Emerson's subsequent references to Christ. In rejecting the ritual of the Last Supper with its prescription, "Take, eat: this is my body" (Luke 14:22), Emerson has merely rejected the vehicle of Christ's metaphor. He has profoundly *incorporated* its tenor. He has "eaten" Jesus as he "ate" Nature, and both values for him are life-giving, are redemptive.[21] Like Nature, Jesus is redemptive because Jesus amplifies the solitary self, making it worthy of reverence, making the famous Emersonian "self" both personal and, by means of this incorporated value, more-than-personal. As in Blake's *Jerusalem,* where, in order to save himself, Albion must reconnect the separate parts of his fallen humanity, redemption in Emerson is *connection.* If one is "redeemed," the "glorified friend" is within one's self.

David L. Smith has pointed out in comparing Emerson and Derrida that "Their real concern is not with getting *beyond* our circumstances, but with the kind of *salvation* [emphasis added] that is available *within* our endlessness—the means of going on with joy" (397). This is a totally *humanized* concept of redemption, what Smith calls the "same old self-redemptive human/divine comedy" (397).

In Emerson's time the "same old" idea was radically new, at least for his audience. But Emerson's version is not unique. Blake's Jesus is equally human. Whether as Orc the crucified rebel, as Luvah the sufferer for love, as Los the prophetic artist, as Albion who is humanity, or even as the compassionate "Chimney Sweeper," Blake's Jesus is always a function of the human imagination. Further, for Blake as well as for Emerson, as both writers get older, that imagination is seen increasingly as the *moral* imagination. The conclusion to be drawn from the figure of Jesus in Emerson and in Blake is that human redemption is exactly and literally that, *human* redemption.[22] Man has the capacity within himself to save himself; the agency of human redemption is not outside but within the human condition. The realization of that fact, however, can only be achieved imaginatively or poetically. In mythic terms, such realization in the human psyche of its own transformation, its own power of self-redemption, is Apocalypse.

"Children of the Fire"

ℰⱭℂℛ

I will not cease from Mental Fight
Nor shall my sword sleep in my hand:
Till we have built Jerusalem
In Englands green & pleasant Land.

—Blake

Other world! there is no other world.
God is one and omnipresent; here or
nowhere is the whole fact.

—Emerson

IN THE YEAR 1319 Dante wrote a "Letter" to his friend and patron, Can Grande della Scala, to whom he had dedicated the *Paradiso* of his *Divine Comedy*. His purpose in the letter is to explain the work, and in the rigidly Aristotelian method and terms which make him a perfect representative of the thought of his age, he discusses "the six things to be inquired about at the beginning of any work of instruction, to wit the subject, the author, the form, the end, the title of the work, and the genus of its philosophy" (Allan H. Gilbert 202). Dante's letter is an essay in practical criticism, answering the question, how should his poem be read. Dante's answer is astonishing.

> For the clarity of what is to be said, one must realize that the meaning of this work is not simple, but is rather to be called polysemous, that is, having many meanings. The first meaning is the one obtained through the letter; the second is the one obtained through the things signified by the letter. The first is called literal, the second allegorical or moral or ana-gogical. In order that this manner of treatment may

appear more clearly, it may be applied to the following verses [Psalms 114:1–2]: "When Israel went out of Egypt, the house of Jacob from a people of strange language, Judah was his sanctuary and Israel his dominion." For if we look to the letter alone, the departure of the children of Israel from Egypt in the time of Moses is indicated to us; if to the allegory, our redemption accomplished by Christ is indicated to us; if to the moral sense, the conversion of the soul from the woe and misery of sin to a state of grace is indicated to us; if to the anagogical sense, the departure of the consecrated soul from the slavery of this corruption to the liberty of eternal glory is indicated. (Allan H. Gilbert 202)

What should startle is the fact that Dante is applying, as a way of reading his own poem, the traditional patristic system of the four-fold interpretation of Scripture, the working (and worked) hypothesis that every line of the Bible has four levels of meaning: literal, tropological, allegorical, and anagogical. The terms themselves differ in the writings of different Church Fathers, but the method is consistent.

Concerning Emerson's theory of interpretation, Alan Hodder has observed:

He never espoused or methodically practiced a multi-leveled method of interpretation such as that adopted by Augustine or Thomas Aquinas, but his own attitude to the interpretation of inspired texts owes much more to the spirit of allegorical and mystical interpretation formulated by the Church Fathers and filtered down into the esoteric wisdom cults of the Renaissance than it does to Protestant exegesis. (144)[1]

What is of interest to the present study, however, is not how Emerson (or Blake, or Dante) interpreted the Bible, but how each thought his own work should be interpreted. Orthodox readers of

Dante seem to have remained undismayed by his claim in the letter to Can Grande della Scala, yet the orthodox should know that Christians before and after Dante's time were burned at the stake for much less radical "heresies." Dante is saying that we should read his poem in exactly the same way that we have been instructed to read the "divinely inspired" *Word of God,* Holy Scripture itself. He is claiming the same inspiration, asserting, in fact, that there is only one inspiration, dissolving the distinction between "sacred" and "profane" writing. The implication is quite clear: if Dante is inspired just as Ezekiel or John was inspired, Revelation is still going on. Blake claims this precise participation explicitly. Implicitly, so does Emerson.

If Redemption is a human function of the human condition, as the previous chapter has suggested, if it is possible for man to be redeemed by himself, then the end of the human story is a happy one. But such awareness of the capacity for self-redemption must be made manifest. That fact must be *revealed.* That revelation, or apocalypse, of man's potential to save himself is Emerson's prophecy, as it is Blake's. For both writers, the mode of Revelation is a "Bard's Song." It is the apocalypse of "Poetry and Imagination."

Statements of the authority of inspiration are ubiquitous in Blake. I shall consider only a representative sample from the engraved works, where Blake is expressing his theory of inspiration in his own canon. In Blake, as in Dante, not only is there no distinction between sacred and profane poetry, the distinction between religious and nonreligious literature is correlatively dissolved. In his very first engraved work, the tractate "ALL RELIGIONS are ONE," Blake delivers what might be called a manifesto:

> PRINCIPLE Ist That the Poetic Genius is the true Man. and that the body or outward form of Man is derived from the Poetic Genius. . . .
> PRINCIPLE 2d As all men are alike in outward form, So (and with the same infinite variety) all are alike in the Poetic Genius

PRINCIPLE 3ᵈ No man can think write or speak from
his heart, but he must intend truth. Thus all sects of
Philosophy are from the Poetic Genius adapted to the
weaknesses of every individual
PRINCIPLE 4. As none by traveling over known lands
can find out the unknown. So from already acquired
knowledge Man could not acquire more. therefore an
universal Poetic Genius exists
PRINCIPLE 5. The Religions of all Nations are de-
rived from each Nations different reception of the
Poetic Genius which is every where call'd the Spirit of
Prophecy.
PRINCIPLE 6 The Jewish & Christian Testaments are
An original derivation from the Poetic Genius. this is
necessary from the confined nature of bodily sensation
(*Poetry and Prose* 1).

There are statements in Blake's "Principles" that resist logical analysis,
but what emerges clearly is his notion of the truth of imaginative literature. His term "Poetic Genius" carries some of the weight Emerson
gives to "Man" or "Soul." Further, Blake anticipates much modern anthropology and comparative religion by his awareness of the common
denominators in what we might call mythology and what he calls
here the "Spirit of Prophecy." Blake's is a more amplified version of
Shelley's assertion that poets are the "unacknowledged legislators" of
mankind, and he echoes Puttenham's and Sidney's Renaissance trea-
tises that affirmed the earliest poets to be priests and lawgivers as well.
For Blake, consequently, imaginative expression takes precedence over
all other forms of discourse: "If it were not for the Poetic or Prophetic
character. the Philosophical & Experimental would soon be at the
ratio of all things & stand still, unable to do other than repeat the
same dull round over again" (*Poetry and Prose* 3). Blake's insistence on
the dependence of both philosophy and science on poetry should be
borne in mind when we read such major Emersonian texts as *Nature;*
the function of the "Orphic Poet" is, quite possibly, to fill the famous

"crack," if there is one, in that text. Blake also here anticipates such twentieth-century thinkers as Bronowski (a physicist as well as a Blake scholar) in *Science and Human Values,* who insists that scientific discoveries are products of the creative imagination.

But Blake is neither philosopher nor scientist, and Emerson is not either. With extraordinary self-consciousness, Blake is an artist and poet, so that even the tractates themselves must be read as poetic works. Blake's self-awareness in the role of poet, especially of poet-prophet, undergoes various metamorphoses but is progressive. The personae change, but the role deepens, until finally in *Milton,* his masterpiece on the subject of inspiration itself, all masks are dropped, and the inspired poet is William Blake standing in his garden at Felpham. But it is instructive to examine the masks.

The "Introduction" to *Songs of Experience* presents us with "the Bard," a figure Blake will use more dramatically later. *Innocence* in its introduction more modestly started with the "Piper." The Piper can guide us through Innocence; the harsh realities of Experience require a tougher poetic voice:

> Hear the voice of the Bard!
> who Present, Past, & Future sees
> Whose ears have heard,
> The Holy Word,
> That walk'd among the ancient trees.
> (*Poetry and Prose* 18)

It is significant that here the Bard has heard the Poetic Genius in the form of Jesus, the "Word" or *Logos* of John's Gospel. It is even more significant that while the Bard *hears* an "ancient" *Word,* he *sees* not just the past out of which that Word speaks, but the present and future as well. "God is, not was," as Emerson points out. The Bard is a prophet, not a transcriber. There is nothing passive about Blake's concept of inspiration.

Blake is never naive or merely fanciful about the dynamics of inspiration (one may perhaps except the experience of the Piper in

Innocence). In *The Marriage of Heaven and Hell,* we get a view of poetic inspiration that is stripped of poetic convention:

> The Prophets Isaiah and Ezekiel dined with me, and I asked them how they dared so roundly to assert. that God spake to them; and whether they did not think at the time, that they would be misunderstood, & so be the cause of imposition.
>
> Isaiah answer'd. I saw no God. nor heard any, in a finite organical perception; but my senses discover'd the infinite in every thing, and as I was then perswaded. & remain confirm'd; that the voice of honest indignation is the voice of God, I cared not for consequences but wrote.
>
> Then I asked: does a firm perswasion that a thing is so, make it so?
>
> He replied. All poets believe that it does, & in ages of imagination this firm perswasion removed mountains; but many are not capable of a firm perswasion of any thing. (*Poetry and Prose* 38–39)

Later, in *Milton,* Blake would write: "The Bard replied. I am inspired I know it is Truth! for I sing / According to the inspiration of the Poetic Genius / Who is the eternal all-protecting Divine Humanity" (*Poetry and Prose* 107–08).

But the genesis of inspiration can be quite prosaic: "I then asked Ezekiel, why he eat dung, & lay so long on his right & left side? He answered. The desire of raising other men into a perception of the infinite this the North American tribes practice" (*Poetry and Prose* 39). Here Blake is observing what an anthropologist would call shamanism in accounting for the prophecies of Isaiah and Ezekiel, and he perceives the analogy between the Hebrew prophecies and native American religious experience, long before William James contemplated his *Varieties.* The dung and the cramps show up in later poetry in Yeats's "rag and bone shop of the heart." But we should not completely forget the dung when we come to Emerson's poetic theory.

[147]

For both Emerson and Blake, poetic inspiration may have very homely origins; it may attain the sublime; it does not come out of the sublime.

Blake varies his personae of inspiration. In *EUROPE a PROPHECY* (1794), the inspirer is a "Fairy," an unusual figure in Blake, perhaps a tribute to the chthonic (or Celtic) element in British folklore which will become more important in his later work, *Jerusalem*. What this particular fairy sings at the beginning of *Europe* is a sophisticated hunk of Blake's epistemology and ontology:

> Five windows light the cavern'd Man; thro,
> one he breathes the air;
> Thro' one, hears music of the spheres; thro'
> one, the eternal vine
> Flourishes, that he may receive the grapes;
> thro' one can look
> And see small portions of the eternal world
> that ever groweth;
> Thro' one, himself pass out what time he
> please, but he will not;
> For stolen joys are sweet, & bread eaten in
> secret pleasant.
>
> So sang a Fairy mocking as he sat on a streak'd
> Tulip,
> Thinking none saw him: when he ceas'd I
> started from the trees!
> And caught him in my hat as boys knock down
> a butterfly.
> How know you this said I small Sir? where did
> you learn this song?
> (*Poetry and Prose* 60)

It is typical of Blake's poetic strategies to follow a comprehensive philosophical statement with a bit of charming whimsy (and such juxtapositions can be found as well in Emerson's essays, much to the discomfort of "serious" readers). Blake may owe the butterfly size of

his fairy to Shakespeare's *Midsummer Night's Dream,* but his address-
ing of him as "small Sir" is quintessential Blake. What this "small Sir"
has been singing is quite simply Blake's view of the fallen senses and
their fallen limitations, their ability—notwithstanding such limits—
to catch glimpses of the "eternal world," and an astonishing pre-
Freudian view of sex (touch) as potential liberation and resurrection
of the fallen human body, a potential thwarted by the neurotic
pseudo-pleasures of repression. But that is just the beginning of this
beginning. When the "I" of the passage (William Blake as William
Blake, and if so, the kidnapper of the inspirer, the thief of inspiration)
has captured the fairy, he demands, "Then tell me, what is the material world, and is it dead?" Of course, for Blake, it isn't, and the fairy's
bargain is that if Blake will "Feed [him] on love-thoughts" and "give
[him] now and then / A cup of sparkling poetic fancies," when he is
"tipsy," he will show Blake "all alive / The world, when every particle
of dust breathes forth its joy." The fairy's gift, then, is visionary revelation about the nature of the Blakean (human) universe. Blake takes
him home, like a pet, and then "My Fairy sat upon the table, and dictated EUROPE" (*Poetry and Prose* 60). This is quite a piece of
dictation for the fairy, since *Europe* is one of the darkest and most difficult of Blake's minor prophecies, and one which ends with an
evocation of the French Revolution which is ambiguous and unresolved. Blake engraved the poem in 1794; disillusionment with the
outcome of that political revolution had clearly already set in.

Sometimes Blake uses no persona for the figure of inspiration.
The "Preludium" to THE (FIRST) BOOK OF URIZEN simply uses "I":
"Eternals, I hear your call gladly, / Dictate swift winged words, & fear
not / To unfold your dark visions of torment" (*Poetry and Prose* 70).
Sometimes the persona has little or no status as a mythic character
even when named, such as "Eno," the "aged Mother," whose "speech
[breaks] forth" to give us THE BOOK OF LOS (*Poetry and Prose* 90). It is
in *Milton* that Blake gives us his most elaborate and conceptually
most probing figure of inspiration, both in theory and in practice. *Milton* is a "brief" epic, on the scale of *Paradise Regained.* Any

detailed consideration of it would go far beyond the scope of this study, but any consideration of how inspiration works in Blake cannot ignore it.[2] Further, it ends with one of Blake's two major descriptions of Apocalypse (the other being the conclusion of *Jerusalem*).

Blake's "Preface" to *Milton* clarifies and redefines the concept of the "Poetic Genius" he expressed in his earliest tractate. Its first two prose paragraphs deserve quotation, for they constitute Blake's mini-history of inspiration. The remainder of the "Preface" is the lyric, "And did those feet in ancient time," whose last quatrain is one of the epigraphs to this chapter, and which is independently too well known to need commentary.

> The Stolen and Perverted Writings of Homer & Ovid: of Plato & Cicero. [*not* Blake's "Representative Men"] which all Men ought to contemn: are set up by artifice against the Sublime of the Bible: but when the New Age is at leisure to Pronounce; all will be set right: & those Grand Works of the more ancient & consciously & professedly Inspired Men, will hold their proper rank, & the Daughters of Memory shall become the Daughters of Inspiration. Shakspeare & Milton were both curbed by the general malady & infection from the silly Greek & Latin slaves of the Sword.
>
> Rouze up O Young Men of the New Age! set your foreheads against the ignorant Hirelings! For we have Hirelings in the Camp, the Court, & the University: who would if they could, for ever depress Mental & prolong Corporeal War. Painters! on you I call! Sculptors! Architects! Suffer not the fash[i]onable Fools to depress your powers by the prices they pretend to give for contemptible works or the expensive advertizing boasts that they make of such works; believe Christ & his Apostles that there is a Class of Men whose whole delight is in Destroying. We do not want either Greek or Roman Models if we are but just & true to our own

Imaginations, those Worlds of Eternity in which we
shall live for ever; in Jesus our Lord. (*Poetry and Prose* 95)

Blake is always huskily emphatic in defining battle lines. Here
they are drawn so explicitly as to make these two paragraphs *his*
"American Scholar," or at least his "British Artist" Address. Blake
turns the Augustan ancients vs. moderns debate on its head: the
"ancients" as "classical" models, Greek and Roman, are not ancient
enough; the biblical authors are, as he affirmed much earlier, "An
original derivation from the Poetic Genius." It is in reconnecting
with those originals that the "Young Men of the New Age" will find
their true artistic integrity. The problem with the Muses, for Blake, is
that they were the daughters of Mnemosyne, or Memory. Memory is
not good enough; Ezekiel and John saw what they saw face to face;
they record it as direct experience—immediate, not mediate, inspiration. It should not surprise the reader of this study at this point to
find Blake's advocacy of "being just & true to our own imaginations"
sounding a lot like Ralph Waldo Emerson.

Having formally rejected the classical Muses or "Daughters of
Memory" in his Preface, Blake begins his mythic and autobiographical epic by invoking instead the "Daughters of Beulah" or inspiration.
But we should remember that Beulah for Blake is a state, however un-
stable, of sexual satisfaction.

> Daughters of Beulah! Muses who inspire the
> Poets Song
> Record the journey of immortal Milton thro'
> your Realms
> Of terror & mild moony lustre, in soft sexual
> delusions
>
> Of varied beauty, to delight the wanderer
> and repose
> His burning thirst & freezing hunger! Come
> into my hand

By your mild power; descending down the nerves
of my right arm
From out the Portals of my Brain, where by
your ministry
The Eternal Great Humanity Divine. planted
his Paradise,
And in it caus'd the Spectres of the Dead to
take sweet forms
In likeness of himself. . . .
. . . .
Say first! what mov'd Milton, who walkd about
in Eternity
One hundred years, pondering the intricate
mazes of Providence
Unhappy tho in heav'n, he obey'd, he murmur'd
not. he was silent
Viewing his Sixfold Emanation scatter'd thro'
the deep
In torment! To go into the deep her to redeem
& himself perish?
What cause at length mov'd Milton to this
unexampled deed[?]
A Bards prophetic Song! for sitting at eternal
tables,
Terrific among the Sons of Albion in chorus
solemn & loud
A Bard broke forth! all sat attentive to the
awful man.
Mark well my words! they are of your eternal
salvation. (*Poetry and Prose* 96)

Blake is creating here an intricate structure for the unfolding of his poem, a deliberate architecture of inspiration-within-inspiration. First the Daughters of Beulah are invoked for aid, but Blake here intends himself to be no merely passive "aeolian harp." He asks his Muses to animate his hand, the nerves of his right arm, and his brain.

Inspiration is an active participation, a commingling or union of inspirer and inspired. The hand and arm are as important as the brain for Blake; he is engraving as well as writing the poem. This initial commingling of the Daughters of Beulah with Blake as poet anticipates the later, climactic commingling of Blake and Milton himself, through the agency of Los.

But within this "invocation of the Muse"—radically original as it is—is another epiphany of inspiration, for the beginning of the story, once it begins, records a prior act of inspiration: what caused Milton to leave Eternity and return to earth was a "Bard's Song." Thus, Milton is inspired by a Bard to inspire Blake to create *Milton*. Curiously, what we have here in one of Blake's major works is a conceptual relationship very much like one we have seen before in Emerson: namely, Milton in *Milton* functions very much like Nature in *Nature*. On one level, *Nature* is about the creation of the book, *Nature;* on that level, *Milton* is about the writing of *Milton*. And we shall see that Blake will carry the idea of *incorporation* at least as far as does Emerson.

At this point, for purposes of both clarity and economy, it will be better to see Blake's *Milton* through Harold Bloom's succinct and illuminating commentary:

> Unlike the Book of Job and *Paradise Regained,* works
> presenting their theodicy through dramatic dialogues,
> *Milton* centers itself on the consciousness of the poet
> himself. The struggle is clearly an internal one, between
> those qualities in Blake that would compel him to sur-
> render his prophetic function, and everything in him
> that desires to follow Milton's heroic dedication as a
> poet. Blake is the Job of his own poem, and confronts
> a tempting Satan [Hayley], whom he overcomes only
> by following Milton's example. Milton, in the poem, is
> shown as casting off his own selfhood, and moving
> toward a visionary emancipation that Blake desires as

his own. It is important to note that Blake does not give us a pattern in which Milton merely assumes Blake's own position. Blake's poem is a genuinely purgatorial one. He wants to be an incarnation of the Poetical Character, as Milton was before him, and for this he needs Milton's aid, or rather the aid of what was most radical and imaginative in Milton. What belonged to religious convention and "moral virtue" in the historical Milton is of no help to Blake, nor was it to Milton himself, in Blake's view. (*Poetry and Prose* 909)

One of the several highly dramatic climaxes of the poem occurs exactly in the middle of the first of its two books, Blake's incorporation of Milton into himself:

> Then first I saw him in the Zenith as a
> falling star,
> Descending perpendicular, swift as the
> swallow or swift;
> And on my left foot falling on the tarsus,
> enterd there;
> But from my left foot a black cloud redounding
> spread over Europe.
> (*Milton* 1:47–50; *Poetry and Prose* 110)

Emerson, as we saw in previous chapters, *ingests* Nature as the Mother and Jesus as a redemptive principle of self-fulfillment. Blake's poetic incorporation of Milton is no less imaginatively daring, but no more so, either. Again, Bloom's commentary provides a helpful guide to this difficult passage:

> Milton, in highest irony, appears to the world, in his return, much as his falling Satan did. Milton enters Blake by the foot because by doing so he alters Blake's *stance,* from Palamabron to Rintrah, from civilizing

poet to redeeming prophet. The union between Milton and Blake is temporal and provisional; hence by the *left* foot. But the first result of such union is negative; Milton is still burdened by the Spectre, and the black cloud may well be Puritan doctrine, as [S. Foster] Damon . . . surmised. (*Poetry and Prose* 915)

The major climax of the poem, however, brings about a positive Apocalypse. In both a dramatic and structural triumph, this second climax occurs near the end of "Book the Second." In it Milton descends into Blake's garden at Felpham (where Blake was suffering under Hayley's patronage), to meet both Blake and Ololon, his six-fold Emanation. Milton's Emanation or Female is six-fold most obviously because Milton had three wives and three daughters, and in a minor triumph of Blake's genuine feminism, it is part of Milton's task of unfinished self-redemption to come to terms with them (her). She appears to Blake as a "Virgin of twelve years" because she is also an analog of Dante's Beatrice, another inspirer. Blake indicates with amusing tact the difficulty of introducing a strange young woman to his wife Catherine: "Virgin of Providence fear not to enter into my Cottage . . . but pity thou my Shadow of Delight / Enter my Cottage, comfort her, for she is sick with fatigue" (*Poetry and Prose* 137). Here visionary epiphany is occurring domestically, just outside the kitchen door. After this moment of gentle domestic irony—a pianissimo before the poem's concluding fortissimo—Milton descends, wins his contest with Satan, and casts out his own errors. Ololon reveals and purges her own sexual fears; she repudiates her own selfhood as part of her reunion with Milton; and she is "purged" of the "stain" of her virginity. These happy resolutions, which one should remember are the symbolic record of Blake's working through the traumas of his own psyche, lead into the final positive apocalypse which ends the poem. Jesus, in an analog of the action of Milton, is reunited with Albion (Humanity) in "death," which is human life, and it is important to note that in *Milton,* in the action of the poem, Milton does not imitate Jesus; Jesus imitates Milton. The positive inspirational symbols of the lark and the thyme are reintroduced. We are situated explicitly in a literal English landscape. The prophet himself has been humanized by empathy. And Blake's apocalyptic images of "harvest" and "vintage" conclude this revelation of psychic and spiritual change. Before all this occurs, however, Blake himself experiences the traditional symptom of inspiration, namely *ecstasy:* his vision has taken him outside himself. His return to himself, the same and also changed, is the literal level of fact that the metaphors of Apocalypse figure.

> And the Immortal Four in whom the Twenty-four
> appear Four-fold
> Arose around Albions body: Jesus wept &
> walked forth
> From Felphams Vale clothed in Clouds of blood,
> to enter into
> Albions Bosom, the bosom of death & the Four
> surrounded him
> In the Column of Fire in Felphams Vale; then
> to their mouths the Four
> Applied their Four Trumpets & them sounded to
> the Four winds
>
> Terror struck in the Vale I stood at that
> immortal sound
> My bones trembled. I fell outstretched upon
> the path
> A moment, & my Soul returnd into its mortal state
> To Resurrection & Judgment in the Vegetable Body
> And my sweet shadow of Delight stood trembling
> by my side
>
> Immediately the Lark mounted with a loud trill
> from Felphams Vale
> And the Wild Thyme from Wimbletons green &
> impurpled Hills

And Los & Enitharmon rose over the Hills of Surrey
Their clouds roll over London with a south wind,
              soft Oothoon
Pants in the Vales of Lambeth weeping oer her
              Human Harvest
Los listens to the Cry of the Poor Man: his Cloud
Over London in volume terrific, low bended in anger.

Rintrah & Palamabron view the Human Harvest beneath
Their Wine-presses & Barns stand open; the Ovens
              are prepar'd
The Waggons ready: terrific Lions & Tygers sport
              & play
All Animals upon the Earth, are prepard in all
              their strength
To go forth to the Great Harvest & Vintage of the
              nations. (*Poetry and Prose* 143–44)

Again, Bloom's commentary will prove helpful:

> Here, in the poem's final vision, Blake comes back to
> himself, triumphantly answering the perplexities of the
> Bard's Song. The Four Zoas and their trumpets mo-
> mentarily impel Blake toward his own Last Judgment,
> but he revives, to await a mortal destiny, following
> Milton in the belief that body and soul must die to-
> gether, and be resurrected together. In the assured
> closing passages, Blake gathers together many of his
> poem's emblems: the Lark and the Wild Thyme as mes-
> sengers of Los; the rising of Los and Enitharmon as a
> wind of possible inspiration; the labors of Rintrah and
> Palamabron. To these he adds the Oothoon of *Visions*
> [*of the Daughters of Albion*], weeping with joy over the
> human harvest she was denied in that poem. Los is
> now altogether transformed from the erring creature of
> the early nights of *The Four Zoas*. Like Amos and the

other prophets, he "listens to the Cry of the Poor Man," and his prophetic anger is bent over London as a cloud of menace, a demand for social justice that threatens destruction if denied. In the closing lines, the Mills of Satan have vanished, and the greatness of the Apocalypse is imminent. It is difficult not to hear the single line of the final plate as a prophetic battle cry, ringing with challenge and with the confidence of the poet-prophet who has been tried severely, and has triumphed over his trials. (*Poetry and Prose* 928)

The theory of inspiration leads to the practice of Apocalypse. I have considered Blake's theory and practice of poetic inspiration, culminating in *Milton*. With those Blakean models in mind, I can now, in that explicitly apocalyptic context, consider Emerson's analogous theory and practice. As in Blake, Emerson's articulation of the theory of inspiration leads him to voice the apocalyptic mode.

"The Poet" is the first of the *Essays: Second Series* which Emerson published in 1844. His statements on poetry and the imagination are scattered throughout the whole body of his prose and verse, beginning with *Nature* in 1836, but this essay, in its concentrated emphasis, is, if such is anywhere, his *Poetics*.

Emerson first distinguishes poetry from mere taste for beauty, then from mere skill or craft. He stresses instead the "dependence of form upon soul" (*Complete Works* 3:3), and that "the highest minds of the world have never ceased to explore the double meaning, or shall I say the quadruple or centuple or much more manifold meaning, of every sensuous fact" (4). Here is a theory of symbolism, with an insistence on the primacy of the "sensuous fact."[3] The connection between the fact and its meanings is the ground of poetry, which is a discovery or unveiling of our real human condition: "For we are not pans and barrows, nor even porters of the fire and torch-bearers, but children of the fire, made of it, and only the same divinity transmuted and at two or three removes, when we know least about it" (4). In other words, being part of the meaning as well as part of the fact, the poet is the person who discovers the other side of the sensuous fact to be its meaning: "The sign and credentials of the poet are that he announces that which no man foretold" (8). The poet gives us an original vision (a prophecy), but that vision consists in revealing ourselves to ourselves. It is the function of the poet to make this announcement, and Emerson, significantly enough, explains that function *mythically:*

> For the Universe has three children, born at one time, which reappear under different names in every system of thought, whether they be called cause, operation, and effect; or, more poetically, Jove, Pluto, Neptune; or, theologically, the Father, the Spirit, and the Son; but which we will call here the Knower, the Doer, and the Sayer. These stand respectively for the love of truth, for the love of good, and for the love of beauty. These three are equal. Each is that which he is, essentially, so that he cannot be surmounted or analyzed, and each of these three has the power of the others latent in him and his own, patent.
>
> The poet is the sayer, the namer, and represents beauty. (*Complete Works* 3:6–7)

A triad is unusual in Emerson's thought, as it is extremely rare in Blake's. Nevertheless, there is a "minor myth" in Blake roughly the equivalent of Emerson's "the Knower, the Doer, and the Sayer." It is Blake's notion of the Strong Man, the Beautiful Man, and the Ugly Man:

> The three general classes of men who are represented by the most Beautiful, the most Strong, and the most Ugly, could not be represented by any historical facts but those of our own country, the Ancient Britons. . . . They were overwhelmed, by brutal arms all but a small remnant; Strength, Beauty, and Ugliness

escaped the wreck, and remain forever unsubdued, age
after age. . . . The Strong man represents the human
sublime. The Beautiful man represents the human
pathetic, which was in the wars of Eden divided into
male and female. The Ugly man represents the human
reason. They were originally one man, who was four-
fold. (*Poetry and Prose* 542–43)

If we line up Blake's mythic triad alongside Emerson's mythic
triad, we discover that Blake's Strong Man is Emerson's Doer; his
Beautiful Man is the American's Sayer; and his Ugly Man is a very
un-Emersonian Knower.

What this juxtaposition of Emerson's and Blake's pair of mini-
myths really reveals is quite simply their mutual talent at mythmaking. As a basic mode of composition, that mythmaking talent is
universally granted to Blake (even by those readers who are puzzled
or disgusted by the myths he makes). It is seldom recognized as a
basic mode of Emerson's thought. In "The Poet," where Emerson
explores the genesis and nature of poetry itself, it is revealing and significant that he employs myth. Greater awareness of Emerson's use of
myth, from *Nature* in 1836 (where epistemological "cracks" might disappear if archetypes are seen to fill them) to "Immortality" in 1861
(which substitutes fables for conclusions), will give a more rewarding
reading of him. It is characteristic then that in "The Poet" Emerson
not only talks about mythmaking; he makes one.

Emerson's view of poetry stresses its substance, not its technical
skill or means. "For it is not metres, but metre-making argument that
makes a poem—a thought so passionate and alive that like the spirit
of a plant or animal it has an architecture of its own, and adorns
nature with a new thing" (*Complete Works* 3:9–10). He takes Coleridge's organicism a step further; far from being a metrical exercise,
the poem creates its own form, fulfills its message by its invention. It
is not mimesis but creation; in M. H. Abrams's terms, it is not
"mirror" but "lamp." Interestingly enough, by Emerson's criterion

Longfellow might have trouble passing; Whitman would get very high marks indeed. What is at stake here is truth, not beauty (although in the myth the poet represents beauty): "The value of genius to us is the veracity of its report" (11). This is a fundamentally different poetics from that of Emerson's contemporary, Poe, whom Emerson was later to describe as "the jingle man." We see here why he could be so disparaging. His distinction is between talent and genius: "Talent may frolic and juggle; genius realizes and adds" (11). An experiment in rhythm is not what Emerson expects from a poem.

On the distinction between "metre" and "metre-making argument," Blake's views correspond quite closely. One of his rare statements on prosody forms a part of the prose introduction, "To the Public," of the first chapter of *Jerusalem,* his last major poem:

> When this Verse was first dictated to me I considered a Monotonous Cadence like that used by Milton & Shakspeare & all writers of English Blank Verse, derived from the modern bondage of Rhyming; to be a necessary and indispensible part of Verse. But I soon found that in the mouth of a true Orator such monotony was not only awkward, but as much a bondage as rhyme itself. I therefore have produced a variety in every line, both of cadences & number of syllables. Every word and every letter is studied and put into its fit place: the terrific numbers are reserved for the terrific parts—the mild & gentle, for the mild & gentle parts, and the prosaic, for inferior parts: all are necessary to each other. (*Poetry and Prose* 145–46)

Not only Emerson in his theory, but also Blake here in both his theory and practice in *Jerusalem* is anticipating Whitman. Of interest too is Blake's term "dictated" to describe the fact of his inspiration, and that he thinks of the overall sound of his large epic as oratory, a form of discourse which Emerson always valued very highly. Underlying the whole note is the same critical priority we have seen in Emerson: in poetry, the *what* takes precedence over the *how*.

Typical of Emerson's rhetorical structure is the fact that in "The Poet" transitions are mostly invisible. But the essay develops by moving on to considerations of what poetry *does,* and what it *does to* the reader, so that the overall structure of "The Poet" follows implicitly that of many older discussions of poetics, moving from considerations of the genesis of the poem, to the poem itself, to the effect of the poem on the audience—or, in Emerson's own earlier terms in the essay, "cause, operation, and effect."

> With what joy I begin to read a poem which I confide in as an inspiration! And now my chains are to be broken; I shall mount above these clouds and opaque airs in which I live,—opaque, though they seem transparent,—and from the heaven of truth I shall see and comprehend my relations. That will reconcile me to life and renovate nature, to see trifles animated by a tendency, and to know what I am doing. Life will no more be a noise; now I shall see men and women, and know the signs by which they may be discerned from fools and satans. This day shall be better than my birthday: then I became an animal; now I am invited into the science of the real. (*Complete Works* 3:12)

The renovation of nature, the reconcilement to life, the discovery of meaning ("life . . . no more a noise"), the breaking of existential "chains"—these are the life-changing effects upon the reader of an inspired poem. How is it that poetry can achieve such wonders?

"Things admit of being used as symbols because nature is a symbol, in the whole, and in every part" (13). Emerson is echoing *Nature* quite closely, but here for a more specialized purpose. Inspiration has become even more democratic than in the earlier work:

"Thought makes everything fit for use. The vocabulary of an omniscient man would embrace words and images excluded from polite conversation" (17). One recalls Ezekiel's dung (and the eating of it) in Blake. How is it that the poet can thus redeem the ugly, or mention the unmentionable? "For as it is dislocation and detachment from the life of God that makes things ugly, the poet, who re-attaches things to nature and the Whole—re-attaching even artificial things and violations of nature to nature, by a deeper insight—disposes very easily of the most disagreeable facts" (*Complete Works* 3:18–19). In Blake's *Milton*, Bowlahoola is the stomach, and Allamanda the digestive tract (*Poetry and Prose* 120–21), and Blake can get considerably more graphic in his imagery of the body. In Emerson's view, "disagreeable facts" are not ignored; they are used by the poet and transformed into coherence in the context of his vision. When Blake writes, "Old Nobodaddy aloft / Farted & Belchd & coughd" (*Poetry and Prose* 500),[4] he is using ugly images to depict a concept which is ugly because it is false: Nobodaddy or God the Father is a fictitious monster, and Blake is prescient enough about modern anthropology to see this particular dead archetype, Jehovah, as a sky or thunder god. The reader's probable response, a laugh, is the enlightened, purged, and innocent "thunder" that explodes the fallacy. The poet is able to transform "disagreeable facts" by his "deeper insight."

For Emerson the poet's "very high sort of seeing" (*Complete Works* 3:26) is more than rational. "We are symbols and inhabit symbols" (20), and the poet perceives that fact. His "seeing . . . does not come by study, but by the intellect being where and what it sees" (26). The *where* is as important as the *what*. If Blake had not suffered his three years in Felpham, he could not have written *Milton,* and that poem ends with a liberated but localized landscape—"Felphams Vale" and "Surrey," "Lambeth" and "London." Poetic inspiration, then, results from a special case of "being there."

Clearly, what Emerson is talking about and Blake is demonstrating as poetry is not fanciful escapism, but "the ravishment of the intellect by coming nearer to the fact" (28). "Ravishment" means delight; it is also a rape. The experience of poetry sows a seed. The effect upon the reader, for Emerson, is *liberation:*

> The metamorphosis excites in the beholder an emo-
> tion of joy. The use of symbols has a certain power of
> emancipation and exhilaration for all men. . . . We are
> like persons who come out of a cave or cellar into the
> open air. This is the effect on us of tropes, fables, ora-
> cles and all poetic forms. Poets thus are liberating gods.
> Men have really got a new sense, and found within
> their world another world, or nest of worlds; for, the
> metamorphosis once seen, we divine that it does not
> stop. (30)

The "metamorphosis . . . does not stop" is not finite. This insight is precisely Blake's when he affirms, but with more of a qualification than Emerson here employs, "If the doors of perception were cleansed every thing would appear to man as it is: infinite" (*Poetry and Prose* 39). Emerson here analyzes the philosophical implications of *metaphor,* which he further describes as "a new witness" (32), and the theological overtones of the latter phrase should not be ignored: the poet brings us a new Gospel.

Why is metaphor so liberating? Emerson is at his most acutely perceptive on this point. Metaphor is liberating because "Every thought is also a prison; every heaven is also a prison" (33). Hence arises the basic human need of the poet's creations: new thoughts, new worlds, new heavens. They create our human freedom.

Emerson ends this remarkable essay of 1844 with a secular "Veni, Creator Spiritus," a kind of summons for Whitman to appear. He will, but not until 1855 and the first edition of *Leaves of Grass.* "I look in vain for the poet I describe. . . . We have yet had no genius in America" (37); and "Yet America is a poem in our eyes" (38). Whitman filled the bill not only symbolically but literally. Not only did *Leaves of Grass* get its best endorsement from Emerson, but eventually Whitman was on hand in all his fleshy person as a real live disciple, at least for a time, sitting at the Emersons' breakfast table in Concord, enjoying the Emerson breakfast of coffee and apple pie. But in its prescription of "metre-making argument" in place of metre, its theory of symbolism, its description of organic form, its advocacy of "America" as a poetic subject, its championing of everyday diction, and its awareness of "dream-power" (40), Emerson's "The Poet" *prophesies* the coming of Whitman. It is in this sense, as the prophet, that Emerson becomes "The Poet" himself.

"The religions of the world are the ejaculations of a few imaginative men" (34). This assertion from "The Poet" links Emerson's thought on poetics—namely, that poetry is Revelation—very closely to Blake's "principle" in ALL RELIGIONS are ONE, that "The religions of all Nations are derived from each nations different reception of the Poetic Genius which is every where call'd the Spirit of Prophecy" (*Poetry and Prose* 1). In a very modern way, this notion establishes the mythic or poetic basis of religion. Both Emerson and Blake retell the myths, and in retelling change them, add to them, transform them into living truth. Emerson explores further the mythic, religious parentage of poetry much later in his career. But it is clear as early as "The Poet" that Emerson's thought echoes Blake's, and that both of them echo Dante's implication in the letter to Can Grande della Scala, that the poetic text is a sacred text.

Emerson's view of poetry underwent no substantial changes during his long life. What he says in "The Poet" in 1844 (delivered as a lecture in 1841) is the same poetics he formulated in a very late essay, "Poetry and Imagination," which he gave in the form of two lectures in 1872; it was published in the posthumously collected volume, *Letters and Social Aims* in 1883.[5] On the whole, "Poetry and Imagination" is more literary, critical, historical, and less philosophical, than "The Poet," but it repeats the same message and can be read almost as an expanded summary of the earlier essay. What is of interest to the present study is its concept of poetry as sacred, or as inspired, endowing poetry with the status of Revelation.

"Sonnets of lovers are mad enough, but are valuable to the philosopher, as are prayers of saints, for their potent symbolism" (*Complete Works* 8:10). The common denominator of symbolism here need not surprise us, but that love lyrics and saints' prayers are equated, even as the sonnets are termed "mad," suggests the Platonic notion of the "madness" of inspiration in the *Phaedrus.* The connection between prayers and sonnets is interesting; either the saints are being devalued or the mad lovers revalued. But a religious, scriptural, Revelatory thread of imagery runs through much of this essay, as in the observation, "American life storms about us daily, and is slow to find a tongue. This contemporary insight is transubstantiation, the conversion of daily bread into the holiest symbols; and every man would be a poet if his intellectual digestion were perfect" (35). The allusions are rich and deep for Emerson—to the Lord's Supper, to food and eating, to the distinctive character of American "insight."[6] The diction of the essay keeps turning up religious terms: "In poetry we say we require the miracle" (16). This aesthetic judgment becomes especially significant if we recall Emerson's rejection of biblical miracles in the Divinity School "Address." They have reappeared, as poetry. "God himself does not speak in prose, but communicates with us by hints, omens, inferences and dark resemblances in objects lying all around us" (12). It is the theory of symbolism or correspondence that we know from as early on as *Nature,* but here natural facts are the images of God's symbolic poem. "Whilst common sense looks at things or visible nature as real and final facts, poetry, or the imagination which dictates it, is a second sight, looking through these, and using them as types or words for thoughts which they signify" (19). So God's poem of the world can be interpreted only by other poets, decoding appearances into realities in a quasi-miraculous "second sight." "The only teller of news is the poet. When he sings, the world listens with the assurance that now a secret of God is to be spoken" (30). What the poet gives us, then, is the *good news,* literally, the Gospel. Finally, Emerson employs a figure for the poet he has used in many other contexts, always a trope of essential import to him: "[The poet] is a true recommencer, or Adam in the Garden again" (31). The poet as the New Adam implies that Paradise has been regained, that the prophecy of Redemption has been fulfilled; this is the message of Revelation.[7]

In *Milton* Blake both theorizes about inspiration and demonstrates it in a work culminating in an explicitly Apocalyptic mode. Emerson delivers his poetic theory most explicitly in his essays, "The Poet" and "Poetry and Imagination." The underlying assumptions in both writers are the same, but Emerson in his prose does not dramatize inspiration or Apocalypse (the poems "Bacchus" and "Merlin" do perform that function). When he is at his most Revelatory, however, Emerson does employ personae of inspiration, the Orphic Poet whose chant ends *Nature* being the most obvious example. It is sometimes assumed that the Revelatory or Apocalyptic mode in Emerson is a feature of his early work which fades or disappears in his later writings, and the earlier essays have virtually monopolized critical attention, although, regrettably, not in those terms. Even recent studies which do not subscribe to Stephen Whicher's hypothesis of Emerson's period of "acquiescence" still seem to focus largely on his writings before 1841.[8] But evidence exists of the visionary (if not Apocalyptic) mode in Emerson as late as the eulogy on Lincoln in 1865. Another late work, and one which employs the rhetoric of Apocalypse, is the essay "Works and Days," from *Society and Solitude* of 1870.[9] Alan Hodder quite perceptively reads *Nature* of 1836 as Emerson's book of Revelation, and he notes earlier readers' awareness of that "source" (4–5).[10] I have read that first book of Emerson rather in terms of the first book of the Bible, as Emerson's visionary account of creation, his Genesis. "Works and Days," late in his career, is a summation and synthesis of much earlier Emersonian thought, and its Revelatory or Apocalyptic mode is eloquently alive and well. Indeed, "Works and Days" is Emerson's account of "a new heaven and a new earth" (Revelation 21:1). It has the added attraction for study that it has been up to now almost ignored.

Emerson begins "Works and Days" by indicating just how radically modern is his revision of John's "a new heaven and a new earth:"

"Our nineteenth century is the age of tools" (*Complete Works* 7:157). The essay begins then rather abruptly as an essay on technology, one of the earliest in our literature.[11] Many more "Apocalyptic" views of technology will be written, optimistic and pessimistic, both hymns and jeremaids, down to Buckminster Fuller and Leo Marx, but Emerson here is almost authoring a genre. These "Works" to be discussed will be technological, not the agricultural ones that occupied Hesiod.[12] The modernism of this essay may be more acutely felt by the twentieth-century reader than it was by Emerson's contemporaries; it is literally prophetic, in that it prefigures a great deal of similar inquiry occurring after his death. It is hard not to read it in the light of certain modern thinkers it seems to preempt. "The human body is the magazine of inventions, the patent office, where are the models from which every hint was taken. All the tools and engines on earth are only extensions of its limbs and senses. One definition of man is "an intelligence served by organs." Machines can only second, not supply, his unaided senses" (157). Emerson's observation here, that technological gadgetry is an extension of human faculties, quite amazingly anticipates the popular modern theories of McLuhan in *Understanding Media: The Extensions of Man*. It is also significant that Emerson's view of "tools and engines" as "extensions" of human "limbs and senses" is thoroughly Blakean.

Emerson goes on to survey the "tolerable apparatus" which his century had "inherited" (158), then regards the inventions of his own time. He catalogs the physical transformations of his world: "the sewing machine, the power-loom, the McCormick reaper, the mowing machines, gas-light, Lucifer matches" and "steam, the enemy of space and time" (158). He notes the social revolutions created by rubber (160) and "the ocean telegraph, that extension of the eye and ear" (160–61), the latter example (it was achieved in 1858) an updating addendum to the 1857 lecture. He senses what some later commentators on technology have felt with less optimism, that technology seems to have a life of its own: "invention breeds invention" (161). Emerson's optimism here is based on the actual physical improvements in human lives that such inventions have either caused or promoted. "Our politics are disgusting," and Malthus's dire predictions are faulty because he neglected the "augmenting power of invention" (162), but politics is now modified by technology: "This thousand-handed art has introduced a new element into the state. The science of power is forced to remember the power of science" (162). For us, by now used to "nuclear disarmament negotiations," such perceptions can be read only as profoundly prophetic. But the prophetic mode in this essay deepens and intensifies, and, as it does, its optimistic mood subtly changes into a darker one.

> Yes, we have a pretty artillery of tools [the military metaphor indicates a rhetorical shift] now in our social arrangements: we ride four times as fast as our fathers did; travel, grind, weave, forge, plant, till and excavate better. We have new shoes, gloves, glasses and gimlets; we have the calculus; we have the newspaper, which does its best to make every square acre of land and sea give an account of itself at your breakfast-table [McLuhan's "global village"]; we have money, and paper money; we have language,—the finest tool of all, and nearest to the mind. Much will have more. Man flatters himself that his command over Nature must increase. Things begin to obey him. We are to have the balloon yet, and the next war will be fought in the air. We may yet find rose-water that will wash the negro white. (163)

While the style here is worthy of "The American Scholar," the tone is quite different; it moves from mild sarcasm, to a kind of dismay, to a metaphor paradoxical in its context (language as tool), to hideously accurate political prophecy (the future war "in the air"), to harsher sarcasm on the problem of racial intolerance in America— unsolved in 1857, unsolved in 1870, unsolved today. In a typical shift, once again, Emerson in the structure of his essay has moved from one dialectical pole to its opposite. It is at this point that the essay more drastically changes its mode by introducing a revisionist myth. That myth will be the structural and conceptual fulcrum of this essay.

> Tantalus, who in old times was seen vainly trying to quench his thirst with a flowing stream which ebbed whenever he approached it, has been seen again lately. He is in Paris, in New York, in Boston. He is now in great spirits; thinks he shall reach it yet; thinks he shall bottle the wave. It is however getting a little doubtful. Things have an ugly look still. No matter how many centuries of culture have preceded, the new man always finds himself standing on the brink of chaos, always in a crisis. Can anybody remember when the times were not hard, and money not scarce? Can anybody remember when sensible men, and the right sort of men, and the right sort of women, were plentiful? Tantalus begins to think steam a delusion, and galvanism no better than it should be. (163–64)

We need to remind ourselves that this is the voice of Emerson in 1857 (and later), not 1836. It could be confused easily with his earlier voice: it has that strength, that depth of resonance. The concept expressed by his myth, technological man as Tantalus, may well be one of the finest epiphanies in all of Emerson.

So the mood has turned in the movement of this essay. "Many facts concur to show that we must look deeper for our salvation than to steam, photographs, balloons or astronomy" (164). The negative pole in "Works and Days" descends as deeply as it does in "Experience" or "Circles." In a passage from the lecture, omitted in the essay, Emerson had written, "I dreamed I stood in a city of beheaded men, where the decapitated trunks continued to walk" (395). It is St. John as Baudelaire, and as the Eliot of *The Waste Land*. Where is the famous Emersonian optimism? Where, indeed? Dialectically, in another part of the essay, of course, but as always that optimism is severely qualified by a balancing rigor.

The pessimism about technology continues. "Machinery is aggressive. The weaver becomes a web, the machinist a machine" (164). Emerson had raised this danger and uttered this warning as early as 1837. Here it has become more urgent. "If you do not use the tools, they use you" (164). Many years before he had written, "Things are in the saddle, / And ride mankind" (*Complete Works* 9:78). He had not changed his mind.

At this point in the essay Emerson makes his major transition. "If, with all [man's] arts, he is a felon, we cannot assume the mechanical skill or chemical resources as the measure of worth. Let us try another gauge" (166). "Works" has occupied the first third (significantly, not the first half) of the essay. Now Emerson turns to "another gauge." His reason for the rhetorical shift is bluntly philosophical: "T'is too plain that with the material power the moral progress has not kept pace. It appears that we have not made a judicious investment. Works and days were offered us, and we took works" (166). The implication is that we cannot have both. We can have *techne* or we can have *time*. The passage is haunted by echoes:

> I . . . watched the pomp,
> Forgot my morning wishes, hastily
> Took a few herbs and apples, and the Day
> Turned and departed silent. I, too late,
> Under her solemn fillet saw the scorn.
> (*Complete Works* 9:228)

Again, he has not changed his mind. Technology has tried to make "a new heaven" out of the old earth. In doing so, Emerson is prescient enough to tell us, it may have instead created a new hell. We need "another gauge."

"Works and days were offered us, and we took works." Emerson becomes profoundly Apocalyptic in spelling out just what it is that we have rejected. There are two startling etymologies in "Works and Days." The first concerns the meaning of "day":

> The new study of the Sanskrit has shown us the origin
> of the old names of God,—Dyaus, Deus, Zeus, Zeu
> pater, Jupiter,—names of the sun, still recognizable
> through the modifications of our vernacular words,
> importing that the Day is the Divine Power and Mani-
> festation, and indicating that those ancient men, in
> their attempts to express the Supreme Power of the
> universe, called him the Day, and that this name was
> accepted by all the tribes. (166–67)

In choosing *techne* over time, our time, human time, what we have
rejected is God.

At this point Emerson alludes to Hesiod's ancient poem, *Works
and Days*. He praises the Greek writer for "piety" and "prudence."
"But he has not pushed his study of days into such inquiry and analysis as they invite" (167). Emerson accepts that invitation. "He only is
rich who owns the day" (168). Without the human realization of time,
the technical transformation of the world remains a mere poverty. But
if the days are divine, they must be revered as divinities, and here
Emerson echoes in prose his own poem: "The days are ever as divine
as to the first Aryans. They are of the least pretension and of the greatest capacity of anything that exists. They come and go like muffled
and veiled figures, sent from a distant friendly party; but they say
nothing, and if we do not use the gifts they bring, they carry them as
silently away" (168). The crux then is the human use of time, which
remains an ambiguous gift or ambivalent potential. At this point the
essay changes its mode again, and moves into a bardic or prophetic, a
Revelatory, eloquence. Now with echoes not of his own poems but of
one of the most lyrical passages in Ecclesiastes (3:1–8), "To every thing
there is a season, and a time to every purpose under heaven," Emerson describes certain days, units of time redeemed from time: "One
author is good for winter, and one for the dog-days. The scholar must
look long for the right hour for Plato's Timaeus. At last the elect
morning arrives, the early dawn,—a few lights conspicuous in the

heaven, as of a world just created and still becoming,—and in its wide leisures we dare open that book" (169–70). One must perhaps return to the celebrated passages in *Nature* in 1836 to find parallels to this eloquence. But it continues: "There are days which are the carnival of the year. The angels assume flesh, and repeatedly become visible" (170). In this paradoxical apotheosis of human time, the celebration, the "carnival," is not a farewell to the flesh, as the literal meaning of the term dictates, but a welcome of new flesh, of new incarnations. The incarnated angel as a metaphor for the joyful realization of human time is one of Emerson's most beautiful figures, both imaginatively superior to and philosophically more liberating than Wallace Stevens's "necessary angel." These fleshy angels of human exultation are Blake's angels.

"The days are made on a loom whereof the warp and woof are past and future time" (170). Just such a sentence makes one understand why Barish echoes Packer in describing Emerson as "simply the best American writer" (253). Here in these passages is the old Emerson as the young Emerson; he himself demonstrates here the timelessness of human time; he has lost nothing. As if he himself is aware of that fact, he now echoes the most visionary moments in *Nature*:

> The days are made on a loom whereof the warp and woof are past and future time. They are majestically dressed, as if every god brought a thread to the skyey web. 'T is pitiful the things by which we are rich or poor,—a matter of coins, coats and carpets, a little more or less stone, or wood, or paint, the fashion of a cloak or hat; like the luck of naked Indians, of whom one is proud in the possession of a glass bead or a red feather, and the rest miserable in the want of it. But the treasures which Nature spent itself to amass,—the secular, refined, composite anatomy of man, which all strata go to form, which the prior races, from infusory

and saurian, existed to ripen; the surrounding plastic
natures; the earth with its foods; the intellectual, tem-
peramenting air; the sea with its invitations; the
heaven deep with worlds; and the answering brain and
nervous structure replying to these; the eye that
looketh into the deeps, which again look back to
the eye, abyss to abyss,—these, not like a glass bead, or
the coins or carpets, are given immeasurably to all.
(170–71)

Here the "transparent eyeball" is fulfilled and justified; here something is looking back.

Appropriately for a book of Revelation, those *angels* that incarnated themselves in the carnival of the year reappear, and *miracle,* no
longer "monster," but now "one with the blowing clover and the
falling rain"—is made manifest: "This miracle is hurled into every
beggar's hands. The blue sky is a covering for a market and for the
cherubim and seraphim" (171). Perhaps only Emerson could include
a "market" and the "seraphim" in the same comfortable sentence.
And now Emerson provides the second of the two startling etymologies in this essay, this one arresting perhaps because he has never
provided it before, not in *Nature* of 1836 (where it might have opened
an inquiry that would have filled the "crack"), not in "The Method
of Nature" of 1841, not in the "Nature" of the *Essays: Second Series* of
1844: "It is singular that our rich English language should have no
word to denote the face of the world. *Kinde* was the old English term,
which, however, filled only half the range of our fine Latin word,
with its delicate future tense,—*natura, about to be born,* or what
German philosophy denotes as a *becoming"* (172). *"Natura, about to
be born" or "becoming":* it is a concept that might have in itself united
the ME and the NOT ME in his first book.

"Works and Days" is a retrospective of Emerson's thought as
well as an original prophecy. Daringly here, the old dialectical
method returns; there are contraries, polarities, even in this late text,

and Emerson almost shockingly brings together in one paragraph, in one sentence two of his most highly charged archetypal images: the positive term "food" and the negative, "illusion": "Such are the days,—the earth is the cup, the sky is the cover, of the immense bounty of Nature which is offered us for our daily aliment; but what a force of *illusion* begins life with us and attends us to the end!" (172).

The image of the earth as cup and the sky as its cover is Blake's image of the "Mundane Shell." Within that fallen perspective, illusion is coextensive with life-giving food. Emerson asks, "Where is the old eye that ever saw through the deception?" (172). He has momentarily forgotten it; it is his own, in *Nature*. In this paragraph life is "a gale of warring elements," and the catalog of illusions here is short but eloquent: "a rattle, a doll, an apple, for a child; skates, a river, a boat, a horse, a gun, for the growing boy; and I will not begin to name those of the youth and adult, for they are numberless" (172–73). Significantly, he names the children's toys; the adult ones are anonymous. But why does this passage on illusions occur here in this essay and now at this point? "This element of illusion lends all its force to hide the values of present time" (172). We saw in an earlier chapter that Emerson's "illusion" is Blake's "Vala," the whore of fallen perception. In Revelation, she must be stripped of her veils, as Babylon or Mystery is seen as such, stripped and destroyed, in John's book (Revelation 17, 18). The rest of Emerson's essay Apocalyptically removes the illusions attached to time. If illusion hides "the values of present time," the naked truth is the Revelation of those present values: "The world is always equal to itself, and every man in moments of deeper thought is apprised that he is repeating the experiences of the people in the streets of Thebes or Byzantium. An everlasting Now reigns in nature, which hangs the same roses on our bushes which charmed the Roman and the Chaldean in their hanging-gardens" (174).

The rest of the essay lyrically expounds the concept of the "everlasting Now": "One of the illusions is that the present hour is not the critical, decisive hour. Write it on your heart that every day is the best day in the year. No man has learned anything rightly until he knows that every day is Doomsday" (175). Emerson is as revisionist in his theology here as he was in the most radical passages in the Divinity School "Address." When is Judgment Day? *Today* is Judgment Day. Emerson is telling the same story that John did in Revelation, and it is still a story with a happy ending, but he is redefining its terms.[13]

"Works and Days" is about not only the "infinitude of the private man," but the infinity of the present moment, the infinite value of each moment of human existence. It is in this context that Emerson remembers Jones Very: "I knew a man in a certain religious exaltation who 'thought it an honor to wash his own face.' He seemed to me more sane than those who hold themselves cheap" (177). And it is in this context, also, that the Emersonian view of the past becomes as uncompromising as it was in "The American Scholar" and in "History": "Zoologists may deny that horsehairs in the water change to worms, but I find that whatever is old corrupts, and the past turns to snakes" (177).

If the first illusion about time was that "the present hour is not the critical, decisive hour," then a second is that time is quantitative rather than qualitative, or, in Emerson's words, "that there is not time enough for our work" (177–78). This illusion or problem is almost universal in ordinary human psychology, and Emerson's philosophical correction here is both immensely valuable and sharply astute, using as it does to make its point both a pair of apostles and a Native American chief (and two apostles and an Indian chief will beat any skeptic's hand in philosophical poker):

> A snake converts whatever prey the meadow yields
> him into snake; a fox, into fox; and Peter and John are
> working up all existence into Peter and John. A poor
> Indian chief of the Six Nations of New York made a
> wiser reply than any philosopher, to some one com-

plaining that he had not enough time. "Well," said
Red Jacket, "I suppose you have all there is." (178)

In a definition of time in human terms, the quantitative term
"enough" becomes meaningless. We have all the time there is.
The arithmetic of Emerson's expository points is always somewhat ambiguous, a distinctive feature of his rhetoric and still another
refutation of quantity as value, and in "Works and Days," he is both
characteristic and contextually appropriate. "A third illusion haunts
us, that a long duration, as a year, a decade, a century, is valuable"
(178). If the reader has failed to count to three, or fails to see the
distinction between the second and third illusions, that is also appropriate to the reading of an Apocalyptic text; John's sevens and
twelves in Revelation are symbols, not digits. In discussing the third
illusion concerning time, Emerson reaffirms the value of quality over
quantity. "We ask for long life, but 'tis deep life, or grand moments,
that signify" (178). And perhaps only an older thinker could observe:
"Life is unnecessarily long. Moments of insight, of fine personal relation, a smile, a glance,—what ample borrowers of Eternity they are"
(178). It was a Blake younger than the Emerson writing here who had
said, "Eternity is in love with the productions of time" (*Poetry and
Prose* 36), but the philosophical insight is the same.
The qualitative value of time is intrinsic to its present realization.
"He only can enrich me who can recommend to me the space between sun and sun" (179). The distinction between time and eternity
becomes dissolved: "These passing fifteen minutes, men think, are
time, not eternity" (179), and that perception is illusion or mistake.
Emerson's "fifteen minutes" here are Blake's "Eternity in an hour"
(*Poetry and Prose* 490), Americans by all accounts moving faster than
their British counterparts. But Emerson, like Blake, is by no means
being whimsical here. "And him I reckon the most learned scholar,
not who can unearth for me the buried dynasties of Sesostris and
Ptolemy, the Sothiac era, the Olympiads and consulships, but who

can unfold the theory of this particular Wednesday" (179). Like the "space between sun and sun," like "these passing fifteen minutes," Emerson's emphasis on "this particular Wednesday" suggests the need for a study of Emerson which has not yet been written but which may be urgent, namely Emerson's *Existentialism*.

Being in time is being in a particular moment of time. It is also being in a particular place; *being-there* is always *being-here*. So correlative to Emerson's theory of time in this essay is a Revelatory theory of place. If the present is better than the past, it follows that "here" is more valuable than "there":

> This mendicant America, this curious, peering, itinerant, imitative America, studious of Greece and Rome, of England and Germany, will take off its dusty shoes, will take off its glazed traveller's-cap and sit at home with repose and joy on its face. The world has no such landscape, the aeons of history no such hour, the future no equal second opportunity. Now let poets sing! Now let arts unfold! (180)

Here is again the "declaration of independence" of the "American Scholar," but in a more philosophical context.

There is no Orphic Poet in "Works and Days." No such persona is needed. Emerson here speaks Orphically in his own voice, without a fictive mask; he is Blake in his garden at Felpham. The whole second part of this essay (its last two-thirds) is an Orphic chant.

"Life is good only when it is magical and musical" (180). Emerson talks of "timing" and "consent" in our not anatomizing life. Then he completes an implied syllogism: "You must treat the days respectfully, *you must be a day yourself,* and not interrogate it like a college professor" (180; emphasis added). Earlier he had given the etymology of "day": a *god*. Now he urges us to become a day— logically, to become divine. Again, this is a Revelation of human transformation, an invitation for the human to participate in the divine. The logic is symbolic and visionary, not Aristotelian, not that of a college professor, and Emerson underscores his method by a lyrical rather than logical antithesis: "The world is enigmatical . . . and must not be taken literally, but genially" (180). He "explains" by metaphor and image: "We must be at the top of our condition to understand anything rightly. You must hear the bird's song without attempting to render it into nouns and verbs. Cannot we be a little abstemious and obedient? Cannot we let the morning be?" (180). The "bird's song" is also the "Bard's Song," and a number of Emersonian scholars, college professors all, have rendered it into most unlyrical nouns and verbs. The subtext of this essay is a set of directions on how to read the text.

The problem of syntax (nouns and verbs, not to mention conjunctions) is the nonmimetic connections it makes. "Everything in the universe goes by indirection. There are no straight lines" (181).[14] Emerson quotes a "foreign scholar" who "made a week of [his] youth happy by his visit":

> "Just to fill the hour,—that is happiness. Fill my hour,
> ye gods, so that I shall not say, whilst I have done this,
> 'Behold, also, an hour of my life is gone,' but rather, 'I
> have lived an hour.'" (181)

Here in its concluding paragraphs, "Works and Days" becomes a hymn to spontaneity. Emerson contrasts Newton, the spontaneous thinker, with "the savant" whose "performance is a memoir to the Academy on fish-worms, tadpoles, or spiders' legs; he observes as other academicians observe; he is on stilts at a microscope." In contrast, for Newton, "science was as easy as breathing; he used the same wit to weigh the moon that he used to buckle his shoes" (183).

Emerson's essays often frustrate the reader accustomed to conventional expository form. Often they seem not to conclude, but merely stop.[15] I suggest that they be read as prose poems.[16] But "Works and Days" satisfies even conventional rhetorical expectations, a curious structural irony for an Apocalyptic work, but rather like that of Shakespeare in finally observing all three of the classical unities in, of all plays, *The Tempest*. Emerson does not give us merely one summary conclusion; as if making up for earlier omissions, he gives us two. The first reviews the concept of time:

> In stripping time of its illusions, in seeking to find what is the heart of the day, we come to the quality of the moment, and drop the duration altogether. It is the depth at which we live and not at all the surface extension that imports. We pierce to the eternity, of which time is the flitting surface; and, really, the least acceleration of thought and the least increase of power of thought, make life to seem and to be of vast duration. (183)

"To seem *and to be* [emphasis added] of vast duration": the writer of Revelation is not playing a game of psychological impressionism; his message is metaphysical vision. "Mark well my words," the Bard in Blake's *Milton* repeatedly announces, "they are of your eternal salvation."

Second, Emerson summarizes his entire essay in its final paragraph:

> And this is the progress of every earnest mind; from the works of man and the activity of the hands to a delight in the faculties which rule them; from a respect to the works to a wise wonder at this mystic element of time in which he is conditioned; from local skills and the economy which reckons the amount of production *per* hour to the finer economy which respects the quality of what is done, and the right we have to the work, or the fidelity with which it flows from ourselves; then to the depth of thought it betrays, looking to its universality, or that its roots are in eternity, not time. Then it flows from character, that sublime health

which values one moment as another, and makes us
great in all conditions, and as the only definition we
have of freedom and power. (185)

"Freedom and power" are thus the last words of the essay. In its
whole context they can be related to the two terms of the title only
with profound irony. Nineteenth- (and twentieth-) century man
sought power through works, through technology, and was already in
Emerson's time well on the way to creating a new hell rather than a
new heaven on his earth. We were offered works and days, Emerson
tells us, and as part of the operation of the Fall we chose works. But
the second half (or rather two-thirds) of the essay reverses this pessimism: it is still possible to choose days, and in doing so, we are able
to experience eternity in time. That choice creates human freedom,
which is the real human power. Time in this context has nothing to
do with the clock (although each sensuous human "day" is divine),
and everything to do with the human awareness of human "infinitude." Like that in Blake's *Milton,* Emerson's Apocalypse in "Works
and Days" is not an end but a beginning.

This apocalyptic redefinition of space-time Blake had already
announced in *Milton:* "The Satanic Space is delusion" (36: 20, *Poetry
and Prose* 137). Further,

> There is a Moment in each day that Satan
> cannot find
> Nor can his Watch Fiends find it, but the
> industrious find
> This Moment & it multiply, & when it once is
> found
> It renovates every Moment of the Day if rightly
> placed. (*Poetry and Prose* 136)

Blake is expressing in these lines quite exactly Emerson's view of
the human capacity to transform temporal experience. The radical

redefinition here is simply the perception that time is a human phenomenon:

> But others of the Sons of Los build Moments
>   & Minutes & Hours
> And Days & Months & Years & Ages & Periods;
>   wondrous buildings
> And every Moment has a Couch of gold for soft
>   repose,
> (A moment equals a pulsation of the artery)
> And between every two Moments stands a Daughter
>   of Beulah
> To feed the Sleepers on their Couches with
>   maternal care.
> And every Minute has an azure Tent with silken
>   Veils.
> And every Hour as a bright golden Gate carved
>   with skill.
> And every Day & Night, has Walls of brass &
>   Gates of adamant,
> Shining like precious stones & ornamented with
>   appropriate signs:
> . . . .
> Every Time less than a pulsation of the artery
> Is equal in its period & value to Six Thousand
>   Years.
>
> For in this Period the Poets Work is Done;
>   and all the Great
> Events of Time start forth & are conceived in
>   such a Period
> Within a Moment: a Pulsation of the Artery.
>
> The Sky is an immortal Tent built by the Sons
>   of Los
> And every Space that a Man views around his
>   dwelling-place:

Standing on his own roof, or in his garden
                on a mount
Of twenty-five cubits in height, such space is
                his Universe;
And on its verge the Sun rises & sets. the
                Clouds bow
To meet the flat Earth & the Sea in such an
                ordered Space:
The Starry heavens reach no further but here
                bend and set
On all sides & the two Poles turn on their valves
                of gold:
And if he move his dwelling-place, his heavens
                also move.

. . . .

As to that false appearance which appears to
                the reasoner,
As of a Globe rolling thro Voidness, it is a
                delusion of Ulro
The Microscope knows not of this nor the
                Telescope. they alter
The ratio of the Spectators Organs but leave
                Objects untouchd
For every Space larger than a red Globule of
                Mans blood.
Is visionary; and is created by the hammer of Los
And every Space smaller than a Globule of Mans
                blood. opens
Into Eternity of which this vegetable Earth
                is but a shadow.
                (*Poetry and Prose* 126–27)

    The earth is "flat" for Blake (or, as he puts it elsewhere, "one in-
finite plane," a cosmic Möbius strip), because that is what we
experience; no human being has ever stood upon a round one. This
is human space. And if time is also a human phenomenon ("A

Moment equals a pulsation of the artery"), this fact represents our freedom from the external machine. The implication for human action is indeed Apocalyptic. As Emerson put it in 1836, "Build therefore your own world."

For both Emerson and Blake that human world is not a *given;* it must be *built.* The building of our own world is the labor of Los, the work of the imagination. The realization of this possibility is Revelation. The function of the Poet, for Emerson as for Blake, is to show us that we already possess the key to open the gate of the New Jerusalem:

> I give you the end of a golden string,
>   Only wind it into a ball;
> It will lead you in at Heavens gate,
>   Built in Jerusalems wall. (*Poetry and Prose* 231)

We must bear in mind, however, that "Jerusalem" was "builded" *here,* among these Pennsylvania hills, and that if the New Jerusalem is to be rebuilt, it must be *here* as well, wherever we happen to find ourselves; for, as Emerson tells us, "There is no other world" (*Complete Works* 10:199). The "new heaven and the new earth" must be created imaginatively out of the here and now. "Where do we find ourselves?" Emerson asks at the *beginning* of "Experience." "In a series of which we do not know the extremes, and believe that it has none" (*Complete Works* 3:45). But at the *end* of "Experience" he affirms, "We must be very suspicious of the deceptions of the element of time. It takes a good deal of time to eat or to sleep, or to earn a hundred dollars, and a very little time to entertain a hope and an insight which becomes the light of our life" (85). That "very little time" is Blake's "pulsation of the artery." It is enough, if for no other reason than it is "all we have," as the Indian said to the complainer. Emerson continues in that same conclusion, "In the solitude to which every man is always returning, he has a sanity and revelations which in his passage into new worlds he will carry with him" (85). "Revelations" (the plural is significant) and "new worlds"—perhaps we have more than enough.

The poet as prophet, whether Emerson or Blake, confers upon us an enormous gift of freedom, and with that gift comes an equally profound debt of responsibility. Like the visionary creation of one's own world, like one's own tragic and fortunate Fall, like one's own Redemption of one's self (for which one is *absolutely* responsible), the Apocalypse—if it is to occur—must happen inside one's own head. Emerson and Blake beckon us to follow, not them, but rather our most authentic selves in the quest of that fulfillment.

Conclusion: "Prospects"

꿍ᑲᘊ

*I am inspired I know it is truth! for I Sing / According
to the inspiration of the Poetic Genius.*

—Blake

I am in all my theory, ethics and politics a poet.

—Emerson

IN "THE TRANSCENDENTALIST," a lecture of 1842, Emerson
makes clear that he does not regard himself as a "Transcendentalist."
After defining transcendentalism as "Idealism as it appears in 1842"
(*Complete Works* 1:329), not "new views" but the "oldest of thoughts"
in a current "mould," he goes on to contrast idealism and materialism, leaving little doubt that his sympathies lie on the idealist side.
But here again we find the familiar Emersonian dialectic of structural
method: the two philosophical schools are played off against each
other in a merely exploratory introduction. If his strongest personal
statement places him emphatically at the idealist pole ("You think me
the child of my circumstances: I make my circumstance" [334]), that
significant first person singular pronoun is revealingly dropped by the
end of the introduction, and "Transcendentalists" are discussed in the
third person, singular or plural.

The Transcendentalist is "he" (336), "they" and "these" (341), and
"they" (342, 344, 345, 346, 348). With still greater distancing, suggesting some condescension, the Transcendentalists are "these children"
(348) and "these persons" (352), "this class" (354, 355) and "these of
whom I speak" (357), where the "I" is explicitly distinguished from
the "they." This distinction becomes even more of a divorce with,
"When I asked them concerning their private experience, they an-

swered somewhat in this wise" (352). The only section of the main body of the lecture (everything after the first five paragraphs) which employs the first person singular (350–53) prompts Edward Waldo Emerson to issue a careful disclaimer on his father's behalf:

> The change to the first person in this paragraph—very likely due to a sheet introduced after the main part of the essay was written—does not mean that Mr. Emerson states here his own views. In this and what follows he only continues to be a mouthpiece for the views of these "children" with whose faith he admits a sympathy, but it is a measured one. (*Complete Works* 1:449)

After a century and a half of textbook and anthology clichés to the contrary, it may be time to take Emerson at his word: he is *not* a Transcendentalist. What, then, is he? This study has suggested one possible answer. The quotation from Emerson at the head of this chapter indicates that he would agree, and its context dissociates him not just from Transcendentalism but from "philosophy" itself. Again, Edward Waldo Emerson's note provides relevant information: "Mr. Emerson, when called a philosopher, said, 'I am in all my theory, ethics and politics a poet'" (*Complete Works* 1:446). Such self-evaluation on Emerson's part might place studies with titles like *Emerson's Epistemology* in a somewhat dubious limbo; it leaves this study in comfortable concord.

In all his "theory, ethics and politics" Emerson is a "poet"; the three categories comprehend his whole work. This authorial judgment means that *Nature* is poetry; that both series of *Essays* are poetry; that *Representative Men* is not biography but biographical poetry; that the later essays and lectures are still poetry; that *The Conduct of Life* is a collection of poems, not a set of directions in a how-to-do-it self-help manual; that even *English Traits* may be an idiosyncratic Byronic narrative poem, Childe Waldo's Pilgrimage.

But what kind of a poet is Emerson? "Now every one must do after his kind, be he asp or angel. . . . The question which a wise man and a student of history will ask, is, what that kind is?" (*Complete Works* 1:341). I have suggested that Emerson is a mythic poet, and that the myth he employs illuminates the whole spectrum of the human condition.

That large and radically humanistic myth can be described in different ways, but that its terms are both human and cosmic, no serious student of Emerson can doubt. As a rhetorical convenience, I have used the four human-cosmic archetypes of William Blake's analogous myth as a descriptive framework. For both Emerson and Blake "there is one story and one story only," to wrench Robert Graves's fine line far out of its context. That story in Emerson's version has been described as "universal biography." The mythic archetypes serve the rhetorically convenient function of providing universal "handles" or hooks, and they are universal because every individual human being repeats as an individual that mythic history. In humanity's story, every human being, first as the child (then hopefully later as the poet) remakes the world, creates the world anew in personal vision. Second, that child-visionary falls into self-consciousness and sexuality. Third, she (or he) discovers the possibility of Redemption from the sexual and conceptual divisions created by the Fall. Fourth, that realization of Redemption, made manifest or revealed imaginatively, is human Apocalypse.

Blake tells this story over and over again, with differently named characters for the different parts of the human psyche, with variations and inconsistencies, but the pieces are pieces of the same large whole. Emerson tells the same story for the most part without named characters, but his "I" in his long time takes many parts, and in Emerson's version (as in Blake's) the surface inconsistencies reveal the deeper integrity of that mythic whole.

The story reaches a happy resolution (rather than an end), but that resolution is not achieved by ignoring pain, suffering, frustration, or even contradiction. The danger of misinterpretation of the myth, in Emerson as in Blake, results from taking one part in isolation from its very large context. A reading of "The Lamb," extracted and isolated from the rest of Blake's canon, will bog down in mere pietistic non-sense. It is equally the case with Emerson: a view of "Self-Reliance" alone may discover mere crass conservatism. Often both writers, to prevent such partial readings, try to mirror the complexity of the whole mythic spectrum in a single work, such as *Milton* or *Jerusalem,* or *Nature* or "Circles" or "Experience." When commentators have extracted concepts from these works, rather than contemplated images in them, the integrity of those works has suffered. If "Fate," for example, were read as the complex mythic poem it is, the image in the line, "Let us build altars to the Beautiful Necessity" (*Complete Works* 6:49) would prevent some of that essay's more popular misreadings. Out of the context of the rest of Emerson's mythic spectrum, we forget what the image of altars means to him, though he has been consistent about those cold sacrificial slabs ever since he turned his back on them in "The Lord's Supper" and in the Divinity School "Address." "Fate," if read as a mythic poem, reveals itself to be a hymn to freedom, a freedom not of course unconditioned, but rather as existentially conditioned as the victories of the spirit achieved through the negativities and anxieties of "Experience" or "Circles."[1]

This study has taken Emerson at his word, that he is not a philosopher, that he is a poet. It has looked at his images, with the help of analogous Blakean models. And it has discovered in Emerson a literary artist—not a minor (or confused) philosopher, but a major (and consistent) poet.

Dialectics is not myth, is not archetype. This study began by scrutinizing "Emerson's inveterate habit of stating things in opposites," to use Matthiessen's honest but misleading phrase. Perhaps it is not that Emerson states "things" in opposites, but rather that he structures images in a polarized arrangement to express the one thing he wishes to say. Emerson is not, any more than Blake, a "dialectician" or dialectical philosopher. What these two literary artists do is to let their imaginations play with contraries until that interplay generates the meaning of the poem. This dialectical method is simply that—a means, not an end. Such writing reveals not conceptual dialectics but the dialectical imagination at work, at play, creating imaginatively the singleness of vision which each of these two writers uniquely possesses.

When he attended Longfellow's funeral, Emerson, after visiting the coffin twice, asked his daughter, Ellen, "Where are we? What house? And who is the sleeper?"[2] The questions may accurately serve as evidence of senility. But, if they are removed from the biographical pathos of Emerson's last days, they stand as Orphic utterance. This occurred in 1882, not long before his own death, but he had been saying ever since "The American Scholar" in 1837 that the ordinary life of most human beings was "sleep walking" (*Complete Works* 1:107). The interrogation might have been uttered by his own Bacchus or Merlin, or perhaps by his Sphinx; it indicates that Blake's "Poetic Genius" is still alive and well in him. The Sleeper is Albion, is Humanity, and Emerson had spent a long life of thinking, speaking, and writing in an effort to awaken that sleeper.

"Where are we?" He knew. He had said, "Where do we find ourselves? In a series of which we do not know the extremes, and believe that it has none" (*Complete Works* 3:45). The beginning of "Experience" is quite possibly the most existential passage in nineteenth-century American literature.

"What house?" It does not matter, of course, what roof or masonry, what floor boards, what wallpaper or what walls. ("Hear the rats in the wall," he had said, near the end of, appropriately, "History" [*Complete Works* 2:39].) It does not matter because "Every spirit builds itself a house, and beyond its house a world, and beyond its world a heaven" (*Complete Works* 1:76). It did not matter in 1882. He had built his "own world."

Blake looked around at the horrors of the slums of London and heard "mind-forged manacles" (*Poetry and Prose* 27). The profound optimism of Blake, like that of Emerson, is based not on deafness toward "every cry of every Man" and "every Infants cry of fear," nor blindness toward "swine, spiders, snakes, pests, mad-houses, prisons, enemies" (*Complete Works* 1:76). But Emerson, like Blake, sees what the manacles are really made of. If the human mind forges them, the human mind can *break* them. Emerson, like Blake, urges us to free ourselves.

Another prophet once wrote, "But in the last days . . . they shall beat their swords into plowshares, and their spears into pruninghooks . . . they shall sit every man under his vine and under his fig tree; and none shall make them afraid" (Micah 4:1–4). The prophets Emerson and Blake share that vision, with one Romantic revision: those will not be the "last days"; those will be the *first days.*

NOTES

INTRODUCTION: "DISCIPLINE"

1. James Russell Lowell, "Emerson the Lecturer," 45, quoted in David Leverenz, *Manhood and the American Renaissance,* 42; Jonathan Bishop, *Emerson on the Soul,* 6, in Leverenz 42; Eric Cheyfitz, *The Trans-Parent: Sexual Politics in the Language of Emerson,* 10, in Leverenz 43. Joel Porte reviews a similar set of complaints in "The Problem of Emerson," 85–90, calling attention to what David Robinson has described as the "bafflement . . . among Emerson's interpreters, who feel that they have not gotten to the essential Emerson" (*Apostle of Culture: Emerson as Preacher and Lecturer,* 1). F. O. Matthiessen, *American Renaissance: Art and Expression in the Age of Emerson and Whitman.*

2. Ralph Waldo Emerson, *The Complete Works of Ralph Waldo Emerson* 1:10, 70–72. All subsequent quotations from Emerson's essays, lectures, and poems are from this edition, cited hereafter as *Complete Works.* M. H. Abrams, *Natural Supernaturalism: Tradition and Revolution in Romantic Literature;* Harold Bloom, *The Ringers in the Tower: Studies in the Romantic Tradition;* Northrop Frye, *Fearful Symmetry: A Study of William Blake.*

3. Armida Gilbert, "Emerson and the English Romantic Poets."

1. THE DIALECTICAL IMAGINATION

1. On an experimental list of essay topics for his forthcoming book, *Essays [First Series],* Emerson paired "Art" with "Nature," although he later omitted "Nature," reserving it for the 1844 *Essays: Second Series.* See Ralph Waldo Emerson, *The Journals and Miscellaneous Notebooks of Ralph Waldo Emerson* 7:498, *n.* 498–99, cited hereafter as *Journals and Notebooks.*

NOTES TO PAGES 8–19

2. Lawrence Buell in "Ralph Waldo Emerson," also observes the first series of *Essays* as "twelve pieces on moral, religious, and intellectual concepts arranged in groups of two, each pair surveying common or analogous subjects from contrasting or complementary angles" (53).

3. David V. Erdman, ed., *The Complete Poetry and Prose of William Blake,* 19. All subsequent quotations from Blake are from this edition, cited hereafter as *Poetry and Prose.*

4. Emerson, *Complete Works* 9:35. Leonard Neufeldt, *The House of Emerson,* has observed Emerson's "preference in Coleridge's poetry for pieces such as the conversation poems" (147).

5. Hyatt Waggoner, *Emerson as Poet,* asserts that neither the first nor third line of the poem "can be scanned by any traditional prosodic system" (153), which is debatable. See Richard R. O'Keefe, "Scanning 'Hamatreya': Emerson as Miltonic Prosodist," 1–2.

6. *Journals* 9:321. Thomas Wentworth Higginson, "Emerson's Oriental Texts," 81; Richard Bridgman, "The Meaning of Emerson's Title, 'Hamatreya,'" 24; Kiffin Ayres Rockwell, "Emerson's *Hamatreya,* Another Guess," 24; Mohan Lal Sharma, "Emerson's HAMATREYA," 63; Alice Hull Petry, "The Meeting of the Twain: Emerson's 'Hamatreya,'" 48.

7. Robert J. Gangewere, ed., *The Exploited Eden: Literature on the American Environment,* 84–86.

8. Perhaps more deeply analytical of Emerson's thought than Whicher's *Freedom and Fate* is David L. Smith, "Emerson and Deconstruction: The End(s) of Scholarship": "Emerson's world . . . is characterized by an irreducible doubleness. Experience is split between moments of insight and long stretches of sleep; between visionary wealth and an all-embracing poverty. Ecstatic insight renders ordinary consciousness paltry and mean. Ordinary consciousness takes its revenge by convincing us that ecstasy is merely a quirk of the digestion or blood. Moreover, this basic doubleness of the faithful and skeptical moods is reflected in virtually every department of Emerson's thinking. Variety and unity; Understanding and Reason; fall and apocalypse; nominalist and realist; conservative and transcendentalist; the party of the past and the party of the future; the many and the one; fate and freedom—all of these agonizing contraries were codependent facts in Emerson's experience, and as such they endlessly galled him into irritation and wonder" (385).

9. Studies pertinent to the problem include Frye, *Fearful Symmetry;* Kathleen Raine, *William Blake;* Harold Bloom, *Blake's Apocalypse: A Study in Poetic Argument;* Robert F. Gleckner, *The Piper and the Bard: A Study of William Blake;* Leopold Damrosch, Jr., *Symbol and Truth in Blake's Myth.*

10. An exception among recent critics is Julie Ellison, who rejects, in *Emerson's Romantic Style* the term "dialectic" altogether. For Ellison, Emerson's prose "accumulates but does not progress" (76).

11. Further clarification of the term "dialectical" as it is used in this study may prove helpful. It is *not* employed in the narrowly technical Hegelian sense that Leopold Damrosch, Jr., invokes in order to reject, in *Symbol and Truth in Blake's Myth:* "Blake's system is often called dialectical, but it is so only in a special sense, envisioning truth as the *simultaneous* union of all particulars rather than as the sequential development that we ordinarily expect in dialectic" (28).

Damrosch explicitly contradicts Jacob Bronowski's earlier view, in *William Blake: A Man Without A Mask:* "Blake made for himself, *twenty years before Hegel,* the dialectic of Hegel's formal thought" (93; emphasis added). Bronowski sees Blake's dialectic as closer to Marx than to Hegel: "this is the full meaning of the dialectic of contraries, in Blake and in Marx: that no revolution is the last" (134).

The third term in this dialectical footnote is Harold Bloom. Closest to this study's use of the term is his, and Bloom employs it in writing about both Blake and Emerson, respectively, in such essays as "Dialectic of *The Marriage of Heaven and Hell*" and "Bacchus and Merlin: The Dialectic of Romantic Poetry in America," both from *The Ringers in the Tower.* Bloom observes that Blake's dialectic in *The Marriage* is "a dialectic without transcendence" and that "by the 'marriage' of contraries Blake means only that we are to cease valuing one contrary above the other in any way" (57). Instead of Hegel, Bloom's philosophic parallel for Blake is Husserl: "Blake more than anticipates Husserl here; he gives a definitive statement of the phenomenology of existence, the ceaseless dialectic of daily appearance" (60). Bloom uses the term with roughly equal frequency about Emerson. "Throughout Emerson's great period (1832–41, with a sudden but brief resurgence in 1846) there is a dialectic or interplay between the assertion of imagination's autonomy, and a shrewd skepticism of any phenomenon reaching too far into the unconditioned" (292). And Bloom analyzes in some detail Emerson's "oscillation between poetic incarnation (Bacchus) and the merging with necessity (Merlin)" (305). It is this last sense, then, Bloom's "interplay" or "oscillation," that comes closest to what this study means when it uses the term "dialectic."

2. EYEBALLS, WINDOWS, AND THE WORLD'S BODY

1. Evelyn Barish, *Emerson: The Roots of Prophecy,* 177–84, reveals new medical evidence to suggest that Emerson's temporary blindness, as well as his lameness of hip and difficulties in breathing, were all "aspects of the same illness" (178), a form of tuberculosis (182), a disease tragically frequent in his family. This study in no way wishes to deny the physical reality of Emerson's illness; it merely suggests a psychosomatic component which throws its own light on some central images in his texts.

2. Michael Davis, *William Blake: A New Kind of Man,* 14.

3. Sherman Paul, *Emerson's Angle of Vision,* recalls the "good-natured" sketch by Cranch; the vituperation of the Rev. Henry A. Braun, whose review of *Nature* in *The Catholic World* used the passage as evidence of Emerson's "insanity"; and the accusation of oversimplification by *The Westminster Review* of London (84–85).

4. T. S. Eliot, "The Dry Salvages," 27.

5. Harold Bloom, Introduction, *Ralph Waldo Emerson: Modern Critical Views,* 6.

6. Richard Tuerk, "Emerson's *Nature*—Miniature Universe," 110–13.

7. Kenneth Burke, "I, Eye, Aye—Emerson's Early Essay on 'Nature,'" 875–95. This essay is not representative of modern commentary on *Nature.* Packer, Bishop, even Whicher, are more central. Burke's essay, however, is often cited by later commentators, for example: Bloom, "Emerson: The American Religion," *Emerson: Modern Critical Views,* 107; Cheyfitz, *The Trans-parent,* 112, 173n.5; Ellison, *Romantic Style,* 139; Hodder, *Rhetoric of Revelation,* 64; John Michael, *Emerson and Skepticism,* 36; Van Leer, *Emerson's Epistemology,* 42. It was also reprinted in Merton M. Sealts, Jr., and Alfred R. Ferguson, *Emerson's Nature: Origin, Growth, and Meaning,* 150–63. Burke's essay has thus had an influence disproportionate to its merits.

8. A fact observed by, among others, Tuerk, "Emerson's *Nature,*" 110.

9. Relevant studies, pursuing a wider "angle of vision" than does the present study, include Neufeldt, *The House of Emerson;* Sherman Paul, *Emerson's Angle of Vision;* James M. Cox, "R. W. Emerson: The Circles of the Eye,"

45–60; Damrosch, *Symbol and Truth in Blake's Myth;* idem, "Vision and Perception," 11–37; Thomas Weiskel, "Blake's Critique of Transcendence," 117–32; Donald D. Ault, *Visionary Physics: Blake's Response to Newton.*

10. Typical of the critical reaction against Frye's "holistic" reading is Damrosch's deconstructive appetite for inconsistencies; these two approaches, synthetic and analytic, suggest ironically the labors of Los and Urizen, respectively.

11. Bloom, "The Central Man: Emerson, Whitman, Wallace Stevens," *The Ringers in the Tower,* 223–24.

12. "All history resolves itself very easily into the biography of a few stout and earnest persons" ("Self-Reliance," *Complete Works* 2:61).

13. The position I take on the "noble doubt" passage in *Nature* differs substantially from that of John Michael in *Emerson and Skepticism,* 36–39. Strenuously supporting his thesis of the influence of Hume on Emerson, Michael exaggerates the importance of that particular passage in *Nature* at the expense of its context. "Hume's influence can be seen in *Nature.* The shadow cast by what Emerson once called Hume's 'malign light' is most evident in the passage that is physically and thematically the book's center . . . the 'noble doubt,' in which he gives his ideal theory its most explicit formulation" (37). The passage occurs in Chapter 6 of an eight-chapter book, so it is most certainly not physically the book's "center." As to the status of the passage as *Nature's* thematic center, it is arguable whether *Nature* has any thematic center at all. But for Michael, "Emerson's formulation of unanswerable doubt suggests his resignation and despair" (39). "Unanswerable doubt . . . resignation and despair" are a strange description of Emerson's rhetorical shrug, "What difference does it make?" Put back into its context, the passage becomes part of what this study describes as the dialectical interplay of the motifs of *Nature,* a position Michael himself seems to come around to later in his book, when he states, "In Emerson, it is never the resolution of the conflict that signifies, but the interplay of the opposed views that create the conflict" (154). Amen.

A dialectically corrective view of *Nature* is Alan Hodder's Emerson's *Rhetoric of Revelation.* Reading *Nature* as Emerson's book of Revelation, Hodder finds its "characteristic movement" to be "forgetfulness turning to recall" (1), but also that "Emerson's lapses have the license of method" (3). Further, he persuasively argues that the famous "crack" in *Nature* is "*the* condition which *Nature* strives to overcome," not only a "crack between

NOTES TO PAGES 72–102

chapters in a book," but between "world and spirit," between "the reader and the text, the sign and its significance, the reader and the self. The world we start with is fractured and fissured all over. It is the task of *Nature* to close all these gaps. *It does not do so philosophically"* (153–54, emphasis added). With the advantage of a mythic perspective, Hodder avoids falling into Michael's philosophical traps.

Hodder probably, Emerson certainly, and John Michael possibly would enjoy the story of Hume in the bog. David Hume once fell into a bog. An old woman found him and promised to pull him out if he said the Lord's Prayer. He did, and she did, and thus the life of the great skeptical philosopher was saved by the power of prayer (plus feminine muscle). The anecdote is parenthetically but elegantly retold by Virginia Woolf in *To the Lighthouse* (New York: Harcourt, Brace, 1927), 111.

3. CIRCLES, WHEELS, AND CYCLES

1. Dr. Johnson appears, hilariously, in "An Island in the Moon" (*Poetry and Prose* 458).

2. Three commentators who suggest this idea are Neufeldt, *The House of Emerson,* 218; Cox, "Circles of the Eye," 52; Tuerck "Emerson's *Nature,*" 111.

3. John Michael also detects an "agonistic principle" in "Circles," although he restricts it to the application of "the instability of authority in a polemical field" (10).

4. John Michael, in contrast, reads the essay as evidence of Emerson's trauma over human communication: "By the time of 'Circles,' Emerson would see skepticism no longer as a means to a single truth but as part of an agon of personal ascendancy that has no end" (11).

5. Bruno Bettelheim, *Freud and Man's Soul;* W. H. Auden, "In Memory of Sigmund Freud," *Selected Poetry,* 54–58.

6. Harold Bloom links Emerson and Freud with Augustine as "three doctors-of-the-soul," *Poetry and Repression: Revisionism from Blake to Stevens,* 239.

7. Sigmund Freud, *A General Selection from the Works of Sigmund Freud,* 219.

8. Ralph Waldo Emerson, *Journals,* 5:485, quoted in Joel Porte, "Nature as Symbol: Emerson's Noble Doubt," 460.

9. Sigmund Freud, *Civilization and Its Discontents,* 79.

10. For Emerson, as for Blake, "Beulah" is not "Eden." Emerson's "Love," from *Essays: First Series,* one of his shortest essays, moves from lyric description of young romantic love to a lengthy paraphrase of Plato's *Symposium* (on the "ladder of forms") to acquiescence about marital domesticity. Early on in it Emerson confesses, "I have been told that in some public discourses of mine my reverence for the intellect has made me unjustly cold to the personal relations" (*Complete Works* 2:173–74). Even for a fan, this essay is one of his most disappointing productions. The conclusion of this chapter suggests an explanation of that fact.

David Leverenz, "The Politics of Emerson's Man-Making Words," *Manhood and the American Renaissance,* 42–71, discusses Emerson's sexual attitudes from a perspective very different from that of this study. Leverenz offers recycled Whicherisms: "In [Emerson's] later essays, less able to find power surging through his voice" (60), and "the numbed, truculent return of depressiveness in Emerson's later essays" (62). The problem, for Leverenz, seems to be Emerson's response to women: "To achieve a bold male self-reliance presumes a depersonalized female support system" (63). Emerson "relegates women to the margins of his text" (62). He was not a good son: "Emerson seems to have taken Ruth for granted . . . . She was just there, like the dinners" (64).

Leverenz ignores the fact that Emerson was the "care provider" for his mother for the last thirty years of her life, as he seems unaware of the biographical evidence of Ruth Haskins Emerson's coldness as a mother to her young sons, who often went without dinner, facts documented by Barish, 16–23.

Leverenz finds "Experience" to be "insulting to those readers to whom grief and intimacy have meant something" (65). Emerson "universalizes his self-pity and his inability to love Lidian" (69). No evidence is brought forward to support the last charge. Leverenz's conclusion is that "Emerson's partial liberation from male rivalry leads to a politics of man making that trivializes women and feelings" (71). When Leverenz glances at the passage of disillusionment with sexual love in "Experience" (*Complete Works* 3:77), he confides to us, "Whenever I read that passage, I want to write in the margin, 'Poor Lidian'" (69).

One resists, unsuccessfully, the urge to respond, "And whenever I read *Hamlet,* I want to write in the margin, 'Poor Anne Hathaway.'" Leverenz cloaks his own insensitivity to the passage on young Waldo's death in "Experience" with a glib mix of critical clichés and modish ideological trappings. Significantly, such critics as Barbara Packer and Evelyn Barish remain unperturbed by what traumatizes Leverenz. A thorough, probing study of "Experience," one which actually reads the text, is Sharon Cameron, "Representing Grief: Emerson's 'Experience,'" a brilliant exploration of the entire essay as elegy.

4. JESUS LOST AND JESUS REGAINED

1. These assertions are qualified by the context of the present study. A well-established critical consensus (which would include Whicher, Bishop, and Sherman Paul) insists that for Emerson the god of the self, like nature, is a manifestation of the "Over-Soul." This study situates itself, however, within a more recent critical direction, clearly revisionist on this complex problem. Thus Barish stresses that Emerson's "intellectual career . . . was defined by his determination . . . to lay bare the autonomous, unsupported nature of Immanence" (8). "Immanence," especially an autonomous immanence, is the opposite of transcendence. Similarly, Packer, analyzing at length the "axis of vision" formula from *Nature,* is forced to conclude: "One cannot really call the formula a program for uniting subject and object, since it denies, at least implicitly, that what we call 'objects' really exist, just as it denies the existence of any essential difference between the inner light and the light of higher laws, the god within and the God without" ("The Instructed Eye," 220).

Emerson's only reference to an "Over-Soul" occurs in the essay of that title: "The Supreme Critic on the errors of the past and the present, and the only prophet of that which must be, is that great nature in which we rest as the earth lies in the soft arms of the atmosphere; that Unity, that Over-Soul, within which every man's particular being is contained and made one with all other" (*Complete Works* 2:268). The language here, especially in the last phrases quoted above, suggests a collective, not a transcendent entity. Given the number of times the term appears in his work (a total of twice), it might be said, statistically speaking, that the "Over-Soul" in Emerson has about as much importance as "guano." See Robert Detweiler, "The Over-rated Oversoul," 307–10.

2. Edward Waldo Emerson cites Sampson Reed's *The Growth of the Mind* as his father's introduction to Swedenborg's thought, and he

deemphasizes (quite accurately, from the viewpoint of this study) the Swedenborgian influence. "[Emerson's] recoil from all the parson and sexton and controversial elements of Swedenborg's writing, the Hebraism and prosiness of expression and the wearisome length, is sanely expressed with a kindly humor" (*Complete Works* 4:323). In the essay on Swedenborg referred to, in *Representative Men*, Emerson's initial praise gets drastically qualified in its later pages: "Swedenborg and Behmen both failed by attaching themselves to the Christian symbol, instead of to the moral sentiment, which carries innumerable christianities, humanities, divinities, in its bosom" (135). For Emerson, Swedenborg suffers from a "theological cramp" (137), and, "with all his accumulated gifts, paralyzes and repels" (143).

3. "It seems quite unlike his usual method," Edward Waldo Emerson (*Complete Works* 9:550). Philip F. Gura, in *The Wisdom of Words: Language, Theology, and Literature in the New England Renaissance*, reminds us that "what Emerson was in fact doing here as he stressed the spirit above the letter of the law was turning the Unitarians' exegetical principles against their own (to him) insufficient creed: He decided that their commonly accepted practice of Communion was not in line with the deeper, more intuitive truths of the Christian religion. Having outlined his objections to the rite on *exegetical* grounds, Emerson politely retreated" (78–79). The same point is made by John Michael in *Emerson and Skepticism*, 15–17. Wesley T. Mott, *"The Strains of Eloquence": Emerson and His Sermons*, clarifies the same point in slightly different terms: "Christ was best appropriated for the nineteenth century not through dead sacraments but as an immediate spiritual essence" (161).

4. That statement in *Nature* prefigures Emerson's assertion in the Divinity School "Address," that "Jesus Christ belonged to the true race of prophets" (*Complete Works* 1:128).

5. This negation is by no means merely a Unitarian (anti-Trinitarian) emphasis. If Emerson had been expressing orthodox Unitarian theology in the Divinity School "Address," there would have been no resultant furor. The negating of the father is significant in the present study of mythic contexts, but Evelyn Barish, in a recent and brilliant psychoanalytic biography, has brought forward such illuminating facts as Emerson's disembowelment of the manuscript of his father's sermons as both "Oedipal" and "cannibalistic" (*Emerson: The Roots of Prophecy* 3, 32).

6. The poem has been the object of extensive, even exhaustive critical commentary. Relevant specific observations, some of them taking very dif-

ferent views of the poem from the one elaborated here, include the following: Gleckner, "Point of View and Context in Blake's Songs," 40; Gleckner, *Piper and Bard*, 110; Hirsch, 26, 186; Hazard Adams, *William Blake: A Reading of the Shorter Poems*, 261; Porter Williams, Jr., "'Duty' in Blake's 'The Chimney Sweeper' of *Songs of Innocence*," 292–96; Martin K. Nurmi, "Fact and Symbol in 'The Chimney Sweeper' of Blake's *Songs of Innocence*," 252.

7. James Harrison, in "Blake's *The Chimney Sweeper*," is correct when he observes that "what Blake is doing here . . . is to create a rhythm for the poem as ingenuous as its tone" (3), but it is important to note that the rhythm of the poem is not uniform.

8. This study uses the word "miracle" to mean only, but exactly, what Blake meant by it when he defined the term in his "Annotations" to Bishop Watson's *An Apology for the Bible* (*Poetry and Prose* 616–17). Blake rejects the orthodox meaning of "an arbitrary command of the agent upon the patient." He stresses "belief," or the active participation of the "patient," and cites both Paine and himself as miracle workers in this sense. Blake would agree with Emerson in the Divinity School "Address," that "the word Miracle, as pronounced by Christian churches . . . is Monster" (*Complete Works* 1:129). In "The Chimney Sweeper," the miracle occurs through an act of love, the imaginative union of the speaker and Tom.

9. At least two commentators see the speaker of the poem as "Christlike," but that is not the conclusion of this study. Hirsch remarks that "the speaker relates his Christ-like sufferings with an acceptance like Christ's own" (184). But the *speaker* does not suffer in this poem. Williams also thinks that "the sweeper is a symbol of the suffering Christ" (95). But in this poem it is Tom who suffers, not the speaker. These readings ignore the poem's action and confuse its characters. This study suggests as an identity of the speaker not the "suffering Christ" of orthodoxy but rather Blake's "Jesus," the redemptive, creative human imagination.

10. Cox, Neufeldt, Packer, and Smith make, to one degree or another, persuasive qualifications of Whicher's hypothesis. Among recent critics, John Michael is most explicitly anti-Whicher.

11. Jerome J. McGann, *The Romantic Ideology: A Critical Investigation*, offers some theoretical exposition of this conflict: "The polemic of Romantic poetry . . . is that it will not be polemical; its doctrine, that it is non-doctrinal; and its ideology, that it transcends ideology" (70). Clearly, McGann speaks as the academic, not the poet.

12. Evidence derived from the journals for dating "Immortality" is suggestive but inconclusive: a paragraph from 1865 finds its way into it (*Journals and Notebooks* 9:81); so does a sentence of 1863 which Emerson translated from the French (333); in 1869 its title is included in a list for the proposed new volume of essays, which would become *Society and Solitude* of 1870; it was not, however, included in that volume (*Journals and Notebooks* 16:148). This evidence suggests that certainly the essay is late, but just how late remains a matter of conjecture.

13. Robert E. Burkholder, "Emerson, Kneeland, and the Divinity School Address," 7.

14. Something like pioneer scholarship in this area has been performed by Lawrence Rosenwald, *Emerson and the Art of the Diary*. One may disagree (completely) with Rosenwald's thesis that "Emerson's journals are his authentic work, his greatest formal achievement, his true and adequate genre" (xii) and still discover a wealth of valuable insights in this original study. For Rosenwald, the journals did have an audience: "New England Transcendentalists . . . passed their diaries around as scholars pass around drafts of essays" (10). Thus for him "the diary [is] a text for the inner circle" (12). More relevant to the context of the present study is Rosenwald's observation, "Emerson in the journal names four possible audiences: oneself, a friend, a few friends, and God" (78).

15. *Emerson and Skepticism,* throughout, but especially "The Skeptical Origins of Emerson's Authorship," 3–33.

16. "The material resists reading" (Barish 4).

17. For example, there are no references to "Jesus" or "Christ" in Jonathan Bishop, *Emerson on the Soul.*

18. Barish finds the early sermons "starkly rationalistic" (203).

19. Two recent critics who have devoted considerable attention to Emerson's "Jesus" are Wesley Mott and David Robinson. For Mott, "Emerson's Jesus may have been stripped of 'supernatural' power. But transformed as he was into the stuff of Unitarian and, later, Transcendental myth, Jesus remained in a most important personal way for Emerson the essence of wisdom, righteousness, sanctification, and redemption" (33). David Robinson, writing on a sermon of 1830, "The Authority of Jesus," makes a central point with relevance for Emerson's later thought as well: "[Emerson's] argument is that Jesus's claim for man's devotion is justified by his embodiment of the moral law available to every human. Christ thus derives

his authority from a preexisting law; he does not, by his authority, establish that law" (57).

20. Detweiler, in Burkholder and Myerson, eds., *Critical Essays on Ralph Waldo Emerson*, 307–10, provides the statistical evidence.

21. The emphasis on Emerson's ingestion in this chapter and in the previous one may seem excessive. The importance of this trope finds support, however, from Barish, with a different point of view pursuing a different line of inquiry, who cites evidence from family letters and other documents demonstrating that as a child Emerson often simply did not have enough to eat (Barish 26–27, 55).

22. Blake is, if anything, even less "Trinitarian" than Emerson. In *The Marriage*, he tells us: "In Milton; the Father is Destiny, the Son, a Ratio of the five senses, & the Holy-ghost, Vacuum!" (*Poetry and Prose* 35). From Blake's point of view, the dialogue between "God" and the "Son of God" in book 3 of *Paradise Lost* would constitute a grotesquely empty fiction, a conversation between Nobodaddy and his Spectre, a chat of spooks.

5. "CHILDREN OF THE FIRE"

1. Hodder suggests as the *loci classici* for the four-fold theory of biblical exegesis the following texts: Augustine, *De Doctrina Christiana*, II.10, III.27; Aquinas, *Summa Theologica*, I, Q. 1, Art. 10 (166).

2. Studies of Blake's *Milton* which go far beyond the single motif explored in this study include the following: Susan Fox, *Poetic Form in Blake's Milton;* John Howard, *Blake's Milton: A Study of the Selfhood;* Peter Otto, "Visionary Deconstruction: The Bard's Song in Blake's *Milton*"; Denis Seurat, *Blake and Milton.* Valuable and profoundly sensible insights can be found in Diana Hume George, *Blake and Freud,* especially on the problem of Blake's often misunderstood feminism. Frye's chapter on *Milton* in *Fearful Symmetry,* "Comus Agonistes," remains permanently illuminating, perhaps indispensable.

3. Gura observes that "Emerson became interested in language as a form of vatic inspiration" and that he "saw how within the language of nature there was an infinite variability of forms available to express man's thoughts, religious or otherwise" (77). However, supporting his own thesis, Gura goes on to ignore the "otherwise" in "The Poet" and to read it in exclusively religious terms. The essay for Gura represents "Emerson's most thorough

reworking of theological language and dogma into the poetic" (92), a finding congruent with this study's, but with a reversed emphasis. Thus Gura goes so far as to describe "The Poet" as a "reworking of the morphology of conversion into an esthetic experience" (101), a judgment which distinguishes between terms which this study would roughly equate. When Gura goes still further in his religious emphasis and finds that in "The Poet," "Emerson remains very much the mystic, finally denying the intrinsic value of the things of this world and seeking instead a transcendent relation to his surroundings" (104), he moves in a direction opposite to this study's, which continues to stress immanence over transcendence, evidenced in "The Poet" by Emerson's own emphasis on the "sensuous fact."

4. This is probably as good a place as any to point out that Blake's language, here and everywhere else, is *not* that of a "mystic." The most sensitive and sensible solution of that old false problem is Frye, *Fearful Symmetry,* 431–32.

5. These dates are those provided by Edward Waldo Emerson (*Complete Works* 8:357–58). Emerson recycled some passages from "The Poet" in the later essay.

6. It is in the context of insight or second sight that Emerson in this very late essay quotes "the painter" William Blake, from a passage in Gilchrist that would obviously have caught Emerson's eye: "I question not my corporeal eye any more than I would question a window concerning a sight. I look through it, not with it" (28). The passage from Blake and its connections to Emerson's earlier thought have been discussed at length in an earlier chapter of this study. This reference, among others, has been noted by Armida Gilbert, 55.

7. The Americanism as well as the nonhistoricism of such concepts finds emphasis in R. W. B. Lewis, *The American Adam:* "The American was to be acknowledged in his complete emancipation from the history of mankind. He was to be recognized now for what he was—a new Adam, miraculously free of family and race, untouched by those dismal conditions which prior tragedies and entanglements monotonously prepared for the newborn European" (41). For Lewis, Emerson is "the archetypal man of good hope" (40), certainly an incomplete image; in the context of this chapter Emerson is rather the poet of "good news" or Gospel, and ahistoricism is the appropriate mode of Revelation, which announces the end of time.

NOTES TO PAGES 167–168

For Sacvan Bercovitch, *The Puritan Origins of the American Self,*
Emerson's "exegetical approach is above all prophetic, his Romantic
apocalypse of the mind a guide to vaster prospects ahead, because *his* scripture is the New World" (159). Bercovitch observes that "the Romantic
tenets of Emerson's thought" are adjusted by Emerson to "the tenets of
early New England rhetoric. Characteristically, the self he sought was not
only his but America's, or rather his *as* America's, and therefore America's
as his" (165).

These interesting and valuable observations by Lewis and Bercovitch
pursue a different line of inquiry from that of the present study, that of a political, cultural, "American" myth, rather than the archetypical one traced in
these pages.

8. Such non-Whicherite critics as Barish, Cheyfitz, Cox, Hodder,
Michael, and Packer devote most if not all of their critical attention to early
Emerson, and especially to *Nature,* which still seems to get examined more
than all of the other essays put together. Much of Emerson's later work is still
being ignored, even by very recent criticism. A valuable exception is the
recent work of David Robinson.

9. Edward Waldo Emerson dates the essay from its lecture version of
1857 (*Complete Works* 7:393).

10. The earlier discoverers of the book of Revelation in *Nature* were
Jones Very, Thomas Carlyle, and Oliver Wendell Holmes.

11. John F. Kasson in *Civilizing the Machine: Technology and Republican Values in America, 1776–1900,* places Emerson centrally in the context of
that book: "To preserve the poet's eye in an age of technology would become
for him a central concern" (116). Kasson notes that Emerson "Grew increasingly concerned about technology's dominance in society" (124), and
"though in the flower of his transcendental revolt he had celebrated technology as a stimulus to creative vision, in his later career he emphasized
more its tendency to debase the imagination" (131). Kasson concludes: "The
answer for Emerson, then, was not to renounce technology, but to subordi-
nate it to the imaginative and moral life" (131). These observations will not
surprise the student of Emerson, and they are in close agreement with this
study's reading of "Works and Days."

12. The references to Hesiod occur later in the essay (167). The lecture
of 1857 opened with this paragraph, omitted from the later publication:

[205]

One of the oldest remains of literature is the poem of Hesiod, called *Works and Days*. It is not much read in these times crowded with books and manifold spiritual influences; but it has had its day, and has furnished its share of the general culture; in as much as passages from it have passed into the public mind, and make part of the proverbs of mankind. I borrow from it only its title, to offer from this text a lesson to this day and hour. (*Complete Works* 7:393)

Emerson's phrasing, to "offer . . . a lesson" from a "text," suggests that the preacher was still alive within the lecturer.

13. In a very recent and brilliantly perceptive study of "Works and Days," David Robinson discusses the essay as an example of the later Emerson's "pragmatism" ("A Theory of Wednesdays: Emerson's Later Ethic of the Ordinary," unpublished MLA paper, Chicago, 30 Dec. 1990). "Pragmatism" seems an oddly inaccurate label, belied as it is by Robinson's own philosophical diction, which is quite explicitly existential: "But the classical echoes and the emphasis on the problems of technology cannot mask the modern *angst* latent in the essay" (12). Angst is quintessentially Existential, and not at all pragmatic. Similarly, Robinson observes that "The 'brink of chaos,' Emerson's familiar existential edge, is the outer limit or circumference upon which we must play out our self-creation" (13). Also, paraphrasing Emerson on time in this essay, Robinson quite accurately observes, "The day, the hour, all measures of time, are the situations of acts. Here only is the spirit available. Any sense of the moment which fails to attribute a radical freedom to it ties it to a past that freezes its latent spiritual import" (13). "Situations of acts" and "radical freedom" are common key terms in Existential thought; to pursue Emerson's direction in this essay requires not William James but Sartre and Heidegger. It might also be noted that although Professor Robinson titles his paper "A Theory of Wednesdays," neither that phrase nor its philosophical implication is in Emerson's text. Emerson writes, "the theory of this particular Wednesday." A "theory of Wednesdays" is conceptual and essentialist, an abstraction; a "theory of this particular Wednesday," on the other hand, is experiential, phenomenological, Existential. Robinson's fine essay does however perform a most valuable service in bringing "Works and Days" to the attention of a wider

audience. He cites Neufeldt (83–99) as virtually the only earlier discussion of it. Neufeldt's treatment is efficient summary, making connections with Emerson's earlier thought, but retaining the overall noncommittal character of his whole book. Robinson, in contrast, rethinks, explores, and discovers.

14. "The voyage of the best ship is a zigzag line of a hundred tacks" ("Self-Reliance," *Complete Works* 2:59).

15. Standard discussions of Emerson's aesthetic theory and practice include Vivian C. Hopkins's *Spires of Form: A Study of Emerson's Esthetic Theory* and John Q. Anderson's *The Liberating Gods: Emerson on Poets and Poetry.* These studies do not connect Emerson's aesthetic with a mythic perspective, as has been the aim of the present study.

A critic who does read Emerson in terms of myth is R. A. Yoder. In *Emerson and the Orphic Poet in America,* Yoder sees Emerson's "old fable" of the "One Man" as a "version of the traditional 'universal man,'" and that "this myth reaches out to the extremities of Emerson's own writing, from the early sermons on 'The Genuine Man' and 'The Miracle of Our Being' through the idea of the scholar to the conception of the poet as liberating god and the most complete or representative of men" (xi). Further, "Emerson thought of poetry as prophecy in the Renaissance sense of an unbroken tradition of revealed truth" (xii). For Yoder, "Orpheus . . . is a name for the Universal Man or Central Man of Emerson's own mythology" (70). Although Yoder restricts himself to one classical archetype, Orpheus, his mythic treatment is closer to this study's emphasis than it is to the abstract conceptualizing of Hopkins and Anderson. Yoder even makes some brief comparative references, in passing, to Blake (34–36, 38). This scholar's richly suggestive approach (like those of Packer, Hodder and Bloom, a mythic reading of Emerson) is nevertheless self-limiting in its echoing some basic notions of Stephen Whicher.

More recently, Ellison employs a more sophisticated rhetorical analysis to vent disapproval. Her chapter on the essay, "The Poet" (114–40), argues her thesis that "Alternation between these ['sublime transcendence and ironic descent'], not a developing argument of 'dialectical' synthesis, accounts for the progress of the essay" (126). Readers who expect "developing argument" in Emerson will always be frustrated, but polemicists inevitably find polemics, attractive or not: "His poetics are polemical; freedom is always freedom *from* and power, always power *over*" (130). These are predictably fashionable terms in the current climate of academic opinion, and when Ellison sets out to seek "the defensive and aggressive functions of Emerson's irony, his repetitions, and his contradictions" (114), she finds them. "The Poet" moves Ellison only to derision; for her the essay concludes with "trappings of sublimity" and "conventional flourishes" (139). If one approaches an essay by Emerson expecting "argument" (he once said, "I never argue"), whether "developing" according to some abstract rhetorical pattern or not, frustration can be the only possible reader response. The tone of irritability in much recent Emersonian criticism may be a clue to an inappropriateness in its approach. The present study has suggested an alternative: to look at Emerson's prose not as argument but as myth, not as logical constructs, but poetic ones. Such a critical approach will leave some problems of interpretation unsolved, perhaps untouched; but it may suggest a corrective and more rewarding direction. It may be time to stop fussing over the mechanics of the wagon and to start admiring the light of the star.

16. This study is not unique in analyzing Emerson's prose as poetry. Elizabeth Palmer Peabody, as early as 1838, read *Nature* as "A Prose Poem" (Burkholder and Myerson, eds., 26, 31), and as recently as 1971 Harold Bloom described "The Poet" as "more a hymn of praise than an essay" (*Ringers in the Tower* 229). In contrast, most Emersonian criticism, past and present, has sweated and strained in the Quixotic task of wrestling logically with Emerson's poetic, nonlogical forms. This study attempts to supply an appropriate critical paradigm to support such insights as those of Peabody and Bloom.

Neither is this study unique in its attempt to redefine the modality of Emerson's essays. Rosenwald sees them as secondary in importance to "his greatest formal achievement" (xii), his journals, so that the essays become for Rosenwald drafts in an endless process of objectifying the self (65–83). Robinson (*Apostle of Culture,* 158–85) finds a five-voiced authorial polyphony operating among the personae of the essays, an artistic emphasis close to this study's, and his "Orphic," "colloquial," "dramatic," "assertive," and "Evangelical" voices (176–84) compel him to regard Emerson's "essays as art, rather than philosophy or theology, and to associate them with the poem rather than the treatise" (174). Robinson reaches this conclusion in spite of his overall thesis that "much of the sermon remained in the lectures, and much of both sermon and lecture remained in the essays" (166). It seems that poetry, like murder, will out.

CONCLUSION: "PROSPECTS"

1. Some support for the view suggested in these pages of an "Existential" as opposed to a "Transcendental" Emerson can be gathered from several recent studies. Cox concludes: "Reading Emerson at his best is always a reminder as well as a recognition that *I am*" (60, emphasis added). Smith discovers that Emerson's "real concern is not with getting *beyond* our circumstances, but with the kind of salvation that is available *within* our endlessness" (397). Barish asserts that Emerson's "intellectual career . . . was defined by his determination to demonstrate the irrelevance of claims for evidence, to lay bare the autonomous, unsupported nature of *Immanence*" (8; emphasis added). Further, and more beautifully, she shares with us her excitement that "Emerson understood that the true mystery was not in the abyss, where consciousness ceases and death begins, but here in the humming room where life spins itself out" (258). Further support for an Existential rather than a Transcendental Emerson can be found in Michael Lopez, "De-Transcendentalizing Emerson."

2. Rusk, *The Life of Emerson*, 506, quoted in Philip Young, "Small World: Emerson, Longfellow, and Melville's Secret Sister," 397. Young compassionately reads the questions as evidence that Emerson's "body outlived his mind." A second childhood closes the natural cycle in the figure of a circle, appropriately enough. But taken out of their context, the questions express Emerson's mind as freed from that circle, as inhabiting the words themselves that speak to us in his and our *now*.

WORKS CITED

Abrams, M. H. *Natural Supernaturalism: Tradition and Revolution in Romantic Literature.* New York: Norton, 1971.

Adams, Hazard. *William Blake: A Reading of the Shorter Poems.* Seattle: U of Washington P, 1963.

Allen, Gay Wilson. *Waldo Emerson: A Biography.* New York: Viking, 1981.

Anderson, John Q. *The Liberating Gods: Emerson on Poets and Poetry.* Coral Gables, FL: U of Miami P, 1971.

Arendt, Hannah. *The Human Condition.* Chicago: U of Chicago P, 1958.

Auden, W. H. *Selected Poetry.* New York: Modern Library, 1958.

Ault, Donald D. *Visionary Physics: Blake's Response to Newton.* Chicago: U of Chicago P, 1974.

Barish, Evelyn. *Emerson: The Roots of Prophecy.* Princeton: Princeton UP, 1989.

Bercovitch, Sacvan. *The Puritan Origins of the American Self.* New Haven: Yale UP, 1975.

Bettelheim, Bruno. *Freud and Man's Soul.* New York: Knopf, 1983.

Bishop, Jonathan. *Emerson on the Soul.* Cambridge: Harvard UP, 1964.

Blake, William. *The Complete Poetry and Prose of William Blake.* Ed. David V. Erdman. Rev. ed. Commentary by Harold Bloom. New York: Doubleday, 1988.

Bloom, Harold. *Blake's Apocalypse: A Study in Poetic Argument.* Ithaca: Cornell UP, 1970.

———. *Poetry and Repression: Revisionism from Blake to Stevens.* New Haven: Yale UP, 1976.

———, ed. *Ralph Waldo Emerson: Modern Critical Views.* New York: Chelsea House, 1985.

———. *The Ringers in the Tower: Studies in Romantic Tradition.* Chicago: U of Chicago P, 1971.

——, ed. *William Blake: Modern Critical Views*. New York: Chelsea House, 1985.

Bridgman, Richard. "The Meaning of Emerson's Title, 'Hamatreya.'" *Emerson Society Quarterly* 27.2 (1962): 16–24.

Bronowski, J. *William Blake: A Man Without a Mask*. London: Secker and Warburg, 1944.

Buell, Lawrence. "Ralph Waldo Emerson." *The American Renaissance in New England, Dictionary of Literary Biography*. Vol. 1. Ed. Joel Myerson. Detroit: Gale Research Co., 1978.

Burke, Kenneth. "I, Eye, Aye—Emerson's Early Essay on 'Nature': Thoughts on the Machinery of Transcendence." *Sewanee Review* 74 (Oct.–Dec. 1966): 875–95.

Burkholder, Robert E. "Emerson, Kneeland, and the Divinity School Address." *American Literature* 58.1 (Mar. 1986): 1–14.

Burkholder, Robert E., and Joel Myerson, eds. *Critical Essays on Ralph Waldo Emerson*. Boston: G. K. Hall, 1983.

Cameron, Sharon. "Representing Grief: Emerson's 'Experience.'" *Representations* 15 (Summer 1986): 15–41.

Cheyfitz, Eric. *The Trans-parent: Sexual Politics in the Language of Emerson*. Baltimore: Johns Hopkins UP, 1981.

Cox, James M. "R. W. Emerson: The Circles of the Eye." Bloom, *Emerson: Modern Critical Views* 45–60.

Damrosch, Leopold, Jr. *Symbol and Truth in Blake's Myth*. Princeton: Princeton UP, 1980.

Davis, Michael. *William Blake: A New Kind of Man*. Los Angeles: U of California P, 1977.

Detweiler, Robert. "The Over-Rated Over-Soul." Burkholder and Myerson, eds., 307–10.

Edmundson, Mark. *Towards Reading Freud: Self-Creation in Milton, Wordsworth, Emerson, and Sigmund Freud*. Princeton: Princeton UP, 1990.

Eliot, T. S. *Four Quartets*. New York: Harcourt, Brace, 1943.

Ellison, Julie. *Emerson's Romantic Style*. Princeton: Princeton UP, 1984.

Emerson, Ralph Waldo. *The Complete Works of Ralph Waldo Emerson*. Ed. Edward Waldo Emerson. The Centenary Edition. 12 vols. Boston: Houghton, 1903–04.

———. *The Journals and Miscellaneous Notebooks of Ralph Waldo Emerson.* Ed. William H. Gilman et al. 16 vols. Cambridge: Harvard UP, 1960–82.

———. *The Journals of Ralph Waldo Emerson, 1820–1876.* Ed. Edward Waldo Emerson and Waldo Emerson Forbes. 10 vols. Boston: Houghton, 1909–14.

Fox, Susan. *Poetic Form in Blake's Milton.* Princeton: Princeton UP, 1976.

Freud, Sigmund. *Civilization and Its Discontents.* Trans. James Strachey. New York: Norton, 1961.

———. *A General Selection from the Works of Sigmund Freud.* Ed. John Rickman, M.D. Garden City: Doubleday, 1957.

Frosch, Thomas R. *The Awakening of Albion: The Renovation of the Body in the Poetry of William Blake.* Ithaca: Cornell UP, 1974.

Frye, Northrop. *Fearful Symmetry: A Study of William Blake.* Princeton: Princeton UP, 1947.

Gangewere, Robert J., ed. *The Exploited Eden: Literature on the American Environment.* New York: Harper, 1972.

George, Diana Hume. *Blake and Freud.* Ithaca: Cornell UP, 1980.

Gilbert, Allan H. *Literary Criticism: Plato to Dryden.* Detroit: Wayne State UP, 1962.

Gilbert, Armida. "Emerson and the English Romantic Poets." Diss. U of South Carolina, 1989.

Gilchrist, Alexander. *The Life of William Blake.* 1863. London: John Lane Company, 1907.

Gleckner, Robert F. *The Piper and The Bard: A Study of William Blake.* Detroit: Wayne State UP, 1959.

———. "Point of View and Context in Blake's Songs." Bloom, *Blake: Modern Critical Views* 35–41.

Gross, David. "Infinite Indignation: Teaching, Dialectical Vision, and Blake's *Marriage of Heaven and Hell.*" *College English* 48 (Feb. 1986): 175–86.

Gura, Philip F. *The Wisdom of Words: Language, Theology, and Literature in the New England Renaissance.* Middletown, CT: Wesleyan UP, 1981.

Harris, W. T. "The Dialectical Unity in Emerson's Prose." Burkholder and Myerson, eds., 215–21.

Harrison, James. "Blake's *The Chimney Sweeper.*" *Explicator* 36.2 (1978): 2–3.

Higginson, Thomas Wentworth. "Emerson's Oriental Texts." *Critic* 12 (Feb. 1888): 81.

WORKS CITED

Hirsch, E. D., Jr. *Innocence and Experience: An Introduction to Blake*. New Haven: Yale UP, 1964.

Hodder, Alan D. *Emerson's Rhetoric of Revelation: Nature, the Reader, and the Apocalypse Within*. University Park: Pennsylvania State UP, 1989.

Hopkins, Vivian C. *Spires of Form: A Study of Emerson's Esthetic Theories*. Cambridge: Harvard UP, 1951.

Howard, John. *Blake's Milton: A Study of the Selfhood*. Rutherford, NJ: Fairleigh Dickinson UP, 1976.

Kasson, John F. *Civilizing the Machine: Technology and Republican Values in America, 1776–1900*. New York: Grossman, 1976.

Konvitz, Milton R., ed. *The Recognition of Ralph Waldo Emerson: Selected Criticism Since 1837*. Ann Arbor: U of Michigan P, 1975.

Leverenz, David. *Manhood and the American Renaissance*. Ithaca: Cornell UP, 1989.

Lewis, R. W. B. *The American Adam: Innocence, Tragedy, and Tradition in the Nineteenth Century*. Chicago: U of Chicago P, 1955.

Lopez, Michael. "De-Transcendentalizing Emerson." *Emerson Society Quarterly* 34.1, 2 (1988): 77–139.

Lowell, James Russell. "Emerson the Lecturer." Konvitz 43–49.

McGann, Jerome J. *The Romantic Ideology: A Critical Investigation*. Chicago: U of Chicago P, 1983.

McLuhan, Marshall. *Understanding Media: The Extensions of Man*. New York: McGraw, 1965.

Matthiessen, F. O. *American Renaissance: Art and Expression in the Age of Emerson and Whitman*. New York: Oxford UP, 1947.

Michael, John. *Emerson and Skepticism: The Cipher of the World*. Baltimore: Johns Hopkins UP, 1988.

Miller, Perry. *The Transcendentalists*. Cambridge: Harvard UP, 1979.

Mott, Wesley T. *"The Strains of Eloquence": Emerson and His Sermons*. University Park: Pennsylvania State UP, 1989.

Neufeldt, Leonard. *The House of Emerson*. Lincoln: U of Nebraska P, 1982.

Nurmi, Martin. "Fact and Symbol in 'The Chimney Sweeper' of Blake's *Songs of Innocence.*" *Bulletin of the New York Public Library* 68 (1964): 249–56.

O'Keefe, Richard R. "Scanning 'Hamatreya': Emerson as Miltonic Prosodist." *Emerson Society Papers* 3.2 (1992): 1–2.

[213]

Otto, Peter. "Visionary Deconstruction: The Bard's Song in *Milton*." *PQ* 66.2 (1987): 207–30.

Packer, Barbara. *Emerson's Fall: A New Interpretation of the Major Essays.* New York: Continuum, 1982.

———. "The Instructed Eye: Emerson's Cosmogony in 'Prospects.'" Sealts and Ferguson, eds., 209–21.

Paul, Sherman. *Emerson's Angle of Vision.* Cambridge: Harvard UP, 1965.

Peabody, Elizabeth Palmer. "*Nature*—A Prose Poem." Burkholder and Myerson, eds., 24–31.

Petry, Alice Hull. "The Meeting of the Twain: Emerson's 'Hamatreya.'" *English Language Notes* 23 (Mar. 1986): 47–51.

Poirier, Richard. "The Question of Genius." Bloom, *Emerson: Modern Critical Views* 163–86.

Porte, Joel. "Nature as Symbol: Emerson's Noble Doubt." *New England Quarterly* 37 (Dec. 1964): 453–76.

———. "The Problem of Emerson." *Harvard English Studies* 4 (1973): 85–90.

Raine, Kathleen. *William Blake.* New York: Praeger, 1971.

Robinson, David. *Apostle of Culture: Emerson as Preacher and Lecturer.* Philadelphia: U of Pennsylvania P, 1982.

———. "A Theory of Wednesdays: Emerson's Later Ethic of the Ordinary." Paper presented at MLA, Dec. 30, 1990, Chicago.

Rockwell, Kiffin Ayres. "Emerson's *Hamatreya,* Another Guess." *Emerson Society Quarterly* 33.4 (1963): 24.

Rosenwald, Lawrence. *Emerson and the Art of the Diary.* New York: Oxford UP, 1988.

Rusk, Ralph. *The Life of Ralph Waldo Emerson.* New York: Columbia UP, 1949.

Schorer, Mark. *William Blake: The Politics of Vision.* New York: Henry Holt, 1946.

Sealts, Merton M., and Alfred R. Ferguson, eds. *Emerson's Nature: Origin, Growth, Meaning.* Carbondale: Southern Illinois UP, 1979.

Seurat, Denis. *Blake and Milton.* London: S. Nott, 1935.

Sharma, Mohan Lal. "Emerson's HAMATREYA." *Explicator* 26 (Apr. 1968): 63.

Smith, David L. "Emerson and Deconstruction: The End(s) of Scholarship." *Soundings* 67.4 (1984): 379–98.

Tanner, Tony. "Emerson: The Unconquered Eye and the Enchanted Circle." Burkholder and Myerson, eds., 310–26.

Thorslev, Peter L., Jr. "Some Dangers of Dialectical Thinking with Illustrations from Blake and His Critics." *Romantic and Victorian: Studies in Memory of William H. Marshall.* Ed. Paul W. Elledge. Rutherford, NJ: Fairleigh Dickinson UP, 1971: 43–74.

Thurin, Erik Ingvar. *Emerson as Priest of Pan: A Study in the Metaphysics of Sex.* Lawrence: Regents Press of Kansas, 1981.

Tuerk, Richard. "Emerson's *Nature*—Miniature Universe." *American Transcendental Quarterly* 1.1 (1969): 110–13.

Van Leer, David. *Emerson's Epistemology: The Argument of the Essays.* Cambridge: Cambridge UP, 1986.

Waggoner, Hyatt. *Emerson as Poet.* Princeton: Princeton UP, 1974.

Weiskel, Thomas. "Blake's Critique of Transcendence." Bloom, *Blake: Modern Critical Views* 117–32.

Whicher, Stephen. *Freedom and Fate: An Inner Life of Ralph Waldo Emerson.* Philadelphia: U of Pennsylvania P, 1953.

Williams, Porter, Jr. "'Duty' in Blake's 'The Chimney Sweeper' of *Songs of Innocence.*" *English Language Notes* 12 (1974): 92–96.

Wood, Barry. "Dialectical Method in the Strategy of Emerson's *Nature.*" *PMLA* 91 (May 1976): 385–97.

Yoder, R. A. *Emerson and the Orphic Poet in America.* Berkeley: U of California P, 1978.

———. "Emerson's Dialectic." Burkholder and Myerson, eds., 354–67.

Young, Philip. "Small World: Emerson, Longfellow, and Melville's Secret Sister." *New England Quarterly* 60.3 (Sept. 1987): 382–402.

INDEX

෨Ⓒ෨

Abrams, M. H., 2–3, 47–48, 160
Absolute value, 13
Academic conservatism, 124,
    201n.11
Adam, 51, 99
Addiction, 81
Aeschylus, 81
Aesthetic theory, 207n.15
African American. *See* Negro
Agons, 81, 83, 197n.3
"Ah! Sun-flower" (Blake), 69–76,
    77, 79
Albion: as "Eternal Man," 34, 51, 52,
    54–55, 57; Jerusalem and, 74; Jesus
    and, 117, 140, 155; Lincoln as, 63;
    separateness and, 104; as universal
    humanity, 33, 49, 59, 67, 140, 190;
    Zoas and, 58, 61
Alcohol, 81
Alienation, 55, 104
Allamanda, 163
Allegorical meaning, 142, 143
Allen, Gay Wilson, 30, 98
All Religions are One (Blake), 7, 54,
    144–45, 165
America, 164, 165, 166, 204–05n.7
America (Blake), 7, 62
American Renaissance, The
    (Matthiessen), 28
American Romantic poets, 3
"American Scholar" (lecture), 38, 59, 61,
    98, 99

American Scholar, The (Emerson), 7,
    56–57, 63, 106, 109–10, 116, 169, 176
Anagogical meaning, 142, 143
Analytic, 196n.10
Anapestic rhythm, 70, 120–21, 201n.7
Anderson, John Q., 207n.15
Androgyny, 16, 89
Angels, 173, 174
"Angle of vision," 46, 126, 195n.9
Apocalypse, 188; Blake on, 49, 167, 184;
    as Christian mythic archetype, 3;
    Emerson on, 4, 47, 167, 184; in
    Jerusalem, 150; in *Milton,* 150, 155,
    156, 158; reproduction and, 101–02;
    self-redemption and, 141, 144, 185; in
    "The Mental Traveller," 23; theory of
    inspiration and, 158; "Works and
    Days" and, 5, 167, 168, 171, 175
Apple, 97, 98
Aquinas, Thomas, 143
Arc of a circle, 72, 74
Archetypes, 188, 205n.7; analysis of, 3;
    Blake's use of, 3, 4, 21, 163; Christian
    mythic, 3; Emerson and Blake
    parallels, 4; as Emerson's poetic
    devices, 2, 160; sexual, 89, 93
Arendt, Hannah, 67–68
Argument, 207–08n.15
Art, aesthetic experiences with, 33
"Art" (Emerson), 7
Astrophysical world view, 67–68
Atheism, 127

INDEX

Auden, W. H., 89
Audience: Blake and, 127; Emerson
and, 127–35, 140, 162, 202n.14
"Auguries of Innocence" (Blake), 42,
124
"Axis of vision," 47

"Bacchus" (Emerson), 19, 167, 190
Bacon, Francis, 67
"Bacon Newton & Locke" (Blake),
45, 67
Ballad measures, 21
"Bard," in Blake, 146, 147, 153
"Bard's Song," 144, 157, 179
Barish, Evelyn, 80, 173, 195n.1, 200n.5,
209n.1; on Emerson's health, 195n.1;
on Emerson's hunger, 203n.21; Freud
and, 89; on orthodoxy break, 138
"Beauty" (Emerson), 39, 91
Becoming, 174
"Being-there," 178
Bercovitch, Sacvan, 205n.7
Bettelheim, Bruno, 89
Beulah, 44–45, 151, 152, 153, 198n.10
Bible, 51, 91, 97, 98, 110, 113; Blake on,
49, 72, 82, 107, 145, 151; divinely
inspired, 144; four levels of
meaning, 143
Biography, 60–63, 196n.12
Bishop, Jonathan, 1
Blair, Walter, 27
Blake, William, 64; Christian mythic
archetypes and, 3, 4, 21, 52;
"contrary states" and, 6, 8;
dialectical method of, 6–28;
Emerson and, 4, 54, 204n.6; father
and, 99–100; feminism and, 155,
203n.2; first vision of, 31–32; four
levels of knowledge, 44–45; letters to
Butts, 43, 44; prose of, 25; as
Romanticist, 2; sexual imagery of,
45, 88–103, 151; worldview, 50
Blank verse, 14, 161
"Blight," 20

Bloom, Harold: on Blake, 26; on Blake
and Swedenborg, 106–07; on dia-
lectical method, 194n.11; on dualism,
64; on Emerson, 56, 59, 208n.16; on
Emerson and Blake, 3, 33–34, 53–54;
on Emerson and Freud, 197n.6; on
Milton, 153–55, 157–58
Body, 82–83
Book of Ahania, The (Blake), 107
Book of Los, The (Blake), 107, 149
Book of Thel, The (Blake), 71, 88
Book of Urizen, The (Blake), 43, 49, 149
Bowlahoola, 163
Braun, Rev. Henry A., 3
Bridgman, Richard, 15
British folklore, 148
British Romantic poets, 3
Bronowski, Jacob, 32, 67, 146, 194n.11
Brook Farm, 16, 20
Brown, Stuart Gerry, 27
Bulkeley, Peter, 17
Burke, Kenneth, 37, 134, 195n.7
Burkholder, Robert E., 127
Butts, Thomas, 43, 44, 60

Cameron, Sharon, 199n.10
Cannibalism, 200n.5
Capitalism, 16
Carlyle, Thomas, 48, 205n.10
Catholic World, The, 195n.3
Cause, operation, effect, 159, 162
Celtic elements, 148
"Central life," 80–81, 86–87
"Central Man" passage, 58–61, 63, 136,
137, 207n.15
Chants, 2
Chaos, 170, 206n.13
"Character" (Emerson), 8, 124–25, 126
Cheyfitz, Eric, 1, 89, 91–92, 93, 96, 100
Child labor, 119, 121
Children of Father Sky/Mother Earth,
15
"Chimney Sweeper, The" (Blake), 8,
99, 117–22, 128, 140, 200–201n.6

INDEX

Christ. *See* Jesus
Christianity, 137; belief in, 130; cultural value of, 114; death and, 121; heresies and, 144; humanist revisionism of, 110–14; love and, 10; man's identity in, 50; in "Mental Traveller," 23; as myth, 112; myths of, 3; orthodox, 48, 49, 51, 99; redemption in, 105; sacraments in, 200n.3; secularization of, 2–3
Chthonic elements, 148
Church Fathers, 49
Cicero, 150
"Cipher," 76, 83
"Circles," 7, 45, 69, 75–103, 170, 189; "Ah! Sun-flower" and, 75; Fall and, 5; God in, 47
Civil War, 62–63
Classical mythology, 48
"Clod and the Pebble, The" (Blake), 9–11, 13
"Clubs" (Emerson), 126
Coleridge, Samuel Taylor, 2, 14, 32, 38, 45, 86, 160, 193n.4
College professors, 178, 179
"Commodity" (Emerson), 38
Communion, 131–32, 200n.3
"Compensation" (Emerson), 7, 75
Conceptual discourse, 2
Concord, 132, 165; founders of, 17; in "Hamatreya," 19, 25–26
Conduct of Life, The (Emerson), 8, 187
Conscience, 102
Consistency, foolish, 6
Contradictions. *See* Dialectical method; Dichotomy; Dualism
"Corporeal Eye," 29, 35, 42
Cosmic personification, 52
Cox, James M., 209n.1
Creation, 4, 49, 68, 188; Blake on, 51; as Christian mythic archetype, 3; Emerson on, 53, 104, 167; Fall and, 50; *Nature* and, 4–5, 47
Crisis, 170

Criticism, 26; of "Ah! Sunflower," 72–74; of Blake, 46, 70; of "Circles," 85–88; of Emerson, 2–3, 46, 55–56, 62, 137, 205n.8, 207–08n.15, 208n.16; of "Mental Traveller," 21
Cultural concerns, 64
Cycles, 74, 76, 87, 95, 101

Damrosch, Leopold, 26, 46, 48, 194n.11, 196n.10
Dante, 58, 59, 136, 142–44, 155, 165
Davis, Michael, 99
Days, 171–85
Death: in "Ah! Sun-flower," 71–72, 73; in "Chimney Sweeper," 121; Emerson on, 53, 209n.1; Eros and, 102; in "Hamatreya," 20–21; in life, 72; in "Mental Traveller," 24
Deconstructionism, 79
Deists, 45
Deity. *See* God
Derrida, Jacques, 140
Despair, 69
Determinism, 77; in "Fate," 6; in "The Mental Traveller," 23; in "Wealth," 6
Deus, 172
Devil. *See* Satan
Dialectical method, 189–90, 194nn.10, 11, 207–08n.15; of Blake, 6–28; in "Circles," 75–76, 77, 80, 82, 84, 87; definition of, 9, 14; of Emerson, 4, 6–28, 79, 169, 170, 186; Miller on, 19–20; in *Nature*, 38, 41, 196n.13; in visionary *v.* nonvisionary, 64; in *Works and Days*, 174–75
Dialectical pairs, 7–8
Dichotomy, 1–2, 4–7, 14, 19; Emerson and, 27, 86; in "Mental Traveller," 22
Diction, 2, 21, 120–21
"Discipline" (Emerson), 40, 91–92
Discursive prose, 2
Divided Man, 57–58, 62, 74
"Divine bard," 111, 113, 114
Divine Comedy (Dante), 142–44

[218]

INDEX

Divine humanity, 112–13, 116–17, 123
"Divine Image, A" (Blake), 9
"Divine Image, The" (Blake), 9
"Divine Marriage," 90–91
Divinity School "Address" (Emerson),
    98, 99, 116, 138, 176, 189; Emerson's
    audience and, 127–35; Jesus in,
    109–12, 124, 200n.4; miracles in, 166,
    201n.8; as prophetic prose, 7; Re-
    demption and, 5, 105, 106;
    Unitarianism and, 200n.5
"Doubleness," 193n.8
Dramatic presentations, 23–24
Dreams, 81, 97–99
Dr. Johnson. *See* Johnson, Samuel
Dualism, 6–7, 19; Blake and, 26, 53–54;
    in Emerson, 86; and Fall, 64; in
    Nature, 100–101
Dyaus, 172

"Earth-Mother," 15, 16, 18, 25
"Earth Song," in "Hamatreya," 14,
    17–19
Ecclesiastes, 172
"Echoing Green, The" (Blake), 70
Ecstasy, inspiration as, 156
Eden, 44–45, 60, 73, 198n.10
Edmundson, Mark, 89
Egotism, 29, 32–33, 40, 97
Eliot, T. S., 33
Ellison, Julie, 194n.10, 207–08n.15
Emanation, 155
Emerson, Bulkeley (brother), 17
Emerson, Edward Waldo (son), 15, 57,
    109, 199–200n.2, 200n.3; dating of
    material, 126, 204n.5, 205n.9; on
    orthodoxy, 123, 137; on
    transcendentalism, 187
Emerson, Ellen (daughter), 190
Emerson, Ralph Waldo, 64; archetypes
    in works, 2, 4; Blake and, 4, 54;
    conclusions about, 5; contradictions
    in works, 1–2, 4, 5, 14; "contrary
    states" and, 6–21; criticism and

scholarship of, 2–3; "doctors-of-the-
    soul," 197n.6; dreams of, 97–99;
    existentialism and, 5; eyesight of,
    29–31, 47; father and, 89, 98–99; at
    Harvard, 29–30; health of, 29–31,
    195n.1; later years, 123–24; lectures, 7,
    108, 133; in the ministry, 29–31, 105,
    108; myths, 2, 47, 52; new approach
    to, 1–2; poems, 2, 3; as prophet, 3, 5;
    sense experience and, 62; sexual
    imagery of, 88–103; transcenden-
    talism and, 5; women and, 198n.10;
    worldview, 50; writing periods,
    55–59, 85
Emerson, Ruth Haskins, 198n.10
Emerson, William (father), 98–99
Empiricism, 85
Energy, 45; Blake on, 74, 80, 82–83; in
    "Circles," 79, 80, 81, 83–85, 87, 88
Engines, 168
English Traits (Emerson), 187
Engraving, 153
Eno the aged Mother, 149
Environmentalism, 16
Epistemological illusions, 16
Epistemology, 32
Eros, death and, 102
Erotic relationships, 9–13
Essays, 2, 7, 25, 27, 56–57, 62, 148,
    208n.16
Essays: First Series (Emerson), 7, 75, 85,
    187, 192n.1, 193n.2
Essays: Second Series (Emerson), 7–8,
    158, 187, 192n.1, 193n.2
Eternal, 49, 51, 52, 149
"Eternal generator," 80, 84
Eternity, time and, 104, 177, 180
Ethical teachings, 114
Ethics (Spinoza), 86
Europe (Blake), 7, 148–49
"Everlasting Gospel, The" (Blake),
    42, 124
"Everlasting now," 175–76
Evil: Blake on, 82–83; Emerson and,
    16–17

Lowell, James Russell, 1
Luther, Martin, 126
Luvah, 62, 74, 117, 124, 140
Lyric mode, "Earth Song," 14–15

McGann, Jerome J., 201n.11
Machines, 168, 171
McLuhan, (Herbert) Marshall, 168,
  169
"Maitreya" (Emerson), 15, 16
Malthus, Thomas, 169
Man: Blake on, 82–83; definition of,
  168; divided into men, 57–58;
  Emerson on, 33–34; God as, 50, 52,
  53, 123; Jesus as, 126, 128, 129, 132–33;
  as Poetic Genius, 145; redemption
  and, 141; sun and, 53
"Man Thinking," 82
Mankind. See Humanity
"Manners," 8
Marriage of Heaven and Hell, The
  (Blake), 7, 10, 48, 203n.22; Emerson
  and, 77, 79, 80, 82–83; Jesus and,
  106–07, 114, 117, 128, 131; poetic
  inspiration in, 147
Marx, Karl, 194n.11
Marx, Leo, 168
Masochism, 10
Materialism, 186
Matthiessen, F. O., 1, 28, 189
Meaning: four levels of, 142–43; in
  poetry, 158–59
Mediator, 127
Memory, 151
"Mental Traveller, The" (Blake), 14,
  21–26, 28, 70, 71, 85
"Merlin" (Emerson), 19, 167, 190
Messiah, 105, 131
Metalogical, 3
Metaphors, 164, 179; eye/sight/vision,
  28, 32–48; of sexual division, 57
Metres, 160, 161, 165
Michael, John, 108, 128, 196n.13,
  197nn.3, 4, 200n.3, 201n.10
Michelangelo, 59, 60, 136

Midsummer Night's Dream
  (Shakespeare), 148
Miller, Perry, 19–20
Milton, John, 63, 153–56, 161,
  203n.22
Milton a Poem in 2 Books (Blake), 63,
  149–58, 163; inspiration and, 146, 147,
  167; as prophecy, 7, 117; studies on,
  189, 203n.2; time in, 181–83
Mimesis, 160
Mind: and eye, 40, 48; reality and, 50
Miracles, 109, 134, 174; biblical, 166; in
  "Chimney Sweeper," 122, 201n.8;
  Christ and, 138; man's life and, 112
Mnemosyne, 151
Modernism, 168
Modes, 2
Monism, 54; Blake and, 26; in Nature,
  101; and "Universal Man," 64
Montaigne, Michel de, 61, 62, 132, 135,
  136
"Montaigne; Or, The Skeptic"
  (Emerson), 8
Moods, 78
Moon, 53, 55
Moral virtues, 79
Morality, 18
Mortality. See Death
Mother-figure, 92–102
Mott, Wesley T., 200n.3, 202n.19
"Mourning and Melancholia"
  (Freud), 89
"Mundane Shell," 74, 175
Muses, 151, 152, 153
Mystics, 204n.4
Mythology, 145, 165, 188–89, 205n.7;
  Blake and, 52, 160; classical, 48, 49;
  Emerson and, 2, 47, 52, 159, 160,
  170, 207–08n.15

Napoleon, 61, 135
"Napoleon; Or, The Man of the
  World" (Emerson), 8
Narrators, 24
Native Americans, 147, 173, 176–77

Nature: aesthetic experiences with, 33;
Blake on, 46; Emerson on, 29, 46,
48, 53; God and, 38, 40; in
"Hamatreya," 16; ingesting of, 154;
reality of, 66; as seductress-whore,
101; as symbol, 162
Nature (Emerson), 29, 32–42, 145,
173–74; archetypes in, 4, 160;
book of Revelation in, 167, 205n.10;
Burke on, 37, 195n.7; Creation and,
4–5; dialectical method in, 38;
divine marriage in, 90–91; eye
references in, 37–42; Genesis and,
167; "Gifts" and, 8; incest in, 92–93;
Jesus in, 106, 109, 200n.4; literary
criticism of, 189, 205n.8; nature in,
153; "noble doubt" passage, 196n.13;
NOT ME/ME, 140; Oedipal complex in, 98–101; "Politics" and, 8; as
prophetic prose, 7, 53–54, 56; as
prose poem, 6, 187, 208n.16;
review of, 195n.3; "Universal Man"
of, 59, 63; visionary experiences
in, 2
Negro, 63, 169
Neo-classic style, 2
Neufeldt, Leonard, 56, 86–87, 138,
207n.13
New Age, 150, 151
New Critics, 19
"New England Reformers," 8
"New heaven and new earth," 167, 171,
181, 184
Newton, Sir Isaac, 51, 67, 86, 179
Nietzsche, Friedrich, 89
"Noble doubt" passage, 66, 196n.13
Nobodaddy, 96, 99, 101, 122, 163,
203n.22
No Exit (Sartre), 70
"Nominalist and Realist"
(Emerson), 8, 125
Nonlogical, 3
Norton, Andrews, 29, 108
Nuclear disarmament negotiations, 169
"Nurse's Song" (Blake), 9

Objective reality, 64–68
Oedipus complex, 89–103, 200n.5
O'Keefe, Richard R., 193n.5
"Old age," 81, 84
Old Testament, 49
Ololon, 155
Olympians, 49
"One Man," 57, 58, 60, 63, 207n.15
Ontology, 32, 49
Oothoon, 157
Opium, 81
Optimism, 102, 104, 113, 168, 169, 170,
190
Orc, 85, 87, 117, 140
Order, 87
Orgasm, 97
Orphic Poet, 2, 63, 77, 79, 145, 178
Orthodoxy, 123, 124, 138, 139
"Out of body experience," 34
"Over-Soul, The" (Emerson), 7, 140,
199n.1
Ovid, 49, 150

Packer, Barbara: on Emerson, 56, 173,
199n.10; on Emerson and Blake, 3,
47, 53, 54, 87–88
Pantheism, 33
Pantheistic apotheosis, 16
Paradise Lost (Milton), 82, 203n.22
Paradise Regained (Milton), 149, 153
Paradox: in "Hamatreya," 19; in
"Mental Traveller," 22; in
"transparent eyeball" passage, 34
Parricide, 92, 93, 99
Past, 176
Patriarchs, 40, 51
Patristic system, 143
Paul, Sherman, 27, 85–86, 138
Peabody, Elizabeth, 111, 208n.16
Perception. *See* Metaphors:
eye/sight/vision
Personification, 52, 64
Pessimism, 171, 181
Petry, Alice Hull, 16

Virgin, 70, 71, 74, 155
Vishnu Purana, 15, 16
Vision metaphors. *See* Eye metaphors
"Vision of the Last Judgment, A"
  (Blake), 34, 42, 60
Visionary experiences, 63, 64; of Blake,
  31; in *Nature*, 2; and science, 68
Visions of the Daughters of Albion
  (Blake), 42, 157
Voltaire, 127

Waggoner, Hyatt, on Emerson, 19,
  193n.5
Walden Pond, 20
Wars, 58, 81
Washington, George, 62
Waste Land, The (Eliot), 170
"Wealth" (Emerson): anti-capitalism
  and, 16; determinism in, 6;
  "Hamatreya" and, 20
"Weed by the wall," 79, 82, 84
Weiskel, Thomas, 75
Westminster Review, The, 195n.3
Wheels, 69, 75, 78, 101
Whicher, Stephen, 2, 85, 86, 96,
  198n.10; on "acquiescent" older

Emerson, 19, 56, 123, 134, 167,
  201n.10; on "Circles," 85, 86; on
  Nature, 96
Whitman, Walt, 161, 164–65
Williams, Porter, Jr., 201n.9
Women, 198n.10
Wood, Barry, 38
Woolf, Virgina, 197n.13
Wordsworth, William, 3, 39
"Works and Days" (Emerson), 5,
  167–85, 205n.11, 206–07n.13
Works and Days (Hesiod), 172,
  206n.12
Worldview: of Blake, 50–52, 55; of
  Emerson, 52–55
"Worship" (Emerson), 123, 125–26

Yeats, William Butler, 147
Yoder, R. A., 27, 207n.15
Young, Philip, 209n.1
Youth, 70, 71, 74

Zeupater, 172
Zeus, 172
Zoas, 23, 49, 63; Albion and, 58, 74;
  as personal projections, 62